JUSTICE COLD WAR

Also by **Frank Sithole**

Justice Cold War (Updated Edition)

Leadership by Design

Fine-Tuning Decades in the 21st Century

JUSTICE COLD WAR

Copyright ©2011 by Frank Sithole

ISBN: 1466323752

To my mother

Bessie,

Without whom I would not be the person I am. I thank my mom for making me feel special from day one, and for encouraging me in times of storms in my life. Great appreciation also goes to my three sisters, Everlet, Phyllis and Virginia. They have taught me the value of family love.

This book is also dedicated in memoriam to my father, Makiseni, who never gave up, overcame tremendous odds to finally connect with Christ, and went to be with the Lord before seeing fruits of this book. My father taught me lessons of manhood that have carried me all my lifetime.

Our family will never be the same without my two brothers, Trynos and Lewis, including my sister Tholiwe, who all had a very short stay on this earth. Their passing on has left a gap in our family. I pray that God's love will bond my family together.

ACKNOWLEDGEMENTS

This book writing took many years to come into fruition. That it has finally hit the printing press is a triumph for the many, many friends who have struggled over the years to tease the text out of me. Because this has been such a long process, the list of those who have helped so much would require a print run in itself. Thank you to everyone who have allowed me to use their stories, who has read the manuscript, made comments, checked the sources and done the typeset.

A huge thanks to Estelle Banda, who was the first to press me on paper, and who has been an example and constant encourager both as critic and loyal friend; Timothy Marsh LeCraw, from Atlanta Georgia, USA, who is always there to sort out the grammar and the other important things in life; his help has been invaluable. This book would never have happened without the gracious firmness of Timothy LeCraw who honed the manuscript into readable text and led me into precision. The patience and love of Mornei, who did final touches on the book cover and made all the difference in getting the book cover done.

Above all thank you to those who have prayed with me and encouraged me over the years.

CONTENTS

CHAPTERS

Tailor designed boxed life

It looked like other ethnic groups took people's lives and packaged them in boxes in order to suit their desire to cause modern day slavery. In order to keep abreast with people's lifestyles and bridge the gap of inequality between the races in both the old and young generations, poor and rich, that seemed to be widening and spelled out a need for good policy makers, it remained for the government to do something. The government leaders blamed the colonial powers for the situations the people were in while the poor masses thought the same minorities in power, which controlled the economy, did not care much about them. By the mere look of things, you could tell that the nation was sitting on a time bomb that was to shock its citizens when it exploded. The country has suffered few times of unrest since its bloody struggle that brought people independence, but did not free them from the injustices that forced the majority into poverty and illiteracy.

How could freedom be celebrated when the masses toiled but were left behind empty handed, with little clue about what was to happen next. Many people saw the African paradise as a symbol of good governance and leadership when it introduced its large-scale plans for infrastructure development and poverty reduction, which looked like successful progress to many in the country and around the world. Surely, this became the best country to live and tour in on the southern hemisphere of Africa. Only time would tell, as the African trend of leadership had always been marred with failure, which contributed to government corruption exacerbated by the residue of colonial policies.

The country had a marvellous potential that was infusing hope to the hearts of its citizens. During the post apartheid era the country was divided into three major subdivisions that were namely: high veld, middle veld and low veld. The high veld linked big cities with its wonderful roads and railway lines that stretched through the middle veld. High veld and middle veld had large, rich soil farms that formed the commercial zones of the country's major cities. Fertile soils were in the high and middle veld areas. The low veld area was where the native reserves were. Not only would you find animals but also large populations of the black majority residing here. This was never by their own choice but the colonial government had pushed them out of the formal economic stream and relegated them there.

Boys and girls walked along these barren stretches of land herding a few animals, going around in search of grazing pasture. All households would have their animals taken into kraals for night keep, as the animals were vulnerable to theft or carnivorous animals. You would think the people around these areas were nomads if you saw their huts and houses. Everything looked unpromising to the rural people even when the new government had taken over the country. Since these things had taken long time to develop, it was going to take a long time to correct them and turn those homes into decent accommodations. Most of these communities had no schools or good health facilities, which made life a mere gift of grace to many forced to live here throughout the harsh conditions of the colonial era. Clean water was a distant dream to these communities that lived under such squalid conditions. Bilharzias and many other diseases affected large numbers of the communities.

The majority of men had to leave the rural homes they loved so much and even turn their backs on parents, wives and children to go and search for jobs in farms, mines and as domestic workers in cities, which is still a widely practised trend today. This was never a good choice for many but a mere means of survival. Salaries paid to these people were unconscionable. In an African family society, the boys are shepherds and the girls take care of the house chores unless the family has no boys, then girls shepherd or herd the cattle. Without education and a decent place to live, life may simply pass the masses by without their realizing its wonderful meaning from the Creator.

You would find most households working on the farms for pennies, and as you draw conclusions, you would begin to see a bleak future for them and the generations to come. The system relegated people to poverty and it left them with no choice but to live under these conditions of glorified slavery. Back in the day, white or some colour that was next to white was associated with wealth and success. What do you do when you find yourself forced to stay where you would not like to stay? Would you be happy? The yoke cannot be broken without bringing people to a fresh starting point of equality, which remains the only solution to break the yoke that is on people's necks even today. All was in the hands of the government; otherwise, many would live not knowing that they were equal with all people on planet earth.

Segregation always has a way of bringing a horrible impact on those it is directed to affect. Leaving those it favoured with an upper hand on the economy, as they would profit at the expense of the poor and helpless. Victims of apartheid suffered cruel effects of skin pigmentation degradation and humiliation that words cannot describe. If we have to be honest, we would agree that the racial system denied blacks an opportunity to live well. The whole world is confused and few leaders have engaged in fighting inequality, which is a travesty of justice. The consequences had mental and psychological effects on both children and elders of these societies, which has today rendered in them a lack of confidence when being among other ethnic groups or races.

Mountainous middle lands had a lot to offer from dairy farming, cattle ranching, crop growing to rearing of sheep, pigs and poultry. It attracted a large workforce from both major tribes of the country, which are Ndebele and Shona. Most people spoke two vernacular languages as well as slang English. The farm bosses portrayed and lived lifestyles of despots with corrupt, unruly attitudes that also ruled at government offices even without them being there. They practised child labour in their farms without fear of labour department officers. The labour officers would get bribes and ignore the pleas and grievances of farm workers. There is a strong revolutionary sentiment in Africa that seems to be gradually setting at liberty the poor masses through modern justice interventions. Most times African laws seem to work only when directed against the poor. That is the problem with wrong ethics and it demonstrates a biased justice system. Rich folks could most times bribe their way out of any situation. These "fat cats" have no handcuff size that fits their hands, as money protects them in their fortresses of greediness in the name of privacy and surrounded by a bunch of shrewd lawyers.

The farming work conditions were of such a complex state that even leaving one farm to go work on another was never an option for many workers. Farmers used the same approach all over the country when dealing with their workers and pinning them down to their system. Trying city jobs was no option for these people, as there were complications involved here, the first one being illiteracy. Going back to rural lands was another nightmare, as the chiefs ruled the people with an iron fist too. When Nelson Mandela said, "I have fought against white domination and black domination," he was speaking about both rural traditional tribal powers and apartheid government. Land was distributed by chiefs to people they knew or who had with them known connections from the same communities. You could get a piece of land to put up a hut if you were lucky and met the chief's demands. Now, the challenge among many that stayed on such unproductive landscapes was day-to-day survival. Most farm households chose to suffer and die in same farms rather than try something new. It looked as if some had been destined to pain and suffering, while a few educated people were in the driving seat of the economy. Tribalism was also an issue but nonetheless all tribes of black people felt the farm owners' racial oppressive tactics equally.

Every farm had its grocery store and sometimes a beer garden for employees owned by the farmer. Workers would buy groceries and drink beer on credit. At the end of the month, some would take very little or nothing home. This was a hand-to-mouth lifestyle. If you did not buy many things up to the end of month, the farm boss would threaten to fire you on suspicion of stealing from the farm. Rarely did these people go shopping or take their kids to school or just go for a family outing or holiday. Farmers made sure that people worked and lived like slaves despite the independence and democracy that had come to guarantee freedom for all. The cry for equality and a better quality of life for all became evident to all in the country of Zimbabwe. Freedom does not come cheap even though many lives were lost during the liberation struggle, which was for emancipation of the black majority; more work needed to be done by governments and the masses at large in order to achieve maximum benefit and a better life for all. War heroes took office in government positions in order to serve people according to their liberation manifestos or freedom charters. During the early years of independence, something seemed to come alive in the hearts and minds of black people, whether living in the farms, rural native reserves or cities. Many blacks went back to school and obviously, those in the cities had an advantage as night schools sprang up everywhere. The government passed a law for all parents to be able to afford education for their children all over the country. This meant that farm kids would see their cruel masters on weekends only or during holiday times, as most farmers made sure fathers worked together with their sons on the farms. It seemed the society was producing economically handicapped men and women.

The times and situations forced blacks to raise their children for other races in order to have workers, as this was the guarantee the system offered the farmers. No blacks could retire from the farms, let alone take an annual holiday leave from work. We would often hear of the farm boss giving extremely heavy work duties to the people and telling of his pleasure trips overseas. When a man could not work because of old age, he was sent away to die in the rural villages. People in farms had to endure the affliction of a cruel racist system, which would later cast them into the hands of ruthless chiefs who tossed the people back and forth whenever they needed land for houses -even in their old age. How can a man start a new life when he is that old and at a stage where he cannot work? The system pushed black people into failure without a way out to a better life. A life of pain and broken dreams was the standard package for these families and societies. Children had to make homes for their parents as that remained the only option available - and only if they got land from chiefs.

Most farmers never allowed workers to own dogs as they complained of a poaching threat. Neither could workers keep their livestock in the farms where they worked. Fishing was not allowed without the bosses' permission. The devastating scenario was that these people never had permanent places to call home. Some would simply move about from one farm to another until old age and then go and die away from the farm.

In every generation, they are those who pave the way for others. These people often pay a price. One man came to live on a farm in the late months of the year 1979. He owned a few donkeys and no other animals apart from these. He came from a midlands farm abandoned by its owner, as war had intensified all over the country. Mark was his name; he was a hero of life and almost everyone in the community fell in love with his spirit. The laws of most farmers never allowed people to own dogs or keep their livestock in the same farms. Mark got a place at Mr. G.W. Smith's farm and brought his family to stay on the farm and he paid rent by taking the farm cattle to the dip tank every Saturday. By a gentleman's agreement with the property owner, it meant Mark was not to work full time or get a salary. All male children were to help their fathers, this was most farmers' law and all the workers followed it. Mark was told by Mr. Smith to allow his donkeys to graze outside the farm, of which the only place available was the railway strip of land. He agreed, as he had no other place to stay and keep his animals or survive with his family. Farm life never allowed anyone but whites to succeed, let alone meeting the needs of one's family. For a change, a man had come to prove to others that all things are possible and the time had come to break the slavery yoke and its mentality.

On the other hand, many people looked at him and thought it was not going to work since no one had done this before. I saw a man rise and fall as he pursued his goal, which was to be free economically and mentally. Few black men would pursue their passion lifestyles when not afforded a chance but Mark strove for his dream. He would often take control of things. Mark had never gone to school and in fact, could not read nor write nor sign a proper signature on his post office bank savings book but would put an "x" mark. His highest achievement was after his retirement from the Rhodesian forces in World War 11, where he served from 1949 to 1951. I looked at the documented piece of paper — a lovely certificate — as I asked him how he felt in the war. Tears and emotions came back as he narrated how his best friend had died in the war as well as many others, as the African armies joined with British forces in a combined effort to protect British interests in those days.

Many times, I would visit Mark when I came from school. I loved to hear his words of inspiring truths. This was a man happy in his heart too. There was one remarkable day when I came from school and this mentor of mine was sitting by his garage as if contemplating his next move. The train had hit one of his donkeys and its right front leg was badly broken. He told me where it was on that rainy evening and in no time, we made our way there. You could tell that the donkey had not moved since he left it in the afternoon.

Neither of us was a veterinary expert; but we prepared four planks of about the same size of 650 centimetres so we could bandage the donkey's leg all around. Many accidents like this would happen whenever he stayed away a little while from his animals during grazing hours. Trains were the biggest threat to his animals even though it was hard to get used to the fact that the rail strip was the only grazing place for the poor donkeys. On arrival at the scene, we took out prepared cloth material that would cushion the leg and started rolling it around the donkey's leg and the planks on top and then tied it.

Looking aside, there were railway technicians driving on the strip road. After seeing us by the donkey, they stopped and came to try to assist. Two held the donkey down, as it wanted to get up; it was struggling in pain while Mark and the technician tried to bandage it. The bandage idea was Mark's but when I looked at it, it seemed to be just a wish that the donkey would live and not die. The trains would make mince meat of the donkeys for a stretch of miles at a time, and this seemed a lucky incident since the animal had survived with only a broken leg. The following day came and the donkey could not eat nor drink water from a dish that we had put before it on the day of bandaging. The donkey made it to sunset but never saw the following day. I had gone to school when Mark went to check it early in the morning and found it dead. On my arrival home from school, I saw that Mark had a sad face; so I suspected before he disclosed the news to me that the donkey had died.

It was important for Mark to have the donkeys as he used to plough for his family and for other people on the no man's land along the railway strip. The railway management also approved of the idea, as they said it prevented wild fires from spreading. He was the first to start ploughing and more people followed suit. He had carts pulled by donkeys to deliver things around the farm communities and the Nalatalie quarry mine. Most farmers did not want to see the donkeys near their farms even when it was just for a delivery. Mark always worked hard and he had a great garden where he grew vegetables for his family and to sell. He also did African traditional carvings for people. I had piece jobs throughout the years with him and that helped me with pocket money. This was a man with many farming skills; the very unfortunate situation was that he could not own any land of his own. If he had had a farm of his own, he could have proven that it is not the colour of people but skill and knowledge, which are the most essential ingredients in success.

Mark had a unique outlook in many ways and things. He took his girls to high school, which many parents would not do, as they complained and gave excuses about girls becoming pregnant before finishing school, and regarded them as second best to boys. This was the view of some parents though pregnancy was not the only risk girls faced. Girls and boys were raised the same in Mark's family. He became a business trendsetter and a hero that changed society and ended up with a political party chair position, which he held for about five years. Societies in these regions needed people like this one—a thoughtful leader who led by example; surely they could not mistake him for another. Mark taught me lessons in life that have carried me for many years. He taught me about having a small body stature with a big heart life. I have learnt that where I find myself does not matter because I can use it as a stepping-stone to get where I want to go.

Mark married Maggie who had a mother living in the city of Bulawayo; she was a strong-willed Ndebele woman. Maggie's father had passed away when she was very small, at about five years of age. She had to leave her mother and grow up in her grandparents home since the bride's price was paid to her mother's family according to tradition. She hardly met her mother while she was growing up until the time came when her grandparents gave her in marriage. The grandparents asked for eleven cows, blankets, and hats, as part of the bride price charge. The relationship was not great between Maggie's mother and her in laws or Maggie's grandparents because even when Maggie was getting married her mother never knew it. When she heard that her daughter was married in her absence, she vowed never to get involved in anything that had to do with Maggie and her children until she received her bride's price share. She claimed her in-laws took all the (lobola) bride price and that she was given nothing, which was true. For more than twenty years, she could not visit her daughter and neither was her daughter welcome at her house. She insisted she just wanted her dues in order to normalize things between the two families.

Mark resolved in his heart to sort out the issue once and for all. He went to the city and bought a pure white jug, a nice blanket and a woman's suit with matching shoes for an undisclosed amount of money, which elders took to Maggie's mother. The elders came back with a thank you note from her. A month later, she visited the farm and saw her daughter and grandchildren for the first time. She claimed that without her fair share paid to her, it was very difficult to relate to her daughter and family. I thought to myself, she must have been the greatest debt collector of the century! She claimed this was her culture and the way things should be. She had a large house that could have helped her daughter's children attend better schools in the city, but her demands ruined it all.

What a privilege it was to have Mark around—this hero with a heart larger than life! Sometimes, he would stumble and fall but he always rose up. I will never forget the day Mark became trapped in the river by the fishing nets and was not sure how to loose himself. Farm people did carry out commercial fishing secretly in Farm Rivers. He called aloud to his son and instructed him to look after the family in case he died in the waters. Finally, he managed to escape the predicament. Many people, who were fishing there and saw him thought he was finished. We were all happy to see him come out of the water safely. Sticking with the norm could not get things done this side of the country. Those who worked full-time jobs received their salaries late every month.

I became Mark's business partner in most of the products he sold. We would sell honey, vegetables, fresh fish and some mushroom in the rainy season. Sometimes, we also stocked game meat from the bush and distributed it to our customers. I mean, stock it from the bush as wild animals were hunted and trapped illegally. Mark taught me how to use nets for fishing and I would take them and catch fish to sell to the teachers on credit, since most seemed to be broke most of the time. Life was good as long as the white man was not around. The moment the white man showed up all hell would break loose. I would meet Mark by the dip tank or by his home and we would finalize our business transactions. At twelve years of age, I was already a great salesperson. Clients would book orders with me as to what they wanted and I would let my partner know. I would deliver the goods and collect the money at month's end. What we could not supply ourselves, we would out-source and then deliver. Not having a full time job became an opportunity to do more for Mark.

Our partnership went from when I was young to when I became a business graduate and later became his business adviser. I always admired how Mark progressed to own his own land, cattle and more donkeys through his untiring industrious spirit. And, with my help, he was able to coordinate all the facets of his business together. I remember when I helped him open a bank account in order to save his first daughter's bride price money. He could not write nor read, so he put an "x" mark, as a signature on his post office savings book. Here I realized that I did not know all there was to know about Mark, since I never knew he could not write his name nor sign a proper signature. He could calculate and add money without a problem and spoke good English. This man never stopped surprising me. Regardless of all his shortcomings, I wanted to be like him. It was my idea that he save money so that when he got land of his own, he could buy cows and prosper even more. By then I was in high school and would work on holidays in order to have enough money during the school terms because resources were scarce. Mark would call me a great man, though I could not believe it myself. I always missed being with him especially during my high school years, since the school was far and I would only see him once or twice a term. His positive attitude and encouraging spirit kept me seeking to spend time with him.

My buddy, my hero & compatriots

Life was what you made it this side of the world. Many people found themselves on the wrong side of the law and would face the wrath of the justice system that was always so strict especial toward the poor. I saw many farm workers go to jail for stock theft related cases, which most of them had never committed. Some farmers would allow workers to keep only ten animals of their own on their farms. One old man lost all his cattle to his boss in court and received a sentence of five years in prison. Coming out of prison, he had lost his wife to another man and eventually got sick and died after a short illness. Lawlessness was common among these communities, even though it went unreported. As long as it had to do with the white man's assets or things, everyone had to think twice about reporting such cases because tomorrow was going to be their payback loot day.

Workers around farms would trap wild animals like buffalo, gazelle and springbok including many others for meat. Traps even caught cows sometimes; once found caught by the traps; they would be released and sent away with terrible scars. The farm owners gave permission for the people to eat dead animals or else burn and bury them. Sometimes, the farmer was told an animal had died and would simply add it to the record book of the dead ones without going to check the carcass. The new beginning resulted in economic liberalization for the poor who received pathetic salaries in both farms and cities.

Law enforcement agencies had no regard or respect for these communities. When they came to make arrests, rarely did they let the people know about their rights. Many people in these communities lost their little assets they had worked hard for and went to prison. Then they came out of prison only to find that the country had very little to offer them even when political independence had been proclaimed and declared. It seemed no workers were content with what they earned though most did not commit crime. With many white farmers, all black workers were thieves or labelled as criminal elements. Some workers would go to jail because the white man said someone stole the generator. Democracy and freedom tastes sour on many White-owned farms of Africa even today.

All the government policies seemed sound and right on paper yet never translated into a reality of a democratic charter chapter of a country enjoyed by all. In time, the country celebrated all people's well being and the masses' livelihood welfare was slowly implementing better development plans. It seemed that the government was not doing much for the marginalized people. That was true in the eyes of these communities, but work was going on on the ground, but the wheels of the law were turning slowly and hopefully at the end of the day, catch up with all lawless people. Farm workers perceived their first enemy to be the Whites, second being the government that they always blamed for not doing anything to protect them from ruthless taskmasters, and which stalled in implementing freedom charter policies of fair land redistribution programmes and black empowerment. Many longed to see a fair land redistribution bill brought into effect, as they thought freedom's fruits rested on the question of land ownership, and considered this to be a point of urgency. The agricultural department in rural areas initiated cooperatives but the land was not productive enough, so such programmes yielded very little fruits.

It was on a Tuesday afternoon at about half past four; I went to Mark's home and sat chatting with his sons and daughters. Maggie had gone to the garden, which was about three kilometres away. Mark had been gone for days and we expected him to come home anytime from his distant fishing trip. Whenever he would return, I would market and deliver the fish on a bicycle to different customers around the community. Suddenly, we saw a grey van approaching the house and pulling off to park by the roadside behind the house. This was a police van and one uniformed officer who was the driver, and his colleague who was in plain clothes came out of the car. They both went to open the back of the van and out came two men handcuffed. It was Mark and his nephew. All four men headed to the yard and Mark greeted us, told us to be calm, and assured us with a soft voice that all would be fine.

When a man is denied the right to resources and to live well, he sometimes resorts to illegal activities in order to make ends meet. People on farms were not criminals but the racial tactics directed toward them had turned many to dubious business practices. The same goes with our current generation where crime has become the order of the day in our communities and nations.

Tears started dropping from Mark's children's eyes. The police harassed, intimidated, kicked and assaulted Mark and his nephew in front of us, which left me in tears and heartbroken too. The police searched different parts of the home and I saw Mark pointing out fishing line hooks to them. The cops finally took the two men back to the van parked by the street. The cops assaulted the men and we saw the nephew, who was a young man, scream and cry bitterly as the cops assaulted him. These cops wanted the fishing nets used to catch the huge amount of big dried fish, which Mark was in possession of on his way to sell them to Shangani mine customers. If the evidence, fishing nets were found in Mark's possession, poaching and the commercial selling of fish without a permit would be the charge.

When Mark was arrested, the police took him to where he was living during the catch of fish by his sister's place. This is where the police officers found his nephew drying some fresh fish. That is why the police arrested the nephew as an accomplice. He was an accomplice who knew very little about the use of fishing nets. After about an hour of assaulting and intimidating the suspects even more worse brutal tactics were introduced. The young suspect was forced under the car that was raved high, and told he was going to be run over if he did not tell the truth. The young man bitterly cried, and even after all that police brutality, the assault did not help in bringing the evidence out. Then the police put their two suspects in the van and drove off.

The police officers of Fort Rixon, Insiza District, were known for their brutality and the notorious handling of suspects by which many could not get a fair trial. When Maggie came back home from the garden, the eyes of her children broke the news. The question in my heart that kept me wondering was, "How would she have reacted if she was there seeing everything take place?" She did not know what to do next but only suggested she would catch a bus the following day to where they had incarcerated her husband. On the next day, we had to go to school, and she went to Fort Rixon. When I came from school, I went to see her and she told me his court appearance was due the following week on Wednesday. It meant that his sons had to take the farm cattle to the dip tank, apologize to the farmer on his behalf, and tell the farmer he had travelled, as this was a family secret. Such was life this side of the country.

The police dropped all charges against the nephew before the court date approached. Mark had insisted to the police that the young man knew nothing about the fish catch and being a minor worked to his advantage. The evidence not being found and the police having taken fish for themselves before the court appearance of the suspect proved to be a disaster. The court dismissed the case and dropped all charges against Mark. After his release, he immediately went to fetch his bicycle at his sister's place and rode home. Mark came home empty-handed after the police took all the fish, but it was a joy for his family to see him back and free again. This was a legal legend in his own right. He could argue his cases with so much wisdom before courts of law. I then realized that this was a generation that lived to learn not learn to do and live. He used to tell me great stories of times he was in jail and how he would talk himself out without a lawyer.

I saw Mark fall and rise in his life as he struggled and battled against many storms of life. If all men had a fighting spirit of that nature, the world would be a better place to live in. I would ride in a cart pulled by his donkeys together with him for long distances. At times, we would travel two nights or so together. His father and mother were old. He had brothers and sisters too. His family knew me well, as in those days it took a society to raise a child. The old man, his father, loved me very much and always blessed me with a few coins whenever he saw me. The first time I met him he was still strong and working in the farm near the city of Gweru.

Not much later, I heard that ghosts had hit him. African traditional mentality can be very ignorant at times. In essence, he had suffered a stroke and his mouth was affected badly. Eventually, he lost his last-born son who was working in the same farm and living together with them. He died in a bicycle accident with a truck coming from a nearby road bar. Life was now a nightmare for these old people. The family got a nephew to stay with them and work in the same farm as there was no way anyone could stay in the farm free or get retirement. This was the order of the day for centuries among farm communities.

Last time I went to see the old man with Mark was four years before he passed on. He was now bed-ridden and could not easily walk nor stand on his own. When we arrived there, we met Mark's mother and chatted with her for some minutes before going into the hut where the old man lay. Mark went in first and spoke to him, then introduced the visitor, which was me. The old man shook and sat up to shake my hand with a smile on his face as he spoke to me. He told me what had happened to him and, as he shook my hand, he held it for a moment and said, "This could be our last moment to see each other on this earth." He told me he felt his time was near for him to go. It was indeed time to leave the earth, as he was in his twilight years. His words were right on point, it surely took us that moment to see each other again and after four years, he passed on. His words haunt me and I had always wished to see him free and living at his own place or land. Mark and his family went to his funeral and buried him in the Gweru city cemetery.

Life was a journey of painful experiences on the farms in the country. A place to call home was scarce to many who died without having a decent place to call home, which is still the case today. Mark would buy donkeys every year to replace those killed by trains. His niece who was married to a cook and was living in one of the farms at Daisy Field had asked us to pass by her place on our way home from Mark's parents' place. She had told him someone was selling donkeys and we passed there considering buying those donkeys. We did find everything ready there. We found the donkeys with two men, who claimed to be the owners of the donkeys. There were two lovely donkeys that Mark paid thirty dollars for each. Immediately we now had a span of four donkeys to pull the cart. We ate a lovely lunch here and as the day got cooler we started our journey of about five hours.

It was after about four years when a stranger arrived by Mark's home and confronted him about the two donkeys he had bought, which had even some young ones by then. The man claimed the donkeys were his and went missing about five years ago. He wanted to get his donkeys back without a problem but Mark refused since he had bought them. The man went away for a month and came back accompanied by the police, who ordered us to round up the donkeys in one place, as the man wanted to identify his donkeys. We did that and the man pointed out the two donkeys which we had brought from the Daisy Field farm.

The police told us to let the other donkeys go back for the graze. Immediately, after a short interrogation, the police charged Mark of stock theft and took him away handcuffed. In the Gweru general police station cells is where they detained Mark. This was the beginning of another dreadful trial case. Stock theft was rife in the country, as unscrupulous people who operated crime syndicate businesses in this illegal livestock market were increasing every day. Sentences on such crimes were now harsh all over the country.

After two weeks had gone by, the police returned with two big police trucks, full of police officers. Dissidents were terrorising the country and that warranted police and soldiers to travel together in large numbers. The third truck had police officers and Mark, including three other men with the man, who claimed the two donkeys were his. This time again the police commanded us to round up the donkeys one place. The two donkeys and its young ones were separated and immediately were driven away by the two other men, who were going with the man claiming to be the owner of the two donkeys. The rest of the donkeys went away for grazing. The police had Mark hand-cuffed and they started assaulting him right there. One cop hit him and he fell before my eyes. I stood helplessly as a boy of fourteen years and just watched the donkeys driven away and Mark whisked away in the police truck without any word from either the police or him.

The police trucks drove away, one with Mark in it. Maggie had gone to the garden again, as this was the only reliable source of her family income. When she got back, she heard the two donkeys and its young ones were no more around. She also heard about how the police assaulted her husband while handcuffed. She would sob and go away from her children and after that, you would see her eyes flooded with tears. I always wondered how she would have felt if she was right there and all these things were taking place before her eyes. Police brutality was common in the country. In Gweru Rural police station, there was a false tomb and a bloody coloured beating stick or knobkerrie. Almost everyone investigated here saw the fake tomb, and were told if they did not tell truth, they would die without remedy.

After a few days, two police officers came by Mark's home looking for me to be a court witness during the trial. I was to prepare to go to Gweru with the officers who would fetch me the following day. The following morning the same police officers came and brought me to the bus stop. The bus came and we boarded, one police officer gave the driver the travelling government warranties. I would see the splendour of the city of Gweru for the first time. When we reached the city, I set foot for the first time on the streets of a city of that size. The officers were kind and they led me to the place of juveniles where I was to stay. They told me I had to stay there until the day I went to court. My heart longed to see my hero and just have a word with him if it was possible. I very much longed to see and talk to him. I stayed at the juveniles witnesses side for three days and nothing happened nor was I told anything nor did I see those police officers until the fourth day.

Here was a place where you would meet many young Ndebele boys waiting to testify in court on various cases involving their parents and relatives. The country had a lot of unrest and dissidents had made the country ungovernable. Most dissidents came from the ZIPRA liberation forces, which were under the ZAPU (PF) party of the late Zimbabwean political hero Joshua Nkomo. This was the second biggest party with the majority of members being Ndebele. The party also dominated in the Matebeleland province as it was mainly comprised of one tribe. When my peers showed me the scars of police brutality on their bodies, I then did not know what to think and great fear took over my emotions. The boys narrated to me about how they saw their fathers assaulted by the police. The dissidents ate in people's homes by force and the police expected the poor farm workers and rural people not give them any food but to simply report them to the police.

 The situation was complex. Dissidents murdered people. These were notorious rebels or dissidents who labelled people who reported them to the police, traitors. The rebels would choose what they wanted to eat and with whom they wanted to sleep among the girls if there were any in the families where they were eating. Some people chose to give dissidents food and keep it a secret. These rebels would commit murder, armed robbery and rape but once the police found out that the dissidents have been eating in the communities, it was another painful round of endless arrests and assaults of these poor people. All I heard, I resolved to keep in my heart as a secret. Life was never easy for people in rural and farm communities.

On the fourth day, at about four o'clock in the afternoon the two police officers came for me. I was being taken back home as there was now no need for me to testify in court, according to them. I bid good-bye to the friends I had met while there and left with the officers. We went to the hiking spot, as many buses had already gone because it was late afternoon. My heart longed to see Mark whom I never got a chance to see or talk with. A livestock truck approached and the police officers stopped it and asked for a lift. The driver allowed us to climb on top of the truck rails on the trailer, as the truck was carrying cattle. The wind blew badly and my eyes were watery during the whole fifty four-kilometre journey. Finally, we were dropped at the bus stop and I went straight with the police to Mark's home where we met Maggie and told her what had happened. The police also told her of her husband's court appearance date. The day came and Maggie made her way to the court in Gweru. It was a dreadful day—Mark got a sentence of one and half months in prison with the option of a fine, which was impossible for he or his wife to raise. I think his sentencing came because he had never received an invoice of purchase for the donkeys, nor, on the other hand, had he had a livestock permit to drive the donkeys to his place after he bought them. In any case, ignorance about the law is not an excuse.

The prison sentence to us who loved him seemed as if it was a decade though we were at last relieved of his predicament. A few weeks passed and our hearts were getting expectant. After a month and a few days, I noticed a man approaching from the bus stop wearing green overall and black gumboots. This was Mark after his release from prison. Life carried on normally and close family members and friends came to meet Mark at his home and gave him a warm welcome.

Now, only his close relatives knew what was happening with Mark. The rest of the people just thought he had travelled. We ran to meet him and the whole family celebrated, Maggie slaughtered her best chicken for him. Mark and I went back into our business as before. The rule was you could do anything you deemed fit in order to earn a living but must make sure that no one found out what you did and reported it to the farmer. If the deal had some illegal elements in it, the rule was just do it and make sure no one catches you. This applied to the white farmers, too, when they used child labour and did not pay people on time but beat them for minor faults at work and fired them, throwing their belongings by the roadside.

The labour department failed to protect farm people and empower them to be self-reliant but left them lifetime beggars and slaves of the rich farmers. Racism was unlawful, yet its proponents embraced it in sophisticated ways and always had a system that maintained the gap between the poor and rich—the twine line never comes to meet here. I was amazed to see that even the black farm owners exploited their own people by adopting the white man's system. Also in town, many black businesses practised this backward act of poorly paying indigenous people and having no regard for the poor, illiterate and the marginalized. Black employers abused the system too.

South Africa was sitting on a time bomb too, as most whites who left the other nations on the continent came to make it their home. The last country on the continent to achieve its independence now became a haven for many racist whites, who had left other independent states of Africa and vowed never to submit nor be under a black man's rule. When they went back to other African states to do business, it was with white folks only. South Africa has continued to be a strong hold of white influence even if not openly practised and easily noticed today. Workers on the farms have been feeling the pain and there was not much the government could do, as it lacked the strength and capacity to address these kinds of issues.

These ruthless farm owners, who couldn't care less about the people's rights, maliciously use the poor illiterate majority of blacks. In 1994, people started having a new hope in a new dawn of democracy. All people from all classes, even the poor and the illiterate rejoiced when they saw a black leader was to lead the country. All welcomed the dawn of democratic South Africa as the dawn of the twenty first century approached. Even if little was on the cards for such communities as these, the hope remained that one day they would surely be free. But the enemies of democracy were preparing for a continued era of enslaving and taking advantage of the poor and the helpless. A new system was designed by racists, which ensured that blacks would continue to suffer though they were supposed to be given freedom and peace.

The folly of many white racists and cultured black conservatives is publicly declaring their position of faith in God yet without good works or fruits. Many of them have used the name of God in vain and this given them respect in the public eye, yet they are wolves in sheepskins. The death of Eugene Terre'Blanche, who had led the Afrikaner wing for years, which is known as (AWB), the wing, has been known for its notorious killings of blacks during apartheid years and for enforcing a strong racial divide among the country's ethnic groups, stunned the South African nation on the 4th of April 2010.

Instead of rallying together behind the new South Africa progress initiatives, this wing continually drifts away from the rest of the society with a philosophy that is total different. The wing has adamantly confessed its disagreement with democracy. Tiaan Theron has said that former white president F.W. De Klerk is to blame since he was the one to lead the transition process during the 1994 elections. He further said democracy would not work for them and that it would be better if they could rule and govern their own land within the same country of South Africa. Maybe something small like Lesotho or Swaziland would do for these people. Adjusting is a big problem for people like these and even accepting the fact that they are equal with blacks is shocking news to them.

When the nation heard that the AWB leader Eugene Terre'Blanche had been murdered, it came as a shock to many citizens of the country. This was a man who had been found guilty of human atrocities during the post-apartheid era and sent to prison for quite some time. When the time came for him to be eligible for parole he was seen praying in court, declaring that he was now a godly, changed man. He claimed that the new had taken over his life and "behold, the old was gone." Some blacks accepted him with love while others watched him closely, waiting to see him bear fruits of repentance first. Did he ever change and bear fruits of repentance? The man had the power and potential to overhaul the AWB wing in the right direction with the meaning of the new democratic dawn if he wanted to. Many questions are still asked, and much said about his style of leadership.

Maybe we should say men who were cowards surrounded him and they could not stand for the vision of a changed man? The truth remains, dead man tell no tales. He had managed to unite Afrikaners for a wrong cause and failed to reconcile them with other ethnic groups for silly reasons based on various racial philosophies. South Africa could have moved smoothly to a democratic state of peace and prosperity if all its citizens had rallied behind the vision of Noble peace prize-winners like F.W. De Klerk, Nelson Mandela and church leaders and other freedom stalwarts.

The Eugene Terre'Blanche murder case had two suspects, Chris Mahlangu 27 years old and a minor of 15 years of age. The murder was brutal and blood spats said to have been visible by many who visited the scene of crime. The Justice act implemented on April 1, 2010 makes it possible to drop charges on a child of that age after all findings are finalized. Was the boy an accomplice in the murder or was he covering up for someone else? The case was postponed on a few occasions during the trial period. A wage dispute is said to have sparked the murder. The minor was confirmed to have indeed worked for Terre'Blanche, but the lawyer who represented him further confirmed that nothing that pointed to a possible wage dispute occurred on the day Terre'Blanche was murdered. The mother of the minor was in court and she testified that she feared for her life. The minor passed his regards to his mother through his lawyer and further appealed to the people not to do his family any harm. It was a traumatic situation for the boy and his family. The brutal murder of the well-known AWB leader left the nation saddened and amazed.

A man known as Mandla Khumalo went to greet the accused. He said he is a former employee of Terre'Blanche, and had worked at the potato farm 18 months ago for R20 a week. Khumalo claimed that Terre'Blanche never paid his workers well. "Let him go and rest," Khumalo insisted. Surely, something is wrong with many whites' attitude towards Blacks in our nation. A minor is not supposed to work, let alone not be paid. There is no justification whatsoever even when it involved adult workers; they deserve a good salary and to be paid on time as well.

The attitude of many white and black farmers is out of date in the twenty first century. The continent of Africa and many developing countries suffer as a result of hatred among ethnic groups, which continues to hold people back from enjoying true democratic freedom and prosperity. The slowness of transformation in the farming industry poses a food security threat in all poor nations and even the rich ones. The big majority of rich whites are still racist and poor blacks continue to suffer because many whites maintain the spirit of apartheid with a new vigour. Thus, some blacks praised the killers of Terre'Blanche, but most people watched with indignation as this can never be a justifiable act.

A police barbed wire barrier Cades was erected to separate black and white community members from each other in front of the court. Police wedged themselves in between the groups, then pushed the black group back and began putting up the barbed wire. The white supporters of Terre'Blanche started singing, "Die Stem." The black crowd sang the old version of "Nkosi Sikelel'iAfrica" in reply. You could tell that the two groups were not tolerant of each other's presence here. A white woman sprayed Kool Aid on a man in the black crowd. Themba Mbatha from Ekurhuleni, Gauteng, the target, said, "We are not here to fight, and the worst thing they did was to separate us with barbed wire."

 He said they came in solidarity with farm workers, because they understood their battles."Terre'Blanche's death is said to have been one of 3000 that have happened since 1994", said Tiaan Theron, a sheep farmer from Beautfort West in Western Cape. Many people feared the murder of Terre'Blanche would raise racial tensions. Surely, people cannot politicize this incident, as it is a criminal activity. What is the root cause of all this? Racial division and the mistreatment of blacks in a nation that was supposed to have been united by now if all parties were genuine and sincere about their reconciliation with each other.

Steyn Van Ronge, a Southern Free State farmer, was introduced to the media on the sixth of April 2010, as the new AWB leader during a press conference at the deceased's home in Ventersdorp. On the 8th of April 2010, thousands of people poured in for Terre'Blanche's funeral at the Afrikaans Protestant Church in Ventersdorp. He was buried in his family cemetery yard, which is not far from his farmhouse home.

The president had already called for calm in the nation and had expressed his opposition to violent action. Unfortunately, leadership of this kind has been severely lacking in other areas until recently. The murder case of Terre'Blanche was thought to pose a threat to World Cup visitors and could affect the joy of celebrating it in peace, but this was not the case. South Africa had to continue going forward and not panic as the road yet to travel was no longer than one lap to go. The world saw a South Africa that was so amazing with so much for everyone and even the world at large. A strong nation makes a move even when many think it is about to fall. It still pulls through. South Africa is a country with many possibilities. The country has been waiting to dine with the world and indeed the time has come, and real people let nothing stand in the way of their future.

Is someone seeing us?

Daisy Field primary school was about forty-four kilometres away from the city of Gweru. The school is situated on a farm that is next to the railway line, it provides primary education to children from the surrounding farms. The humble beginnings of the school are fascinating. One teacher, who taught children under the trees, moved the school up to grade three, which was the highest, having only one classroom with mud stools. In 1980 when I enrolled in it for grade one the school had students who ranged from eight to seventeen years in grade one. This was the same year the country became independent. The government made sure all children attended school. The highest grade being grade three meant that thereafter students would have to find a school elsewhere in order to further their schooling. The distance to Pakama School which most of the students attended after finishing here was about ten kilometres and others travelled greater distances depending on the areas they lived.

The long distance travelled to school was by foot daily except when some motorists would offer us a lifts since they would sympathize with us walking to fulfil our life dreams daily. The one teacher would rotate all three classes of this small school surrounded by big gum trees. Caning in schools was the order of the day. He would visit those gum trees almost daily and most of the children in the class would get a beating. Even his own kids he treated as all the others. A number of students dropped out of school for fear of being beaten, and most found it difficult to be there.

Many boys would join their fathers to work in the same farms where they lived and some joined the army. Girls would most times find short-term marriages with these young men if the girls had dropped out of school. Some girls never attended school at all. The teacher was a strong ZAPU political party leader who used much of the school time to propagate his politic views to students, singing songs of freedom, chanting slogans and dancing. After a year, one other teacher joined him, but nothing much changed as teaching still took place under the trees. We would use the ground to write with our fingers. The history of the school dated back forty years when a physically challenged teacher with one hand pioneered it.

Teachers did not respect the farm communities, so that their brutality in the schools the parents found hard to challenge. The system abused students until finally the ministry of education banned caning and made it a criminal offence in 1991. Rampant teachers' abuse saw large numbers of students drop out of school. Many parents got their teenaged children to quit school and work on farms instead as farm owners never allowed boys to sit home and do nothing. There was no easy option for the children here.

In those days, we never carried books home nor did we use school bags. A plastic paper bag was the only school bag we used whenever we took books home to get them covered. A high level of discipline was the order of the day in schools. Physical and sexual abuse among girls was rampant. The pregnancy rate was high among the primary and high school youth. Some teachers ruined the future of these community girls. The educators would send girls to do chores in their houses and then rape them and easily get away with it since these girls would not report them nor knew the channels of taking their cases to court. Even their parents were of no help since men dominated the societies and treating women as second-class people was common; they had no say in the community. That was how the teachers easily trapped their victims in bed. Family planning back then was unknown to school children or not allowed. In cities baby dumping by schoolchildren became alarming.

If you were late to class, you would join the class by saying, "Excuse me, teacher, I am late." That solved the problem as most of us lived far away. Sometimes we would get a beating for arriving late if others from our neighbourhoods had arrived earlier. This helped to produce great marathon champions among us farm children! Few students had bicycles since most parents could not afford them. We never bought lunch but carried our food in plastic bags. We would hide our food in the bushes before school and on our way home, pick it up and eat it. The school played soccer and netball as its only sport activities, apart from running. This robbed this generation from developing its talents and God-given gifts for sport.

The students had a very low self-esteem, which contributed to such schools coming in last whenever they played in sports competitions with other schools within the province. The better schools practised regularly, and talent development was not just a school programme but career-oriented so that many students excelled in various sports. This saw many kids breaking into professional sports and being successful in their careers. The city and better school teams groomed their players who had talent and many went on to play on great world stages during their sports careers.

If your father worked as a farm supervisor, people would regard you as being from a well-to-do family. Most students had a farm worker mentality that affected their self-esteem. We all highly esteemed and feared the white man who sometimes even beat up their workers who were parents before their kids. The basic teaching of the day was that a black man is nothing, can do nothing and knows nothing except to work for the white man. The black fathers and mothers accepted this servile mentality and passed it on to their kids. The white man had no regard for blacks on his farm so that even the working conditions were terrible. The teachers would tell the farm students that they would never amount to anything and would mock and belittle them. The farm mentality is dangerous when taught to people. It is a terrible thing to send children to school to improve themselves and then have them told they are worthless and will never amount to anything by teachers.

It gives people a negative perception about themselves that persists even when they change cities or continents. Many people with this mentality still believe that without a white minority leading the way, it is impossible for Blacks to make it. They believe Blacks cannot be successful farmers even if given the land and all the necessary resources. This damaging state-of-mind mentality continues today in most parts of Africa and the world among black people. When a white person enters a room or among blacks even in city work places, the atmosphere changes immediately. Unless farm people see white men, they do not believe the farm will be successful. A colour-inferiority complex stands in the way of many black people in Africa as if it is their God. And such low self-esteem destroys what intellectual strength they have.

When we went for sport events, we ate buttered bread slices with the nation's beloved Mazoe juice drink. The enemy to be feared was the teacher at school and the white man at work on the farm. Whites forced us not to call a small white child by name but address them as a small boss or "madam" if a girl. Choice was never an option here but just dancing to the tune of the farmer the order of the day. Most parents knew the value of an education and forced their children to endure the pain of school until the end of the school years. Eventually, it would pay off, they reasoned.

Bullies at schools were the frequent enemies of innocent kids. We could not take our lunch packs near the schoolyard because it was possible that we would not be allowed to eat since the bullies would often take them away from us. Many of them were older than we which gave them an upper hand when squabbles developed. Just going to school at all was the hardest homework to ponder, as it tarnished the joy of learning with pain. Farm parents knew nothing about helping their children with homework. This was because most of them were not educated and neither knew how to read or write. But parents did show much love to their children and families on Christmas day, as almost all farm children dressed in new clothes on that day. They also ate great meals and paraded to special places around the farm chanting Christmas greetings and taking photos if there were camera operators booked for the occasion. Christmas was a momentous occasion here even if many people were not aware of its true heavenly meaning.

Most farm people were religious and spiritually awakened by the little knowledge the farm masters gave in order to subdue them. Even though these people had many forms of worship, they lacked good teaching and revelation about the Biblical God. Polygamy was common here since most of these people came from rural areas where culture reigned supreme. My uncle had five wives and was a devout member of the seventh day Adventist church, but had little understanding about marriage and the Christian life. He would take all his wives in his old car to church every Saturday. He was a farm supervisor and a mechanic. When it came to consulting with medium spirits, he excelled. Such double life styles were common among those who grew up on the farms. All children got special clothing for Christmas and sumptuous meals were cooked and served on the day. Celebrating Christmas day in new clothes was a custom here. My uncle had twenty-six children and most of them were already grown and out of his home.

When going to school, students would hide their lunch packs near bush grasses where they would be sure to be able to locate them when going back home. Meal packs were hidden in such a way that no one would see them except the owners. It was devastating if ever anyone saw where you put your meal, for they would most probably steal it. You would get back and find out that there was nothing there where you had left your meal. Bullies would hide at various points in order to see where the children hid their lunches, and then steal it or simply move it somewhere else after the children were gone. Sometimes criminals would also be a nuisance in this habit of stealing food. Criminals would lay hold of the food in the same way the bullies did. Students at times were instructed by police and parents to walk in pairs or groups when going to school or coming home since crime was another matter of concern. This was because crime against children would get unbearable at times. Students would complain of meals being stolen from the places they would leave them in the bush, but this was common though it varied according to areas.

The school term was ending; all the students were excited about the coming holidays, which meant more time for play. There was no easy solution to stolen meals; this became a crisis at one of the farm areas, which was some distance from us. The parents and students would get angry at this wanton habit of the thieves in the society. It was not easy to bring justice in the situation, as perpetrators were hard to catch and even dangerous when caught red-handed. A week went by, and the school received shocking news about the death of a student from poisoned food. It was not clear whether it was his food or if the poison was a trap to kill the thieves. The student was barely able to walk home after taking the meal, a source revealed. The father quickly put the boy on a donkey cart to rush him to a clinic that was nearly twenty-six kilometres away. He could not approach the farm boss to ring the ambulance or rush his son to the hospital. This could have been because he feared his boss or for some other reason.

Farm bosses were usually hard and difficult to work with. A car would have saved the poor boy's life, as he died after having travelled about ten-kilometres on a donkey cart to the clinic. Until today, the police have an open docket on the case. Learning was important and few children managed to finish grade three here and went on to grade four until grade seven elsewhere. At Pakama primary school, the environment was good as they had nice classrooms and enough teachers some of whom were nice and understood the farm children's situations. The school was opposite the railway workers cottages, but the majority of the children came from nearby farms.

The set up was different here and the gum trees were fewer with more peach and apple trees in the schoolyard. A good number of teachers, who taught in the school, used apple tree branches to cane children. We had to persevere to stay in school here also, attending classes under these harsh conditions. You would see some students run away and never again set foot on the school premises. It all depended on what the school meant to you. This was the state of twentieth century education on this side of the world. Going to school in those days was not for sissies and most failed not because they were dull or slow learners but from fright of abusive educators within the school system. Ironically, now, that school freedom is great students choose drugs and voluntarily become gangsters.

The unbalanced scales of justice

The world is a classroom in which we learn and our experiences a well from which we draw conclusions. All over the world, you will find the poor and the rich. These two kinds of people make up the societies around the globe. Riches or poverty knows no colour. The middle class is comprised of the poor striving to stay afloat on the bread line with the hope of a few goodies. The poor or less fortunate are simply those who cannot earn a living by themselves. These people are below the bread line in terms of economic classification. The problem goes beyond simple scarcity of resources, which many believe is what shuts out the masses from the economic mainstream. Something has happened to them; of course, they do not want to live life unhappy, unfulfilled and without success. I believe they wish above all, to succeed and make it. But the problem they face is bigger than we all think it. It is impossible for them to make it when the main pillars of success-development are not there.

In many parts of the world today, people find themselves dispersed from their native lands against their will or choice. Here their homes are destroyed, jobs lost and professional skills they have mean nothing, as language ends up being a barrier in other countries around the world. Those with money will have to spend the little they have seeking asylum outside their borders with their beloved ones. Most wars fought are to dominate certain classes of people or to liberate and free them from an oppressor's hands.

Unfortunately, the rule of law is usually biased in regard to helping the weak and the helpless, and are enacted for the purpose of baring the masses from equitable wealth distribution with the rest of capitalist society. Unjust laws in trade, mining, farming, fishing and land distribution and ownership are still a problem facing Africa and most parts of the developing world. It seems there is a society that pushes others off to the side because of colour or money. Many African people in Africa are finding life to be hopeless. They are going where they would not like to go, and lose their most valuable commodity, which is the right to own their own land and have meaningful lives.

Modern economies are fine if they do not damage the lives of ordinary people by taking resources from them and giving them all to a few individuals. This inevitably leads to a poor standard of living for the rest of the masses. I do not resent civilization, globalisation and economic development. But when development and growth is at the expense of the poor, you will see a vicious circle of poverty and disease that keeps people trapped in a catastrophic world of shame and underdevelopment that is attended by starvation and hunger. Slums and squatter camps are today erected illegally around big cities by poor mobs that are fighting for survival all over Africa. These people have no financial power but their message is clear and heard by all. All the good land has a rich owner's name on it and even governments cannot easily access the land for use by the poor.

The survival of the poor societies is at the mercy of the rich. There is no job security. And if the poor are hired there is no justice as to what they will be paid. Instead of dying of hunger, men and women have chosen to submit to the modern slavery tactics of the rich. The ones that control the economies have control over cities and countries. That is why Nelson Mandela once said, "If black people cannot control the economy, it means they are not yet free." The plight of the poor in Africa is a nightmare as many live on less than one dollar a day. Millions of poor on a daily basis are not able to meet simple basic needs. The economies seem designed to keep all the weak and less fortunate in the vicious circle of poverty.

Indeed, we can agree that there is little chance for the poor to stand on their own two feet if their government leaders do not do their part in paving the way for equal platforms for all people. The same problems of education and housing are forcing many people into poverty as in the colonial days. If the African child is busy trying to earn a living rather than go to school, it is because he/she cannot afford education. Food and clothing come first and this is what all people must have before we can of schooling and many other issues. With so much challenges lying ahead, African states will have to refocus their policies and constitutions to suit the interests of their national goals. African states are doing very little to get their people invested back into their economies. Unless the governments of Africa get serious about empowering their citizens, the continent will never come out of poverty even with much foreign investment. True economic empowerment results when local people are able to creatively grow their own economies in a way that is comfortable, safe, and constantly improving.

Evil wars have distorted the historic heritage of nations and have given warlords and the puppets of the evil masters' theories an upper hand to strengthen their grip on resources so that the deserving people, who are supposed to benefit from the fruits of freedom and peace do not get their fair share. The large masses whose votes were needed for elections were thereafter dumped, and neglected by the same politicians, who promised all people a better life. Maybe, "all" meant all the rich only. Crying foul in the next election campaign is the usual way for the poor to know their votes are considered important but they are paid back with bad service delivery and false promises.

Most of the faces of leadership are now black on the continent and have in one form or another experienced oppression unlike the white faces that occupied the offices during the apartheid regime. The new constitution should not be a cover up, resembling the blue print of the colonial masters' copy. The residue of apartheid still haunts the nations of Africa and the world today. The enemy of Africa was racism, and now it is economic injustice in the name of globalization, development and foreign investment. This includes even black empowerment incentives and affirmative action programmes which are marred with corruption and nepotism. Apartheid took a few blacks from among the others and used them to benefit the apartheid masters with the lion's share. Black African people speak western languages depending on who was the colonial master in that country in accordance with the manipulative system of the day. Today the educated are sitting in Parliaments using the architectural blue print of the masters of segregation to neglect the people who are supposed to benefit. The poor are getting very little in return for taking part in elections. The corruption rate in Africa illustrates this, as it is mostly linked with tribalism, poverty and bad governance.

History shows that even education followed colour preference on the continent of Africa and the rest of the world. In South Africa, per year, a white student received an R18 000 subsidy while the black child only received a R25 subsidy from the regime government. The so-called superior races of the day were favoured by the entire law system since it was designed by their own. It empowered one race and among Blacks promoted lifting up one gender. Governments must serve as a true foundation if they want to address the questions of poverty, racism or gender inequality in Africa. I believe the sleeping giant is rising up and that the people of Africa will not only have land development but people development, and form a great human capital base. The black child of Africa has yet to equate independence and freedom with self-respect. The people have to design policies that will redress them with respect, honour and dignity. The fight for independence and democracy is almost over now as almost all countries have achieved this goal. But the battle for true emancipation is still going on with the focus now on economic liberation and I believe the people of Africa will win yet again.

Most politicians have defined freedom with only a correct spelling on paper and lip service without a real plan of action. It is time for the African nations to bring substance to their freedom by defining what it needs to be. The founding fathers of Africa only took it so far, and now we must lay one brick on another and build precept by precept on the foundations of this democratic structure. It will soon be fully complete through a just means of leadership. It will take hard work and determination to arrive at this destination, and the only recipe for success is that we help other people not toil alone nor become an obstacle to achieving a prosperous continent. We have to hold hands and move with one purpose and vision to bring freedom to our nations. The greatest blessing is not when a few people make it or succeed, but it is when we all make it. I believe this is the generation to drive it home.

Poverty is increasing instead of decreasing in Africa because of the governments' slowness to change their old leadership styles. Equality comes when people are developed equally and inequality in development is a problem all over the world, as no one seems to get this puzzle right. Most countries are struggling to offer equal education to all their children, which has been the greatest stumbling block to these countries development. The foundation of colonial interests robs people of equal wealth distribution options. Begging from former colonial countries in the name of good trade relations to most leaders of Africa is the best way of running economies. I pray they will soon drop that technique and start utilising their own countries' resources with joy, peace and dignity. Failing to educate a nation and to help people to acquire decent housing is a missing link between economic empowerment and the development of any people. Creative potential resides in all people regardless of where they live and colour. As long as people do not get opportunities to unleash their potential, the potential in them dies unborn.

It does not mean the only people with talent or potential come from abroad. It is a damaging mindset of African leadership that sees potential in other races of people regarding themselves or their own they say, "Will these bones live again?" Start to believe in yourself and others and see them as God sees them. This will make you afford others the same opportunities as all other people. The biggest breakthrough of Africa will be when the potential of all the masses begins to be ploughed back into the formal economy. Now, only a few people are trying to plough back and it is not affording third world nations much in terms of building good economies within their countries.

A worse injustice is the distribution system of the apartheid era where billions in taxes are allocated to rich suburbs compared with just small budgets going to ghettos and black townships. Demographics and population statistics are not used, but rather it is a matter of past implementations, and it has been like that for centuries, which is why today governments keep it that way. That is why ghettos and townships, though highly populated have few resources to help the vast numbers of people. The evil of the apartheid era was that it neglected the blacks and the present generation is reaping the fruits of the racially painful seed sown, which forces it to toil through the searing furnace of joblessness, hunger, poverty and crime. It is tragic that many people who suffered under apartheid can hardly stand on their own two feet economically, even in this day and age. They assert that other races spitefully abused them, told them they were nothing, and groomed them to be a hopeless group of people, lacking even in manners and discipline. High school dropout rates and drug abuse point up the cracks in our societies' foundation. A hopeless generation cannot raise up its own children well but merely perpetuates the same lifestyle for future generations. People can only stop this curse if politicians begin to bring changes and ways of governance ways that are fair and smart. Leaving the masses underdeveloped is a travesty of justice on the continent.

A few greedy rich are responsible for a system that has given the rich easy control over the world's resources and up until now, this has indirectly denied the masses their right to live. When the rich tighten their grip on resources, nations groan as the resources get to a few while the rest of the people starve, which in turn makes good service delivery impossible to reach the poor masses. Ministers are puzzled at the failure of implementation processes in Africa. But you cannot use the same apartheid era ways and still deliver services to people in the current day and age. Unless the root causes of this generation's failure and problems are dealt with, the road to good governance and fair service delivery will continually become more slippery within the poor continent.

It does not take a rocket scientist to tell that service delivery in Africa has been stalled and held back by those colonial entities who went before us in addition to those in power today. The solution to the plight of our generation can only come if we are able to separate the good of the past from the bad. The remedy is to dismantle and transform the old policies of governing that mistreat people, and seek total reform. When equality becomes a reality in Africa, we will then be able to effectively deal with homelessness, poverty, joblessness and many other issues that affect the continent masses.

We need more native sons with new creative ideologies in order to break the enslaving yokes that African nations have been bearing for too long. The once famous and the rich blacks, who now live behind the high walls of posh suburban houses, as if it is because life looks great and tastes better only there, will again inhabit our ghettos and townships only when the environment becomes better for all. Someone programmed it that way and no one seems to have the guts to change it. We need to pool our efforts and resources together in order to overcome this stigma of segregation and poverty. Using inherited policies makes absolutely no sense in most ghettos of Africa and the world's poor places. It is as if the other communities do not matter. Their places are dirty and stinking as if they were meant to be poverty-breeding zones. This is where many people find themselves and it is not what they want, and I believe all who live in such places are crying for change. But change is hard to come by and who can trust any leadership in government to bring change that people want? It is only the voters at times.

Governments have to serve all their citizens not just a few rich minorities. An evil government does not want to give people their dignity and right to life. On paper, all may be regulated well but practical implementation is denied. There is a problem of identity crisis on the African continent and many people seem as if they are just wandering through life. We have many people who do not know who they are, where they come from, and where they are going. Often they have no fixed home. Wanderers cannot participate in building their countries' economy. They are unproductive because they are ill-equipped and have no settled home. This kind of people has no firm place in society whatsoever. They need to be established in order to play an effective role in their countries' development. Only by means of empowerment and justice can they rise up again, otherwise they will be swept by the wayside for the rest of their lives.

Investors tend to invest in countries where conditions are favourable for them and if anything bothers them, you will see them leaving to go to other countries. Indigenous peoples can benefit in their countries if they are empowered and given a chance to play a role in their own economies. The main obstacle is that many black people do not believe they can perform equally well as other peoples. For too long such low esteem has hindered black Africans from being role players in their own economies. I am amazed at the number of black Zimbabweans who believe Blacks cannot farm!

Now that there are not many Whites farming in Zimbabwe, someone has to farm and feed that nation regardless of what anyone says or else it will starve to death. People who say Blacks cannot farm have seen only white folks running farming businesses and have never asked themselves why this is so. They tend to hope for a white man to give them employment rather than to create opportunities for themselves. The heart of a government's leadership must be right, that includes its planning and development strategies in order for it to benefit people equally. This is where everything must start.

I have noticed that every country in Africa is unique. Some countries have produced a variety of professionals while others have just produced just a few. No nation should take from another nation, as this will hamper progress on the continent. Every country must be productive and able to raise its own skilled and educated people. Otherwise, certain classes of people will flock to countries they think have better work opportunities and lifestyles. This creates a problem for a developing continent such as Africa.

That is why xenophobic attacks were based on some taking jobs from others in South Africa. There were two groups of people, who had problems. The first group was those with little education who wanted to earn a living in a tough economy, and the second, the foreign skilled workers who came to South Africa in search of greener pastures. Many of these foreign people have businesses in big cities like Johannesburg and others. When these people could not get employment, they made jobs for themselves and then employed a small number of South Africans. The salaries they paid to their workers were not great, as this remains another weak area: African brothers and sisters not respecting their own people.

I remember looking at the city of Johannesburg during the wave of xenophobia and seeing that trade had come to a halt, as many businesses were under the ownership of African foreign nationals. The rents were very high and the property owners loved it when foreigners would pay those bills without complaints. Locals would not pay that much because they knew the value of their money. Looting took place but many locals had only few days' meals from their loot and thereafter were back to being hungry again. The African child has been poorly equipped to beat hunger and poverty when denied employment. The blame is given either to the government or to someone else for where they are in life. Even if true, we must do something about it in order to move forward.

It may be true that the governments are not doing enough, but what are citizens doing? The educated foreigners who had professional jobs were prospering, yet they watched their local peers remain in ignorance, wandering about on the land without skills or creativity. A snare to any nation is to have many people not working nor given a chance to play a role in their economy. Their foreign peers have managed to acquire better work skills because their governments allowed them to enter school when times were good and those governments' economies were prospering. After a long run, things came to a standstill and the number of people doing nothing increased, as countries could not afford them a better life. The great economies collapse caused by job cuts and job losses affected their countries. The truth is without a skill or qualification one cannot move from one job to another, and also professions and qualifications become of no value when there are no jobs.

Lack of skills and human capital development brings about a situation with a generation of unproductive people, who are weak links in the circle of economic empowerment. And the children of people in this circle also go the same way in the world. A small number of people paying taxes to fund the masses' lifestyle shows that there is a mistaken diagnosis. Governments cannot collect much revenue from a handful of working class people. Neither can the private sector absorb all who need jobs into the workforce. Have African governments done enough to help the economies in their countries? It is not fair for a generation to pay for the previous generation's failures. The next generation will follow suit, which means we will be beset with problems we cannot solve if not careful and will in turn pass them on to coming generations. The World Bank and the IMF, for example, charge compound interest on debts unpaid by borrowers and payment can go from generation to generation.

Nowadays, the IMF and World Bank only cancel a debt loan if the debtor country is too poor and cannot afford to pay it back. The problem in very poor states is the lack of people development. Almost every African state develops people on government bursaries, who in turn do not work for the same governments. Often they go to work for the colonial master countries and language is a major factor here. African states just have to accept the losses as other countries lure their professionals away with better working conditions and pay. Most first world countries have low birth rates and an aging working class that will need replacement soon. Those remaining behind in African countries are a few professionals with a majority of illiterate people.

This is the locust that is eating up African economies. If all people were productive and literate, Africa could quickly go to higher heights. Quality work place management remains poor on the continent. Long queues in our hospitals and government departments show the lack of qualified professionals and staff. This means that a few employees are trying to serve these crowds who come to the departments to get service. Is there enough money to hire more staff? Some will choose to say only God knows. Our economic solution lies in not allowing a few greedy to have all the land and resources while the rest suffer lack and starve to death. Can people do what they do best and make a living? If so, can people have decent places to live and do what they do best? The economic system seems to have changed quickly in Africa as it has exploited the poor and given an excess of wealth to the rich.

South Africa xenophobic disruptions left many black foreigners homeless and others dead and many lost their businesses and assets. They were looted by locals who had little understanding of how big the enemy they faced was, and showed their biased perceptions. Black locals defended their actions and justified them with the perception that foreigners were taking their jobs. Most of the foreign nationals had qualifications and what I call survival skills, which made it easy for them to earn a living in South Africa. If they could not find jobs, they created their own and hired locals, whom in they paid very little. On job interviews many locals, when asked about their salary requirements, would say, "I will take anything." That is the most common answer you would hear from most black locals, as there is a high rate of illiteracy in the country. It is imperative for Africans to begin paying each other what is fair rather than discriminating based on tribe or national status.

An African boss can hire two people, one black and another white and the two can be doing the same job with the same qualifications and years of experience; yet they are paid according to their colour. The white worker is paid more in most cases. Most black men love a white front in their work place, and the white men love a black face if it serves as a front for government tenders or other business favours where they cannot otherwise breakthrough. With the credit crunch hit companies so hard, if you were a black boss in Africa you were the first to be affected. This is the philosophy of the old ways, which says that if black you are not good enough and it still works in most of our organizations today.

The mentality of a superiority complex versus an inferiority complex amounts to brain washing among blacks. People who have an inferiority complex or superiority complex are biased and do not believe they are equal to other ethnic groups or people. It is sad to live life thinking you were created lesser or better than other people. Uncompromising leadership serves all people equally without fear but a cowardly one becomes guilty of doing favours for the dictatorship that put it in power, who are usually the dominant race or corrupt rich. Justice is hard to find here but this system cannot succeed in the twenty first century because people now have eyes to see compared to before when only a few were educated.

The majority of African fathers could not raise up real men or women. They pampered other races' children but turned to their own and taught them they do not matter and will never be equal to other races. Neither was a black child told he or she could amount to anything. This damaged the self-esteem of many black children. As long as the best service goes to a white minority, it is all well as this is the mentality here. It destroyed the zest for life in black children and made them think life is mere existence rather than to unleash their potential to do more. It is a shame to see how colour affects a black child in Africa. When you see blacks working piecemeal lowly jobs of paving and construction for white companies who pay them little, you may understand how deep this problem is in Africa. If a nice car or thing belongs to a white person it is all right, but a black man does not deserve good in the mind and eyes of many Blacks. If you cannot love and appreciate yourself, you will not love your fellow men. An inferiority complex is a result of a damaged ego. It abases you and others like you and lifts up other people because of their colour or status in life.

I have often seen black waiters and servers in my country not willing to serve their own, as they perceive they will not get a gratuity at the end. They must have a sign that says, "No ordinary blacks welcome here, celebrity blacks only." Ironically, a white person will serve a black person well with a smile expecting nothing back and finally get a good tip or gratuity from the same black man or woman. Some Africans, if they cannot serve the supposedly "better race" here, will better fly overseas and stay there illegally among white communities claiming to be a refugee or suffering in their own countries. There are genuine refugees but these are just a burden to add to the number of refugees and in real essence are not.

When a black man works for his own in Africa he will not get what is fair and so only puts in what he thinks his pay is worth. If in London a black person chases the pound in four different jobs and eats only a hamburger a day, he is okay with that as long as he sees many whites. His heart is happy and faith in whites says to him, "You have arrived." This was the mentality instilled in them. I worked for a government department and invited my grandmother to my work place. When I introduced my boss to her, she did not look impressed since he was black. Later at home, she asked me if I had another boss who was white. I said no, and she said Blacks know nothing and are not good bosses. She resented successful blacks and this is simply what she was taught. That is why many black people do not respect even their black presidents and vice versa. Even when a white man pays a black man very little, the black man is still happy and some have even given up their chosen professions to do menial jobs, as good jobs are scarce even abroad.

Rich property owners prey on these poor people and this becomes their target market. Most of these people are usual illegal in countries of work. I was often heart-broken when I saw how foreign construction and restaurant employees were taken advantage of in South Africa. Also on the receiving end were foreign farm workers. They would accept anything and end up getting next to nothing, as ruthless employers would call in their corrupt police friends to arrest all those who were illegal in the country without being paid or before payday. They would work without pay for months. Most foreigners in Johannesburg live in Hilbrow and the surrounding suburbs. Some have acquired fraudulent identity documents while the rest cannot afford the price and have no form of identification.

Those with identity documents apply for flats and then share with others as it is impossible for many of these people to afford the exorbitant rents. From building owners to city council workers, it seems like no one cares or has respect for these communities. The crime is rampant here as all are forced into a survival mode. Hilbrow, Berea, Yeoville, Bez Valley, Jeppestown and down town Johannesburg have had many building hijackings at an alarming rate for too long. Unjustifiable rates and taxes, the abuse of foreigners by police and drug dealers who launder their money through property investments are all shocking to say the least.

Moreover, xenophobic attacks are a sign of the people being vulnerable and left only in the hands of God's mercies lest they die in hunger. It is not even real xenophobia but afro-phobia—directed mainly against African nationals. Political instability in African states is a cause of the many victims of afro-phobia, and the case in which critics of freedom and justice for the poor and helpless challenged the Johannesburg Church Bishop of the Methodists. The continent is looking for men and women to stand up for the cause of freedom. Cowards who want to hide under legalism and the obsolete policies of their countries and organizations will come up short from now on. We will yet see another revolution in which responsible counter parties will take the bull by its horns. Black nations cannot live side by side and walk shoulder to shoulder because they do not understand who they are and who their family is. The curse of this stigma is that anyone black is not good enough. I never saw these attacks affecting other races—only local blacks fighting foreign blacks.

Removing enslaving yokes

Those in authority and in leadership positions owe it all to those who voted them in and these are the masses they serve. It takes a joint effort of families, governments, churches and other organizations to play the important role of shaping people's lives and futures. Let the sole mandate of leadership be to serve people better and with a love for life. Love is the language that the blind can see and the deaf hear. The good heart is the pivotal muscle that drives out of us selfish motives and replaces them with the dynamism of great service to others, which makes us realize we are gifts to others. Can Africa act out its constitutions without fear of the foes of freedom and enforce the laws written in their freedom charters?

Good service delivery in Africa will mean laying a strong foundation of freedom in the twenty first century. The main difference between Africa and the first world countries is that democracy prevails better and justice is administered better abroad, versus the corruption and lack of justice regarding the resources and wealth in the great mineral resource centre that is Africa. The child mortality rate is a matter of great concern in almost all African states and in the developing world. This also goes the same for mothers who die giving birth, all of which shows a great need to educate women and men about contraceptive measures which can save about 100 000 lives a year as statistics have shown. The rich cry foul every time constitutions have to be changed or policies redrafted. Does it mean black leadership has no intelligence or cannot be trusted with this sensitive work? Surely if something has to be changed, it must benefit all people. Constitution is either the heart of freedom or the yoke of slavery put on the necks of people. If changed for the better it can serve all people and if kept unchanged, it only enriches a few. What is it that people and leaders are supposed to do? I guess administering justice well will pay off far better than we all expected.

When two elephants fight, the grass suffers. Why have leaders of Africa not worked as brothers but lived as foes of each other for decades? We have seen severe sanctions levied upon the nations of Africa at times. Where have things gone wrong? Wars and unjustified genocides have left many confused and questioning whether we know what we are doing as Africans and owners of the lovely land. The continent is battling to empower its own and redistribute land and resources, including ores, justly. Someone has made policies that make it hard to get into mining if being a black person. Why is it difficult for poor blacks to acquire land and farms as other races do and have been doing for years? The problems of unavailability of land to millions of people are because of a system that barred blacks from participating in the economic development of their nations.

A good home in a good area is a great asset to people once it is paid off. I just used bank language, as in the end they are the ones who bring fair value when buying or selling through a bank. A house or land is also recognizable collateral for borrowing purposes. Homes for people and education go hand in hand since they are two of the main pillars of economic freedom and development in any society. Every society needs these two things before it can go any further with economic empowerment and liberalisation. Other things are secondary. Without these two pillars, any group of people will always find themselves being victims of the system and having only one leg to stand on, being automatically removed from playing a role in the economy.

The number one thing that has halted development and progress in Africa and the developing world is illiteracy. Whoever owns the bank controls how it should distribute and run the funding of economic affairs including policies. The old dominant system makes it hard for the economy to be free from the hands of its previous colonial architects. A deeper and richer knowledge of economics can help us design a better economic system for the 21st century. We cannot afford to neglect education, which brings knowledge and power to govern properly. People can govern only when they are adequately equipped otherwise it is just hopeless lip service. Africa now needs real economic liberalization and it can only come by empowering the children of the soil for the future as other races have done with their own for centuries. The countries must grasp the concept of globalization in its much-advanced stage of operation today. How can globalisation work well in Africa without her masses having the buying power necessary to participate? Will it benefit the people at this stage? Are the climate and conditions right at this present time? All stumbling blocks must be removed before we can tackle such pivotal economic shift to develop products and ways to benefit nations though the rich try to hold on to power.

Successful leadership has nothing to do with leaders building themselves empires and holding resources. It is odious to pile up wealth unjustly as a leader. Rather one should build a legacy that all generations will look at and admire—a talent and gift of leadership to be treasured throughout many generations. Integrity is the essence of life and faithfulness is its cornerstone. That is why some leaders try to use religion without life or "Spirit" to trick and mislead nations. The desire and cry of every leader's heart should be to remain trustworthy until the end of his or her term of office or retirement. Political leaders should serve their people with all their hearts, doing all that they are supposed to do. They should neither use religion nor blame the past but do something with the time and trust people have given them. Times have changed, and simply using the past or religion as a scapegoat will not bring a halt to poverty and corruption.

Some people pay with their lives and yet some power hungry leaders stay in power and continue in their lies and dictator-like grip. Warlords benefit much as others lose their lives in the name of fighting for a freedom that never comes. The pleasures of wickedness will no longer taste sweet to many leaders in the twenty first century, for it is only greediness and vanity. Power hungry despots are dominating because of the support of a few who want their share of the spoils of war and are greedy for riches. Peace can prevail and wars cease in Africa if fathers and mothers take their place and lead Africa well. For now, many timid cowards are on thrones and hooligans, who instigate wars repeatedly on the continent, surround them. Both the lazy corrupt leaders and the war perpetrators are wrong as both commit evil acts.

Schoolchildren have to understand that time is life. An understanding of life is essential in evaluating events, work and purposes in this world. Dropping out of school will never answer the plight of poverty; disease and suffering that plague this world. Morals make a person. Discipline and work are not swear words. Ignorance is stupid and backward, most things in which we fail and find ourselves struggling today is because our parents' generation stumbled. Two things worked against them, illiteracy and lack of decent housing. Those who got a chance to acquire house bonds and credit worthiness never obtained these two essential ingredients of a happy life as they only fell into the trap of credit debt and bank control that kept them vulnerable all their lifetimes.

Many banks in Africa take advantage of people as they seek to do away with good competition principles and charge high prices for services. These banks charge a higher interest rate to their clients than do their peers in other parts of the world. The banks in Africa have made sure that this market sector remains protected by unjust policies so that their black rivals cannot own a fair share in this market. In South Africa, some banks were blamed for charging the same flat par interest rate to clients as they had fixed the industry under one roof. We see banks repossess houses and movable assets from people constantly. During the credit crunch, it was worse and this is a sign that there is a need to revisit financial institutions' policies and overhaul the industry completely in order to sort out major problems that hinder future development.

I do not mean banks should not take houses and cars back including other assets if people do not pay or when they cannot afford to pay back loans. African bank operations are marred with so many flaws. Are there other options available to meet people's needs without forcing them costly mortgages that they cannot even afford to pay back. Access to land and good jobs is a better answer to the problems people have. Those who cannot pay a bond loan or afford one, are considered a high risk and are left in the hands of unscrupulous business people. Another option would be to apply for city land, which is hard to come by around any African cities. Only now are African cities developing new cluster style accommodations and moving away from the township model. This new model is not cheap, and the size is even smaller than the townships sometimes, the reason being given is that the land is expensive.

African children need to stay away from drugs and become movements instead of monuments. The problem is that we have many people doing nothing or killing themselves through addictions and useless life styles. The result is much waste of talent and life. Some seem to think that life is just occupying space on earth and consuming resources until the end comes. There is no purpose to live for in this kind of lifestyle. Nothing is accomplished or fulfilling here. A big temptation in the world today is the short cut. But if we hold hands and respect ourselves as a people we can overcome HIV and AIDS, poverty and illiteracy. A big crack in the foundation of society today is the prevalence of immorality. Many people regard broken families as a substitute to a normal family because of broken marriages that have turned out to be the norm among many of our societies.

Can the selling of one's body or prostitution be a means of survival for some people? Let us consider its long term fiscal rewards to both them that earn a living through it and those caught in this addiction that has swept society into desolate places mercilessly without notice. The frustration with this old profession—that never operates independently and openly—is the alarming number of youngsters twelve and up who flock to join it in many urban areas. It is an easy way for them to earn a living. I think it is easier to indulge in it than to work for oneself or be self-employed doing honest work. Nevertheless, I understand that in some cases they have looked all around and seen no other way they can save their lives nothing else that can save their lives from hunger. The only lifeline left to them is selling their bodies for cash to buy food, clothes and pay rental rates that are too high.

On the other hand, young men cannot easily sell bodies though some do on a small scale. Young men tend to join older criminals in their different criminal careers. The jails are becoming crowded, and what we need to do is to remove all enslaving yokes off the necks of people. Some are of the opinion that you cannot make it in this life unless you cheat and are dishonest. It is because of this lie that many people go to jail daily.

This way of life is not true and one would realize this if he would stop but check his ways with the truth. Somewhere we will be able to see where we have fallen. If parents are divorced or dead and there is no reliable source of income, there is bound to be a problem with the children left behind, especially if there are no provisions made for their future. Are you disciplined enough to stay out of jail and start earning a decent living? Staying out of drugs, crime and prostitution is a good thing to do and everyone knows it. Let us not just simply judge people but also let us bring solutions to the problems, and they must be solutions which will save our generation and the generations to come.

When a man loves his wife and children and has no job, to take care of the family is an unbearable task. If that woman cannot afford to keep those children under her wings, they will soon become beggars and eventually specialize in all sorts of criminal activities if they do not receive guidance in life. Women have been gender victims too long and many of them love to play the victim role. This has been a fault in the society and because of breakdown among black families in Africa; it is not easy to build right morals in young people. Young and old Women are confused and frustrated in their lives. Without a remedy to their predicaments, they become the prey of heartless drug dealers and pimps. This generation is heading for trouble, as the society seems to continually fall apart. Human trafficking has become the order of the day in many parts of the African continent. All these grievous sins directed toward African women and children portend future serious plight. Africa and many of its third world peers are becoming enslaved again because of poor policy makers.

Why is it so? Is it because poor people do not have much to do with their lives except yield to those who need their services? It seems anyone can have control over them as long as they give them shelter, clothes and food. Teenage pregnancy and violence control our schools and societies, which is a result of drug abuse and infidelity. South Africa gang violence has gotten out of hand. There is a crack in the society and unless the police deal with such cases firmly, the country stands to lose people every day. Strong families form strong communities and strong communities in turn form strong societies of their nations. Are there still noble fathers and mothers in our societies? It seems many are fallen by the wayside and overtaken by pleasures of this life above the call of family duty and purpose in life. Children learn more by what they observe their parents do than by what they hear.

If this generation desires to free itself from all the snares of its failures, it will require radical solutions. It will take getting their hands dirty on some things and accepting that it has a responsibility to account for rather than blame the past generations for problems. It is not too late, Africa can beat the devil of underdevelopment oppression with all its ways that discard men and women daily into rubbish dumps and scrap yards or recycle centre scout sellers, who live unhappy, unfulfilled and unsuccessful lives. Jails are overcrowded, streets are a disgrace with the angels of the night, and on the other hand, hospitals and mortuaries cannot cope with the corpses that flood in there. We need to go back to the drawing board quickly, for surely this generation has strayed. Are we not a people? Surely, we are people and we can make this world a better place to live in if decide to.

Hope in fainting hearts

The final examination written and the year almost ending, all the final year students were gathered in the school hall. The class group was forever going out to face world challenges and the principal had a few words to say. The whole atmosphere was full of emotion and uncertainty about what to say to each other as we exchanged addresses in hope of future contact. There seemed to be a feeling in all of us that we were never going to see some of our classmates again, and indeed, it has turned out that way. "We once met, we shall meet again," this adage gave us hope as we began to bid goodbye to our fellow classmates.

The Principal's speech was short and concise as all the staff gathered in the hall to bid us goodbye in a farewell party. For many of us it was hard to accept the fact that high school life had come to end. Our final year party was marked by low voices filled with hope and a good expectation of the end result of examinations written, which were the culmination of all the years spent in school and, if passed, would be a licence to ride and drive the world in future. This party ended with fantastic peace and joy that affirmed to us that all was over and well. This was the time to turn over a new leaf.

The following day I came to pick up my belongings from the place where I stayed and departed. Many others, who were to leave for their various respective home areas, did so as well. Most of the students who came from outside the Matabeleland province boarded buses to their respective province homelands, towns and cities during that weekend. On arrival home, I stayed there two weeks before I went to my uncle's place. He worked by a ranch, which was forty kilometres away. The ranch owner had a dam construction company and I had done some piece jobs during holidays with his company. He told me to come back when I finished school and so I did, as I would have loved to work for his company. He seemed to be impressed with me and I hoped this would give me a good chance of getting a permanent job here.

Securing a job here would have given me an opportunity to study civil or mechanical engineering with this company. This was a multimillion-dollar company. Studying agricultural management was my other option if things went in that direction. I knew what to expect from the company owner as he was not an easy boss to work for nor to please. You could not just automatically get into your career path without having passed his test, which was to do all kinds of dirty work and then, if you endured and stayed, you might get a better job. I was prepared to start from any position where he wanted me. All his workers would go through this kind of screening process. At six in the morning, I would go and stand next to the working staff at his farm assembly office.

There were a few people here almost daily looking for work. The first day, he asked what level of education I had completed and who exactly I was, since it had been almost a year since I did a holiday piece job there. I think, just by merely looking at me, he could tell I had a vision and was going to get somewhere in life. I knew I would accomplish my mission and purpose on earth. This could have worked against me before the millionaire business owner who had no regard for educated people. Usually, most rich whites never liked educated people, who had not grown up among the farm ranches or in compound families. Employing unknown people posed a threat to companies of this type, as the working conditions were unacceptable and against the country's labour laws. Overtime was never paid and unkind harsh white supervisors subjecting everyone to hard labour rather than simply supervising was the order of the day. If you came from his ranch, and you refused to do something or reported him to the labour department offices, he would make sure what you did affected your whole family working for him and they would all end up losing their jobs.

Men as well as boys worked in companies of this type. In every way, the boss had better control of his workers than in a normal modern working environment where unions educate people of their work rights. Educated people found themselves under this yoke, which gave them a hard time and little chance to change the company operations as most times they would occupy lesser job positions compared to people from the Ranch or with their parents in the company. The Ranch owner told me to come back each day and I only received a "no job" answer every time. I was there every day and saw others being hired and I only was left to go back home daily for a month and half.

One evening, I sat down with my uncle and told him how I felt about the whole matter of job hunting at the Ranch. I had to go sleep early in preparation to walk a long distance the following morning. He could understand my frustration since I had stayed that long without a job breakthrough. I had to prepare to walk a journey of twenty-five kilometres. I had come the same way, so this was not a problem. I had planned to hitchhike home after the long walk. Early in the morning, I started off, walking home. At about eight o'clock in the morning, I had walked fourteen kilometres and I turned off to enter one farm and look for a job, as I was now desperate to raise money for the things I wanted to do before my final school results. I went straight up to the farm office where I met the supervisor who told me his boss had left for town already.

After asking him whether there were any vacancies, he assured me that there were some but added that men had never stayed on that job because it was hard. I asked him what job it was and he told me it was a tree-cutting job. You would dig large trees out by their roots and cut them into pieces making heaps of two meters by one and half meters high. This was a way of clearing pathways for roads on the farm. The pay was four Zimbabwe dollars per heap. No money was paid for digging and filling the soil back. As a country boy, I had done this type of work before and I was determined to take it. I considered nothing too hard or difficult to do. What another man has done I can do it better, was my motto.

The farm owner finally arrived and it was already half past one in the afternoon. He said I could never manage as I was about nineteen years of age. I asked for a chance and he agreed and loaded all the tools on the van and took me to the place on the back of the van. You would never sit in front with the white man since this was taboo. On arrival at the place, he showed me what to do, left me there, and said he would be back at about half past four. I went on with my work and did one heap and half. I felt this was the only chance I had. On his return to fetch me, he was amazed at the amount of work I had done in such a short time. Most older men did only a half or one heap per day.

That evening the farm owner told the supervisor and the other men who worked in the farm that my strength for someone my age was remarkable. Indeed, many came out to see my work and I became the talk of the farm until I left after four months. I was a very hard worker and did what no one else could do. That same evening I bought some bread and milk on credit since I had a heap and a half done which could now be my collateral, and he further told me he could not give me credit if I did not have the work done. The supervisor took me to a big abandoned hall where the community used to hold beer parties on weekends during past years. It had no doors and just looked to be bad news. It was right next to the river and the main road. I entered, rested and made a fire before I ate my food. It was the beginning of January and rainy season and the mosquitoes were very bothersome in here. Later I rolled my single blanket on sack bags and boxes, and lay down to sleep.

Every country boy knows that when looking for a job one must carry a blanket—forget about a pillow, that is luxury! The only risk had been losing my blanket to other men looking for a job. It was possible for some men to turn in, tired and wanting a place to rest in a seemingly abandoned hall, and to steal my spare clothes and the only shoes I had. I never had fear of anyone doing anything to me as I grew up being told that not even a lion can come near a real man, so it was at their own risk if anyone came near my territory trying to do me harm. I was more dangerous than a lion to my foes. Times had very much changed in the late eighties and the country's economy was showing signs of ailing. Job hunters came from all over the nation and were seen everywhere daily. This was becoming like a land of wanderers.

After two weeks working here, a Mozambican refugee and two other local compatriots joined me. The three arrived together and were much older than I was. The farm boss made me the supervisor though I never received any extra salary for that position; nonetheless, I could not turn down the promotion. We were now a band of brothers in the same hall where I lived. None of these men made even one heap a day. They would come and plead with me for rest but I could not allow it, as I knew my goals. My name was talked about so much around the place; it reached an old widow's ears. She lived on the farm with her nephew and she sent him asking to see me.

My surname caused her to want to see me. When she saw me she asked me whether I was related to a man whom she called by name and that man happened to be my father!

This was a relative and she ordered the nephew to help me carry my belongings immediately to their home rather than stay in the hall. It was sad to leave my work mates alone there. But they drank and smoked so much, that in some ways it was a relief even though I missed their company. I worked hard and became the farm's most highly paid worker. My cousin who fetched me from the hall to his home was married to a primary school classmate of mine who had not been able to afford entry into high school. The same went for my cousin whose job was a shepherd on the farm.

It was never easy to bear with the mentality of these kind of people. When the ordinary level results came out I did not go to fetch mine at once but delayed until the end of April. I had made money and could afford to shop for nice clothes and pay my one-term outstanding school fees on the day I collected my results. My results were not that great or as I had wanted. When I wrote my final year exams, I had a lot of stress going on in my life and that affected my performance tremendously. Still, after collecting my results I could now go and explore many more job opportunities. When I went back to the farm, it was only to resign and to collect my belongings to look for greener pastures elsewhere. I had heard a lot about the commercial farms and companies of the Mashonaland province from my work colleagues. Life was great there, according to them.

Having done agriculture and building at school, I was indeed equipped for this great province, which was alleged to have great job opportunities. I had made up my mind to step into new waters and this time it was to be as far as the far eastern high lands of the country. At the same time, I also loved the travelling and exploring opportunities. This has made me a capable executive. On my arrival at the ranch, I went home straight away. I was very tired after walking the long distance from Shangani station. The following morning, I went by the office and told my boss I was resigning and leaving effective immediately. He completely understood my decision and then sat me down in his office and wrote me my first job reference letter by hand. Then he wished me the best in my career endeavours while looking me squarely in the eyes. Though he never shook my hand, I felt his heart open up in love and joy towards me that day. It was as if we gave each other hugs.

A wall of segregation stood between us but nature's rule of love blessed us both alike. All my work mates stood outside quietly and waved hands as I said good-bye to them all. I could not shake their hands and give them hugs as this might have offended the boss after such a nice reference letter he gave me. On the reference letter, he wrote out his heart about me. Surely, I was an outstanding worker, leaving on my own accord to pursue my career interests. He had never shouted at me nor not paid me my dues even when he had an opportunity to do so as we had no written work contract. I really liked this man. My heart went out to the farm workers also, and I wished them well and above all for much focus in developing their lives—my parting gift to them. I had at various times shared my heart with them in relation to life and the importance of focusing on "first things first." The chances of seeing each other again were slim even as it had been with my former peers of high school.

I could look at the sum total of farm life and feel depressed and stressed as I witnessed so many people's lives doomed to this never-ending slavery furnace. It is difficult to know that some people will be spitefully used all their lives to benefit unappreciative masters. It is also difficult to understand this truth without trying by some means to help. Their children would most probably serve the children of the same master with the same heart attitude of the system that says you were born to serve people of my colour. I cannot stand this abuse of farm workers including the women and children. Its effect on me was to bring hatred and a fear of failure in my life. Working for a white or black man on a farm was to be under the yoke of failure in life. You would receive very little salary, called farm minimum wage, and a lot of abuse and hard work. When I considered the salaries paid to farm people, I realized it would make little difference if the farmers only gave the workers food and no money, which is what some farmers still practise in South Africa. The pain of seeing the lives of people failed by others or systems is horrible. The country had many graduates at this time but most had lost hope of ever getting decent jobs anywhere in the country.

After leaving, I wanted to go to Karoi first and see if I could get a job there before heading to Lake Kariba in search of employment. In this mission of job hunting I had always aimed high. I was always optimistic about getting a good job. There was not even one person I knew in the places where I was going but my hope sustained me through all I had to endure. When I arrived at Shangani station, I caught a bus to Chegutu where I was supposed to connect to Karoi. We arrived in Chegutu at about four in the afternoon. The connecting bus was delayed and we stood in queues for quite long while. Finally, it arrived and we boarded. I can speak the Shona language well and I sat next to a woman who was so kind and good to me. She understood my mission well and even told me about a man from Bulawayo who was working in the same farm where she lived. He was the only Ndebele-speaking (my language) man there. According to custom if I met him, he would automatically be like a brother or uncle.

We related to people largely based on language or region or even the faith they upheld. This is how tribalism and nepotism operated at work places within the country. It was always about who got there first and the new employees were supposed to dance to the tune of the senior people. Most mines and companies operated according to these same employment customs. If you were new at a job place, you had to work harder while the senior people could relax and only work when the boss was there. Thus, the new worker or workers would carry the burden of the whole workforce. It was better if the boss had allocated work portions to each worker; but otherwise, they never had any choice, but to do their work fully. Work inspections by farm bosses were strict and cruel at times, as some would get a wage cut for small, silly mistakes done. A wage cut meant, you would have a certain portion of your salary deducted because of a mistake you made or work you did not finish well. The amount of money deducted from your salary at the end of the month was a form of punishment.

The woman told me I could get a job on the farm and that the boss would like me since I came from far away. Being liked because I came from afar didn't mean a better wage package or promotion, it only made the boss happy, as he could abuse me more easily knowing I had come from afar. (It was not going to be easy for me to leave and get home quickly whenever I felt mistreated by the farmer.) The local area folks on the other hand, would immediately leave work if they felt abused or mistreated beyond measure. If fired from a farm, it meant you must leave immediately with all your belongings or else the farm owner would beat you up and put you out on the main road himself. Times were changing, however, even though farmers still took unfair advantage of workers. That was one of the reasons people from far away were preferred in this hidden slavery industry.

After more than twenty years since having left the farm industry I witnessed the same harsh pain in South Africa inflicted on a man who worked on a farm. It was in 2009, and I was driving from Upington to Johannesburg. A hitch-hiking man between Olifantshook and the Kathu area stopped me. I asked him where he was going and jokingly asked him how much he was going to pay me. He told me he was going to the police station and he had no money to pay for a lift. I told him to get in the car and we drove off. He did not look calm, neither did he look sick, but worried. I asked him, what was the matter? He told me his boss had fired him and, after beating him, had pointed at him with a firearm. The reason he was fired was because he had fed dogs twenty minutes later than the usual time on a Sunday.

His boss commanded him to get all his clothes and belongings and leave the farm without his salary. Therefore, he took all his belongings and sat with them by the bus stop while his boss was watching him. But when his boss drove back to the farmhouse, this man hid his belongings not far from where I had picked him up. There is no job security in farms and this is the main reason people have to have two homes that they cannot support. One home is in the rural homeland and one is near the work place, which is unaffordable to many. The system makes nomads out of people who were otherwise normal citizens. I had to go back to help retrieve his belongings to a safer place in Kathu. The man received a salary of five hundred rands (R500) a month with a bag of mealie-meal and a few assorted relish packs. I thought to myself, "Will white farmers ever change their attitude and ruthless behaviour towards black farm workers in Africa?" Nothing much has changed in the farming industry when it comes to workers' treatment and rights and that remains a big threat to Africa's food security.

The Mashonaland trip was a revelation to me. Indeed I resolved to go with the woman I met on the bus and went to the compound where my new relative-to-be was staying. When we arrived at the farm, she asked her husband to take me by the man's hut and the man was happy to receive me. The man that had accompanied me had to leave but was happy to see us so comfortable with each other. It was as if we had known each other for years. This was the magic of tribal love back then. We talked a lot, only to find out that I knew his family and one of my relatives was married there. Tribe and language had bonded us as people, but we were more than that now. I thanked God in prayer for having led me there safely, and then prepared for sleep. We went to sleep filled with much joy and love in our hearts.

In the morning, he took me straight to the farm office where many workers stood waiting to get their daily duties from their boss. He introduced me to the farm owner who hired me immediately. My new job was in the barn on the tobacco floor where I was to be a rough grade checker of different tobacco leaves, and put them in bales according to their group colours. The tobacco barns were so hot inside that I could not stand the heat and smell of the tobacco. There were many men and women working here even though they were paid very little. Some young men had just finished school like me. Among all the young women in the entire compound, not one had finished school and some were in polygamous marriages according to the culture here. Grocery purchases were usually made on credit to workers at the farm store where I bought a few things in cash during my first day at work. The next day it was hard for me to work inside the barn and I asked the boss to give me a different job.

There were two men building a new barn, and I was told to join them as my building knowledge and skill gave me an advantage here. It looked like things were better here until the end of month came and the farm owner counted bricks and paid me about Z$14, which was next to nothing. My salary was less than thirty Zimbabwe dollars and that was the shock of my life. A Z$15 went into my food account bill. There were no salary negotiations when you took a job; you would simply work and see what payment you got at the end of the month. The farm owner asked me what was I eating as my store bill was very low. I had only fifteen Zimbabwe dollars credit for food. Trying to save money here was like a taboo. On weekends, I thought would travel to look for a better job in Karoi town or Chinoyi but all was in vain. This farmer wanted me on the job even on weekends, which made it hard to move around to other places looking for a job. Though depressed, I persevered for few months and then left and went to Kadoma instead of Lake Kariba, which had been my first choice before. I was weary of being taken advantage of because of my skin colour and exasperated by the hurtful abuse.

I wanted a better job desperately. I rented a room in Kadoma and started travelling around Chegutu, which was the neighbouring town, and also other places in search of a job. Corruption was now rampant: supervisors and managers were asking for bribes in exchange for jobs in almost every firm including government departments and mines. I could not afford the bribes and neither was I willing to pay one. After two weeks in Kadoma, I met one of my high school classmates in town. We sat and chatted about many things and laughed a lot too as we shared our experiences with each other. He was not working either and we agreed to launch a strategy of job-hunting together.

A short while later, we came across a man, who had an open cast gold mining company about 70 km from Kadoma. He told us he would buy food and all our basic needs if we would work and stay by the bush where the mining took place. He offered us a straight salary amount, which we accepted. Staying by the bush was not bad since it was not during the rainy season. The mine was also legally registered and we fell for the offer, which was a viable project according to him. He took us to the place in an old battered car that shook badly all the way until we got there. He showed us how to dig and heap stones together for trucks to come and collect for the gold mills. Five people resigned the following day and others would come to join us almost on a weekly basis. Whenever they could not get their salaries, they would immediately resign and leave, as these people had had many experiences with open cast mine owners' greedy ways.

We toiled weeks and weeks here with no salary paid to us. After about six months, we quit without having received a salary. We have witnessed scores of thousands of people in the South Africa Aurora group, whose salaries were unpaid for years, even after its liquidation that itself has been marred with corruption and theft. Pamodzi gold has also failed workers in the same way. It is not that owners of companies and mines do not make money but this is just mere greed. It would be better if governments make it a criminal offence that imposes a jail term for Directors of companies who owe workers salaries. The liquidators have stripped the Aurora group of assets worth $500 million stolen from its mines, with a subsequent inquiry ordered into the matter by the Master of the High Court; we hope to see clarity in this matter. Many people take chances in a recession or challenging economic times, both companies and governments must be alert to deal with such crises and even prevent them from happening at all costs. Where are the unions when things fall apart like this? Most workers have lost faith in the unions of today, which align with politicians more than helping workers.

I would often hear about new job prospects from people but now I wanted to move on to South Africa. The time had come to part ways with my friend, and I boarded a bus straight to Beitbridge a border post town. On arrival here, I decided to look for a job first, as the requirements for me to cross the border were not in place. The place is very hot and people normally slept outside houses during the summer time. Accommodation in the slums was cheap and the cost of living in a town of this type was not expensive. The black market exchange of foreign currency was what benefited most dwellers of this border town even though it was illegal to engage in it.

On the first morning of my arrival, I walked to a bakery where I asked for water from the manager who was the owner's son. He shouted loudly, "Kevin, give this son of Africa some (mvura)," which is water in the Shona language. He was a young man who seemed to be starting to pull ropes in his father's business. After drinking the water, I asked for a job and was short-listed to join the night shift that same evening. If you seek, you will find and this has been my philosophy in life as nothing is impossible with God. My first job was in a bakery as a general night shift worker. The bakery heat reminded me of the tobacco barns of Karoi and only the smell of the two places differed. The barn smell was hard to bear while this one was nice and fresh bread smell good.

When morning came, my hands were sore with bread pan burns. That same morning I quit the job. I quickly applied for my travelling documents which were taking a bit long to come from the Zimbabwe government. I soon worked for a Construction Company and hardly got my full salary every fortnight. When the project was finished, the little I had went to start my small buying and selling business of imported goods. On the other hand, the same construction company got a contract to build the Matopo book centre by the town of Beitbridge. We worked nearly seven months without pay here; most of us left and never even received a cent for our Labour. The people involved in the project management lacked integrity and both the owners of the building and the contractor were to blame.

A week after I had quit my construction job, I came across an advert tagged on a pole. Even though I could not qualify age-wise, I went for it out of a gut feeling and handed in my CV application. The vacancy was for a sales man who had a general high school certificate and who was eighteen years of age. The department store name was Power Sales. Even though I was a year older than the required applicant age, I decided to take the chance. Many other people handed in their applications on the same day with me. When I got there, I realized that the regional Director of the departmental store was in the premises. He pointed at me and spoke with the manager who just nodded his head as I was going out. I felt like God had lifted his finger to point at me and said, "That's you, Frank." This is how desperately I needed a job.

The following day they interviewed the candidates. My time came and after a short interview, the interviewer told me that the branch manager liked me but my age was not what they asked for on the advert. I thought, "What a frustration!" The interviewer excused himself and went to the manager, who stood talking for a few minutes with him and then returned to tell me that my age was no big deal and that the job was now mine. Every day I was to put on a tie and be smartly dressed. I received my salary with no problem and could visit my parents and spoil them! After five months, the casual position was no more, therefore, the contract ended. I had applied for jobs with a few government departments yet no fruits resulted from these efforts.

I had my passport with me this time. I visited South Africa for the first time and it was at Messina, a border town. I fell in love with the country and made it a point that my next stop would be the city of gold, Johannesburg. I knew the problems of staying illegally in South Africa, as I had witnessed scores of illegal immigrants deported on an almost daily basis. That kind of life style inconvenienced those who lived it. At times they were arrested coming home from work and would lose all their belongings to ruthless property owners or criminals who knew them. I then determined in my heart if I was going to live in South Africa, I had to be smart.

One postal address of a friend who was in Johannesburg was all I knew or had here. This classmate from primary and high school had come earlier after dropping out of school. He always bragged about working in South Africa and about the great job that he was doing and his fantastic salary package. I booked a train from Messina and landed in Johannesburg the following morning of 17th of June in winter, then went straight to Fourways where he lived. It was easy to locate him since there were few people who lived around there who were from Zimbabwe. I arrived in Chartwell, Fourways in a taxi and asked to be dropped at 6th street. I walked down the street and saw a man working in a garden outside a yard at a distance of half a kilometre, and went straight to him. As I spoke to him, I heard through his speech that he was a Zimbabwean national.

He took me to his backroom, gave me food, and warned me not to go out as the boss might see me and fire him. Many white men of Africa are the same when it comes to mistreating black workers. These people had no life of their own here. This man knew my school classmate and he pointed through the window at the plot where my former classmate worked, which was about three kilometres away. My former classmate was also a gardener at the other plot and was staying illegally in the country. Amazed to see me, he then immediately denied his promise of having invited me to come to South Africa. He could not even stay with me for one night. He was into heavy drinking and feeling sorry for himself. I think in a way people of this kind got rid of stress and frustration that way. They feet spitefully used and that life has nothing to offer them, let alone being able to help anyone else. I went back with the other man, who was able to arrange an alternative accommodation at the Zevenfontein squatter camp for me. To stay there was my only remaining option.

I had to stay with a band of brothers at the squatter camp. It was cheap to start life from here though crime and many other things were just madness around here. The young men I stayed with took me to a flea market where we sold cold drinks, food and clothes at the stores with the majority of them owned by white folks. This provided me with money for job hunting around the towns of Johannesburg. After a week, I got a job as a sales representative, being paid on a commission basis only. We sold high quality dinnerware sets imported from France. I kept my weekend job and worked my way up. After two weeks of staying at the squatter camp, I met a young man who wanted me to share a room with him.

The band of brothers resented me because I was legally in the country though I did not have the work permit that allowed me to take up employment yet. Having strong roots from my parents' background with South Africa, it was only a matter of time to sort out my papers. I said my goodbyes and still met them by the flea market on weekends. I think the young man asked me to share his place with him because I had bought him a beer and he had heard how different I was from the rest of my compatriots. I don't drink but drinkers are sometimes my friends. The fun part of life at the squatter camp was how zincs made those temporary dwellings we lived in look like great dwellings. The country had a large backlog of requests for housing from its citizens and city accommodation was too expensive for most people like my peers and me.

The same evening I bought the young man a beer, makes me think it is what opened the way for me to sleep by a new place. He instructed me to wait until the boss went out to work in the morning and then I could go out, otherwise we were going to be in trouble. My roommate hid me for about two months here. One day his boss saw me, and right away, he liked me as my roommate introduced me to him as a friend. My friend's boss said if I wanted to stay by his premises, I would have to work one day a week in the garden as room payment. I thought this was fair and it also brought some relief and freedom to me. I chose to work in the garden on Saturdays and to do one day at the flea market, which was only on Sundays. I longed to be at church but believed doors would open for that later and they did.

I would attend a church in the suburbs, which had afternoon services for people who did not understand English. Some Blacks resented those who attended morning services with whites and some whites never felt comfortable when black folks came in their services. But some white folks understood the gospel truth and never had a problem with us as they called us their brothers and sisters. A white man calling you brother when black was hard to come to terms with, as it was unusual for people of my colour and class to be respected by this so called "special" and "superior" ethnic group. A chicken mentality and abuse had messed up our minds. Slowly, the perfect love of God set us free and we began to feel at home. These were different, loving people; you would think they were from a heavenly planet! Great blessings flowing to blacks from white folks and from blacks to whites were hailed as a sign of a new dawn of a nation healing. This was actually the point when I got a changed mind set about whites. I was sick and tired of the groups of youngsters, who had no dreams in life while blaming their colour. The mentality of such people stinks and being around them is asking for trouble. Neither could I fit in their cliques and clubs.

Now I could get a ride from the property owner to work. There was one day when I was coming from a sales meeting in Johannesburg. While going to catch a taxi home when I met some bogus cops, who flashed a fake police card to me and asked for my staying papers in the country, which I had to produce. They searched me and opened my briefcase for search as well. When they saw the beautiful dinnerware samples, they closed the case and forcefully took them from me. This happened on the corner of Bree street and Delvers Johannesburg. I realised later that those were bogus police officers. I had no alternative but to purchase another kit from the company. Not long after that I left my weekend rental place and took a place of my own not far from there. For some reason I felt I needed my space and that my roommate did also. I now needed to focus on my studies and become the person I always longed to be.

We were still friends and would meet often. Within a week of staying by my new place, there was a break in and some of my belongings were stolen. It was chaotic as security was not up to scratch here at the new place. I felt vulnerable again for the second time in the country. A few people lived around here and most of them did not work. Early one morning, the police surrounded the area, searched it, and arrested some criminals that they wanted, who had been on the run for some time. These criminals came from Alexander Township and used the place next door as a hide out. After that incident, I was able to live peacefully until I left Fourways. I saw many people; from my friends from the squatter camp to many that I met along the way on a daily basis some of whom went to jail after committing serious and violent crimes against other people.

I have realized that the people we mingle with in our lives have a great impact on our behaviour and actions. Show me your friends and I will show you where you will be in life tomorrow. Bad company always corrupt good morals. Most of my compatriots here ended up in jail because they had no morals or principles in life. One young man I had stayed with by the squatter camp went to jail for murdering a man during a house robbery. Hopes are dashed when a person loses the focus that is within their inner being. The truth is, when a person begins to be tossed by every wind of life, not sure who he is and needs to do, he ends up sliding on the slippery road with the rest of the people. "IN LIFE, WHAT YOU STARTED AND AIMED TO DO CAN BE ACCOMPLISHED IF YOU KEEP SEEING IT INSIDE YOUR INNER FOCUS." Your inner focus is like inner binoculars held by you, which only you can see through and by their guidance, walk in success and fulfilment in life.

Lawlessness hurts

When evil men rule, people mourn. Lawlessness is the unforgiveable sin of our generation. It has many consequences all over the world. I watched Angolan refuges who flocked into Zambia and Namibia because of renewed fighting between rebels and government soldiers in their country some years back and felt sad to be of so little help to so many people. I went into the camp and saw men and women with broken hands and legs. People were sheltered in tents. There were big signs with organisation names like United Nations and Red Cross and a small clinic inside the camp. Food rations were hard to come by and many children were starving. I began speaking to different people that were at the Nangweshi camp in Zambia and all I heard was how they had lost everything they owned. Some had managed to cross the border in their cars. The enemy was not just the war, as it could not start itself, but the people who had instigated and backed it for years.

The rebels enjoyed the looting of diamonds and the worst criminals were the suppliers of firearms and ammunition. There are two kinds of people who benefit in all the wars around the world: the rebel fighters and the weapons sellers. These last are often the sponsors of wars, and are major beneficiaries of the cruel rewards of conflicts. The accumulation of corrupt wealth at the expense of people's lives is common in our world today. These kinds of people have no regard for the life of others. Neither is justice for people an issue to them.

There are countries that have left the world puzzled as people wonder whether there is anything between the leaders' two ears. Surely, the love of money is a root of all evil here. We have seen it, especially on the African continent, where leaders have led as if they have no talent to lead. The motive is not to help people when many opposition leaders disagree with their governments. It is all about the hidden agendas of those who have an interest in the countries' business and wealth above good governance. There are always fools pushing the wrong political gospel and it makes the countries hard to govern. Almost all opposition party donations come from the enemies of people's freedom as they seek to get their way through sponsorship. Unjustified sanctions are evidence that the nations of the world are biased at times. I believe it is time for African nations to sort out their problems without outside influences. Africa does not only need to vote good men and women into office. It needs more than that: it needs good policy implementation and governance.

Unruly leaders have done much harm on African soil against their own people. What makes African leaders fight long wars and then only after many lives are lost, come and walk side by side and call it unity government? This is an obvious sign of the persuasive influence of a few and not justice. The same issues they never agreed on now suddenly align together. Is it because they do not know what life is worth or what they are doing? No, the problem is Africa is indirectly ruled by foreign influences of colonial entities. They will support whoever wants to do their will even at the expense of people's lives that are taken away by notorious wars. Children recruited to fight in these senseless wars are one example of the injustice of these civil wars. Rebel leaders who involve children as soldiers need to be punished severely by courts of law.

Protectionism, unfair trade with biased economic liberalization in global trade tactics is cruel and not right. The trend of African leadership is like that of colonial interests that barred others from having participation in the world markets or economy streams, and that regime still dominates many countries today. Certain countries could not trade certain things like cars and other products from certain countries or manufacturers easily. There is little access for native indigenous people of Africa to mining rights, farmland utilisation, pharmaceutical industries, and banking including insurance industries investment, just to name a few. The policies involved in the above-mentioned industries are backward and unjustifiable, as they have consistently failed native indigenous people. Those policies rule and are working even when its makers are gone; they serve as a blue print for the will of a few interested in enriching themselves even in the post-apartheid era time by opportunistic means.

The jails of developing nations are full with what I call economic criminal victims. Many sons and daughters of the soil commit crime to live. Otherwise, if they do not pursue crime as a means to earn a living they will die of hunger. Corruption and power hungry leaders indirectly deny many people the right to live. All the xenophobic tactics we saw in South Africa were meant to push one man out of power in Zimbabwe. The strategy was that the masses would push him out after the heat became too intense. Was one man responsible for every problem that destroyed the economy of the country? Perhaps partially, but I am of the opinion that the many sabotage tactics used against the leader and his inner circle meant to make him relinquish power and call it quits are what really ruined Zimbabwe. The people that sanctions were never intended for became the main targets of the west as innocent masses paid the price even with their lives. Why was it like that? The enemy of true freedom has done this to make political changes to their liking.

Today we all live in a global village. We do things together as one family regardless of which part of the world we live in. The stock exchange companies have the upper hand when it comes to dubious dealings and shady profit margins today. Many of its leaders are practising fraud in the name of business investments. The only person who seems to lose money is the vulnerable poor who is the so-called investor who wanted to increase his cash. Companies closing down and liquidations are not the causes of recession, but underlying problems reveal that much damage can continue if no correct procedures are in place to tackle weak and traditional economic growth patterns. Recession is usually caused by a few factors, which are lack of investment confidence and no clear plan to address climate change nor better fair economic development around the globe. The world has always managed to empower a few while neglecting the masses for too long.

Some people have money but are sick and tired of being in losing traps. The racial divide, unfair wealth distribution accompanied by maladministration, corruption and fraud are bringing the world to a standstill of poverty. The suicide rate has been high worldwide and joblessness has become worse since the recession struck recently. Everyone is looking for their fair share but it is hard to come by. In most African work places, people's salaries are still based on colour, which is another matter of concern as I said earlier. This is a shame and an unforgivable sin in the twenty first century.

The workers at the government tender awarding processes are corrupt and those responsible for approving them are involved in kickbacks that enrich the government officials and their close families only. Huge bonuses are paid to parastatal management, banks and mine c-level executives even if financial losses are recorded to be high within those organisations is a sign of weakness in the system. The embezzling of state funds is common place in these challenging times that call for stern law enforcement measures. Funds that are supposed to reach the poor never make it past the hands of greedy politicians. The poverty gap, when not bridged or closed between various classes of people, threatens future developments. If accountability and responsibility, with transparency, were in practice and allowed to reign in Africa, it could be the best continent in the world! The cause of poverty in Africa is lawlessness. If the continent is to heal, it will require all its nations and people to participate in economic building rather than barring them by a system that only allows a few to play a role.

The fair distribution of wealth and services is what many are longing to see happen. The civil wars that we have seen taking place all over Africa are not fought in the poor countries but in the rich ones that have mineral resources and raw products. And the number one cause is the corruption in African states' leadership, influenced by greedy foreigners, who have been policy makers for African resources for far too long. I think it is time for African nations to break the yoke and be free from the slavery mentality of doing things. Africa needs to draft its countries' constitutions independently rather than being led and monitored by the rich developed nations, who are always turning things to their advantage while the African nations lose out. It is also time for the African Diaspora to help and use their knowledge to shape the continent before crises loom out of control. I believe African people can lead and run their continent well in this great democratic dispensation.

Often, what we see in Africa today, even among the war torn rich countries are new black taskmasters taking over in the name of investment, which tends to promote corruption and nepotism. Money often moves from one country to another through dubious means as those in power take it from government budgets. They are walking in the same steps as their apartheid business predecessors. The workers are paid little and there is absolutely no empowerment of the Blacks in these nations. They are just tools of the rich corrupt African business people of the continent. The rich only converge with black business chambers and investment promotion agents to take advantage of the poor.

If true empowerment had been allowed to operate in Africa, we would have had a first world-class continent. The nations of Africa would have afforded to look after their elderly better and to halve poverty and unemployment in a short time. Wars would have been considered outdated if justice had been allowed to prevail.

The burden of homelessness

Modern economy is great if it does not leave people behind but orders its affairs with an inclusive mind for all sectors of society. Unfortunately, it is not like that. Instead of a platform that should be giving equal opportunities to all people, globalisation has only fuelled the will of the rich and given them more of an upper hand in world economies. Globalisation is great for countries ready to benefit from it, but a snare to the developing and third world countries if not handled with caution. Some tend to win while others become losers in one way or another. The lives of rural people are in turmoil as they can hardly participate in farming and agricultural development. In most cases, the land they own is not good for agricultural purposes. Even if it is good land, their crops and harvests cannot get to the designated markets easily.

It is even hard to access a free and fair market distribution system in these countries. As things stand, conditions do not empower the masses but render them vulnerable to joblessness and poverty. And so, many people flock to big cities in search of jobs since there is no way they can survive in their own homelands or places. The rural people and their communities neglected too long is no help to development. When you see one or more beautiful homes in rural areas, you may know that they belong to politicians and businesspersons of the day. It simply tells me that these patterns of development are not valid unless all people get an opportunity to stand on their own two feet with hope for a good financial future.

As many flock to cities they cannot afford to live in, problems start right away, as many will do or take any job offer that comes their way. Indirect economic pressure forces many to labour for almost nothing. Many sons and daughters of Africa do not understand their freedom rights; some just hop from one country to another or from one continent to another in search of greener pastures that many only see and experience in broken dreams. It is a painful thing to find out that where you thought you would have peace you turn out to be a victim of circumstances that are beyond your control. Unaffordable prices for accommodation have made things hard in the cities and have promoted unscrupulous criminal syndicates.

Travelling all in Africa, you will notice squatter camps near almost every big city. Nairobi, Kenya has one of the biggest slum settlements in Africa. Recently a tragedy struck there and shacks burnt down killing dozens of people. The cause of the fire was said to be illegal electric connections, and we see other such problems happening all over Africa. I noticed a housing problem in Johannesburg and Cape Town where increasing numbers of men are sleeping in suburban parks and by city streets or abandoned dwellings. The rich suburb communities would just call police and have the people arrested and charged for loitering. The number of burglary crimes including robbery is alarming in our rich suburbs. So, what we have seen is more boom gates, high walls with security gates erected, sophisticated security measures put in place, and homeowners living in fear of various crimes from the poor. The criminal syndicates in ghettos and townships, live to prey on those they perceive to be rich among them including suburban people. There used to be a dividing wall between the two groups of people. In the old days before committing a crime, the colour of the person was taken into consideration, but now it is just a matter of who has what the criminal wants.

The old style of settling people is coming back to haunt us today. Formerly, Blacks would do harm to other ethnic groups but not their own. This was same with coloureds, Indians and white communities. The system divided the people and I think people never got used to each other. They never have had the opportunity to get to know and accept one another as precious fellow human beings. The enmity brought in through segregation could be done away with through reconciliation and social cohesion. Nowadays, the different ethnic groups would prey on their own without thinking twice—there seems to be a starvation or hunger problem. The better living condition styles are within all race sectors of society. The African governments could afford a nice welfare distribution system for the poor and jobless if they were truly serious about service delivery to their own people.

With the mineral resources and ores the continent has, all things are possible and the solution rests on shoulders of those in power. Most suburbs owned by rich folks do not want to see low-cost housing projects next to them. Neither are other neighbours of a different colour welcome. The wealth distributors who are banks will suffer a drop in property values if the suburb is close to low-cost houses and this order has always promoted the advancement of segregation and capitalism. Those blacks were never poor but the same ruling system of the day made criminals and beggars out of the innocent people of these communities. Now, how can it be possible that when blacks get to live close to other ethnic group areas the property values drop?

I think all our people need to be taught and encouraged not to do crime. Rehabilitation and reconciliation in order to live life with other races in harmony is what both white and black people need. Many blacks cannot live without doing crime because they will die of hunger. They need to be taught skills in order to have good jobs and live normal lives. Rich whites of South Africa must begin to reach out to blacks and pay them a fair wage. Tolerance of other ethnic groups should come from both blacks and whites. There is a new era of truth and reconciliation, which is bringing along with it true healing for the South African nation. While affluent blacks are accepted and absorbed into white communities as rising stars or "black diamonds," the poor majority also needs to be empowered to be on a par with them as well. That tells me all could achieve this, with time and the proper building of our economic foundations, which have to be non-racial, non-abusive and non-segregating. It is amazing that even most financial institutions in Africa are still racially biased when it comes to empowering blacks. How can a homeless person have collateral? Will the children of the poor ever have a fair chance to play a role in their countries' economies?

African governments need to devise strategies of empowerment that will see education reaching all people and the racially biased banking systems removed. Only governments can do this for their people, as no bank changes direction easily on its own. Black empowerment has not done much in terms of Blacks owning shares in banks, insurance companies and the mining industry. Africa and the developing countries have a great opportunity to grow in the insurance sector, as many people do not have insurance in many areas of their lives. The reason this industry has battled to survive on the continent is that insurance is unaffordable or inaccessible. By reversing the old style of doing things, we can introduce new liberating measures of economy building. Two thirds of South African households save nothing of their earned income. The grant system of the country, if it carries on the way it is operating, is not going to be sustainable in the future. The rest of Africa is worse, since saving has become a pipe dream to them. There is a great need to cushion the continent's savings in order to build a prosperous Africa.

When I look at the downtowns of our cities, which are quickly becoming havens of prostitution and drug dealing syndicates, I can see that the continent is sitting on a time bomb of a morally diseased society. During recession period, some parliamentarians pushed to legalize prostitution in the name of helping others earn a living. With a high HIV and AIDS rate, and little being done to fight it, we will need to instil moral value foundations in people. The moral foundations are shaky and changing every time democratic development elements obscure the clarity of modern democratic rights. In order to instil a new era of moral regeneration among the people, this generation will have to leave no stone unturned. The secret of overcoming the moral decay that has taken over our communities lies in discipline.

For many years apartheid governments have not managed to prevent any none white groups from becoming poor. If the governments of today want to win, they must take control from the few rich who maintain the old system by means of investment money. The livelihood of poor Africans and the developing world should not have to depend on the mercy of the rich and the former ruthless laws and policies of a few wealthy interests groups who are not merciful at all but who exploit the poor. Can this kind of economic management justify the democratic independence of African nations? Of course not!

Home, "sweet home," is a place all people long to behold and have. People become hostile when they do not have decent places to live. It ruins the confidence of people and makes them think they do not matter or that they are nothing. If we are to win the battle against homelessness, the culture of the banking system and governments' management of resources will need superior deliberation. Poor government management and unreasonable banking practices are a cause of poverty and lack in many societies. We need to balance the scales and get over it quickly. Two things that apartheid used to keep blacks suppressed were poor housing and lack of good education. The education given to blacks was only to afford them knowledge of a few things—it was greatly inferior to white people's education.

The old system enslaved other races and gave Whites supremacy in society and in the work place. It turned many blacks to begging for a living where they lived in backyard rooms and worked for the superior white people instead of having an equal share with them in economic development. The two above-mentioned tactics destroy people and bury them alive anywhere in the world when enforced. When this kind of system is directed against any people around the world, it always leaves its victims by the wayside of the economy main stream. That the black market is labelled high risk by banks is a sure sign that controllers do not want to change their mentality and allow Blacks to develop economies that are sound and viable. Of course, blacks cannot pay back loans if they have nothing. This is a fact and the issue now is to deal with what makes them not able to afford to pay house bonds and for the rest of essentials in life. African banks' faith has remained in same colour partnerships rather than taking any risk for growth and development and the uplifting of all people.

The price of homes or land is almost unaffordable. The price of a good high school education including tertiary studies in most African states is shocking. Should such important commodities be so highly priced? They are the pillars of development in all countries. It makes it so only those who can afford it stand a chance of enjoying the commodity called freedom. This one colour group of people or only the rich condition of enjoying freedom does not spell out fundamental pillars of democracy and justice and better life for all. Africa needs education and work skills the most, but education and human capital development have remained unaffordable, as well as underestimated and underdeveloped for too long. How could the acquiring of such essentials be so expensive and neglected when these are the pillars of economic growth? The desire of many nations is that the African continent continue to improve. That is why more donations come to Africa than to any other continent in the world.

We could have poverty halved in a short space of time if we addressed the question of land distribution, housing and education well. The farce is that South African apartheid government spent R18 000 on a white child in school and only R25 on a black child. When people have above things, then joblessness and poverty are also solved. Educated people are a creative force in any nation. Real security starts when people own their own homes rather than renting or paying back unaffordable bonds. These two standards are the foundation of a healthy and prosperous nation or country. Unaffordable land and property prices have contributed to high poverty rates in the past in the developing world. I think the developing world now needs people development more than ever. Policy makers and a change of policies, including constitution laws, are vitally important for the developing world to move forward from its stagnant state. Change will come from people who understand the needs of the developing world's people including types of development areas, timeframes and evolving management styles, which have been lacking for too long. Why do African banks charge higher interest rates than their peers overseas or in the first world countries? A good example is a house bond paid more than three to four times while it is cheaper in the first world countries and interest rates are quite low. The same is true of African bank charges when compared with those overseas.

We have seen more children on the streets begging while many others never make it to the streets. Baby dumping by rubbish bins is alarming all over the developing world. Abortion has become the order of the day for many young women of our societies. Bogus abortion doctors with wrong diagnoses are a matter of concern in Africa. There are 5 million girls, who die annually in the world because of unsafe abortions. Sexual education is a key and the best way of addressing the plague. Contraceptives not reaching the people who need them most remains a matter to be addressed with new vigour.

Food prices are sky rocketing to an extent that most people now are living below the bread line. Most are supposed to be farming but for some reason are not and this has resulted in great food shortages on the continent. The illegal occupation of buildings and open land is increasing, including the hijacking of buildings in big cities. Life should not be an issue of the survival of the fittest but it must afford all people the right to live. Countries are stretching out hands with empty baskets to beg support and donations from the rich nations of other continents. The number of orphans is increasing all over the continent of Africa and the developing world. Population growth has decreased due to many factors like HIV and AIDS and more. Many orphans lose their homes to criminal syndicates who pretend to be of help to them and then at the end sell the homes of those same orphans. Large numbers of people suffer because of senseless wars that have destroyed their homes and dispersed them into temporary camps for too long. All these wars and injustices are uncalled for and not worth to have. Hunger and malnutrition linked with other food deficiency illnesses lead to high mortality rates among both children and adults and are hard to beat in developing countries.

Begging can never be forever, so the development of talent and people must be a priority in Africa's goals. The blight of homelessness is bigger than we think. How can people save money when they live from hand to mouth? A home payment should not take all your money but should leave enough for good food, comfort, and security in life. City development plans show little concern for poverty alleviation and empowerment of the poor. Planners and leaders even fear to talk about such issues as it would draw the ire of the greedy rich. Therefore, everyone chooses to let it lie until it explodes in war or revolt. It could be wished that Africa would offer free education and better housing with immediate effect in order to speed up good service delivery and development.

"If wishes were horses, beggars were going to ride." The implementations of these plans are slow and have brought many conflicts of interest to many stakeholders and role players in the different economic sectors. Thus, the high prices of house properties are being determined and influenced by high demand .There are little or no other competitive options for people that are in place. The fact that private schools are taking over and making education unaffordable is a sign of governments' failure to operate efficiently and compete with the private sector more effectively. The government health system is deplorable as it makes the poor suffer from cruelly inadequate service. Rude service from staff and wrong diagnoses, including wrong surgical operations, dominate this sector which lacks expertise and a good workforce. A new hope might dawn if African governments would begin to respect their own professionals and pay them their worth.

Strength of equality

Equality has been dominated discussions for some time now and the weak nations want recognition and good representation in all major world bodies. In South Africa, the month of August is for women and children awareness. The message is very clear; "MAY ALL MEN RESPECT WOMEN AND SUPPORT CHILDREN THEY FATHERED BECAUSE MANY WOMEN ARE STRUGGLING TO EARN A LIVING AND FEED THE SAME CHILDREN." It does not only apply here but in homes, schools, work places, holiday resorts and in the sports world too. People are routinely discriminated against because of their skin pigmentation even if it is indirect and not uttered in words. The second problem is gender equality. I have noticed Blacks being victims of their skin colour in business and in the sports domain. This goes deeper than just skin colour hatred from other races who think themselves superior. How do we get all people of the African continent on the same platform with other races is a question greatly debated about today. It seems every country in Africa has a black economic empowerment programme in place.

Farmers and xenophobic groups have abused black people or workers so badly that at times the continent stood still and watched helplessly, as it witnessed ruthless xenophobic or racist killings of Blacks. In South Africa, the abuses are shocking, especially in farms and other work places. In Mpumalanga province, a farmer tied and dragged a black worker for miles on the back of a van until he died. What a cruel and brutal murder this was! Two South African white police officers were training their police dogs by having them catch and bite two illegal Mozambique men until their ears came off, and were badly injured. The Minister of Police was sued, had to pay for all damages and the two police officers were sentenced to prison. This is simply a racist act, not a political one. Black workers have been shot in farms on the pretext of being mistaken for baboons. Free State white University students gave food soaked with urine to the black cleaning staff. Locals burnt foreigners to death and murdered them for false allegations of taking local people's jobs, which was not true. These are just a few incidents. Some whites and a few rich blacks with no regard for the poor or others have sabotaged and spoken against affirmative action and black empowerment programmes all over Africa. Fronting in tender applications is alarming in our nations. What makes many whites to be so hateful towards less fortunate people of Africa is the teaching they have embraced from their parents.

One woman resigned at work because she would not relieve a black colleague during lunchtime. When the boss called the white woman into his office, as he was tired of her behaviour towards her black workmate, she said she could not believe a black woman could be equal with her. She claimed her parents had taught her that a black person would always be her worker. Her ideology was quite backward and stupid—the result of brain washing and with stale moral views as well. Most companies tell workers that salaries are confidential and if they find anyone having revealed theirs, they can immediately lose their job. The fact of the matter is that even multinational companies do the same. It seems this order started back in the old days and most still think only whites should be in a high salary bracket. Whites are paid more, even when junior to black folks and less qualified. This is the case with most companies in South Africa and in the developing world.

A young white man took a rifle gun and went to stand next to one of the North West province highways in South Africa, and opened fire on every vehicle that had blacks in it. Killing and injuring people because they were black was a heroic act to this young man. Another young man entered a bus at the federal capital, Pretoria, and started shooting at every black person, killing and injuring people. All of the above took place after the start of the democratic elections of our new South Africa.

During the apartheid era, the biological war experts, led by Michael Basson, carried out a strategy under government mandate, which killed blacks only. The aim and mission was that every Black who went into a hospital must not come out alive. People were poisoned and women made barren and many other heinous crimes were also committed. Black people were buried alive in mass graves not only in one country but around the continent as well. Such genocide and shedding of innocent blood on the African continent are the result of a mindset of inequality. This mindset has continued to the present day in African countries and in the world. It is only true equality and respect for life that will bring wars and killings of people to a halt.

Does Africa manufacture all the weapons used on its soil? No, the developing world does not make weapons but those who want wealth or ores from her, even at the expense of innocent lives, bring the weapons. Weapons are big business today in the developing world. Many ports of entry and harbour law enforcement agencies have confiscated many dangerous weapons imported by illegal arms syndicates destined for African shores to destroy innocent lives. Accompanying a mentality that has no regard for other people is war for resources and raw material ores. Racists do not believe the developing world's people have the right to their diamonds and minerals including the land and its development. This is a big problem, which has brainwashed even black people's minds to resent their own when they begin to prosper as in their minds prosperity is for other races only. A prosperous black man is a suspect and suspected of criminal activities in the eyes of many poor blacks. It is very common for the developing world's police to put rising Black stars under surveillance without a cause. That is why black sons and daughters of Africa struggle so much to get their hands on anything.

It is not only policies barring them from getting involved and playing major roles in their economies; it is also wars and a mentality that agrees with the enemy word that says they cannot amount to anything in life. Every time Africa finds people who try to correct the evil of racism or apartheid once and for all, those leaders are likely to be assassinated or sabotaged by people through rigged elections. It all depends on who has the pin. What is wrong with Africa? For centuries, other races that suppressed blacks kept telling them that they were weak in the brain and that seemed to be the accepted truth. Well, no one would waste time pinning down someone weak and useless unless insane. I feel it is time to take charge and break the stigma of racial divide if we want to have sustainable growth in our economies. If we lay true foundations of freedom now all will be well with us and generations to come will enjoy the fruits.

The issue is simple, if we leave out other role players we will be doomed to fail. The more people who participate in the economic mainstream, the healthier are those countries' economies. Our poverty is uncalled for in Africa and unnecessary as well. I am sorry to offend those that say a black man cannot farm. Give him all the knowledge and necessary implements and see the best harvest records on the continent! Remember, what another person has done you can do better. Farming is what blacks specialized in for centuries until the whites came and made land inaccessible to the majority of blacks but only available to a few whites who received huge subsidies from governments and got richer and richer. Largely this is still the issue on the continent. How can certain races claim to be the only ones who can farm for the nations and neglect the potentials in other people? To beat poverty we will need to refocus our economic planning and policies on empowerment values that are inclusive of all people.

It should not please just a few but rather allow all people to taste the fruits of freedom. Starting from farm workers and those in remote rural areas, the taste of freedom must be real to all. As long as the poor are living on the wayside, there will never be a dream continent of joy, peace and prosperity for all Africans. Even our universities do not reflect our nations because of the capitalist divide we have. Students from poor backgrounds and homes, having no opportunity to better their lives through expensive tertiary education, turn to governments for bursaries, which is a big problem since it is impossible to help all. In 2014, Mugabe bursary scheme had about 4000 Zimbabwe students in South African universities. Their government failed to pay tuition fees and female students were reported to have turned to prostitution in order to keep themselves in class. Problems of this nature are widespread in Africa and the developing world. This has led to a call for free education all even but in vain, as some claim bursaries already sponsor students from poor backgrounds. Corruption robs many of their right to resources of this nature. Whatever the government contribution, it is just a small drop in the ocean. Privately owned and run universities and colleges in Africa have more control than the governments they operate under can dictate to them. African states have not done well in building what is their own and what they can control well because of the influence of the rich greedy mentality that aims for maximum profits even when it is folly to do so.

When soldiers are in training, they start on the same footing until the end, as this is the base of a strong battalion. You cover your colleague's back regardless of colour and likewise they do the same for you. This is a band of brothers and sisters bound with codes, which cannot be broken. The training makes all strong and fit. During pass out time all celebrate the moment and are ready to prove their point out there. This is by providing their citizens with great protection and peace. A strong army is one that is fit and knowledgeable about their weapons. For the same reason, to give blacks a fair opportunity and chance, the continent will flourish better and faster if all start with an impartation of knowledge first. Now on paper, everything always looks great but implementation is what is important including consistently fast tracking it with goals in place for meeting deadlines. Common business sense tells us that when too many people are poor, buying power and consumption are low. When consumption is low, production has to be low also. Thus it means those in business are prevented from making huge profits and others are not given the privilege of supporting them.

The economy will only involve a small fraction of the nation and leave the majority outside in economic unproductiveness. Actually this is how poverty cycles around. Relatively few participants in countries' economies have caused this world's great recession. The greedy rich reaped huge profits by defrauding investors who, in turn, invested money with shady companies. When people got tired of being cheated, they quit and left the economies with little investment confidence. Jobs were lost and the credit crunch came in. Building what we were supposed to have kept and treasured is never going to be easy. The companies and people have billions sitting in banks and not circulating as the business climate has sent panic all over the world. Only new change that people can trust will make them change their attitude. Upright business ethics and policies must be put in place, even when there is a price to pay. In the long run it will be better when it is done right.

It takes more than revolutionary ideas to get over the wave of recession disaster. Why did the world's economists not see such a terrible recession coming? The problem is that economists and advisors are stuck to bookish norms that could not translate into the twenty first century management plan that is progressive and rewards equitably. The other reason could be that they operated in an old style of economic development that catered to only a few and that blinded them from seeing the potential buying power of the poor masses if only the poor were equipped and helped out of poverty. Many economists settle for what is a good idea and miss what is the best idea.

There are deeper issues of concern about true equality. When people are equally developed, they in turn become great assets to their countries. It is easier to make money among people with jobs and healthy businesses than in poverty-stricken societies. Where there is more money going around, it means there can be greater profit margins. That is why the truly rich non-racist billionaires have understood the power of developing talent and investing in people. This is their future guarantee to more riches. How could this have slipped out of the minds of business leaders and owners including politicians in the world? When people earn a living through salaries, businesses win since people will spend and governments get tax revenue to develop their countries' infrastructure.

Arrogance has failed people. Greedy companies paid bribes to improve profit margins. And private interests and profits are put above peace and the lives of people. Tax evasions and investment incentives are abuse that is rampant all over developing countries and is a sign that the developing world needs new mechanisms to overcome illegal money exports. If African states empower their citizens well, they will have sustainable economies. Bloodshed has to end now in Africa and in the third world nations. Wars cost developing states a lot and are costly to maintain whether from the rebel or government's side. If that money is ploughed back into the economies, many people would benefit. The evil war architects always have money ready to bring their goods of interest home. The foolish greedy will put people's lives on the line because someone has a figure on the table to get a few ores for next to nothing. Wealth and money are the root of many evils and only true justice can stop this sinister scourge.

The sleeping giant, which is the African children of the soil, is rising up and many are about to see its banner of prosperity flown high. The continent does not have to go on in poverty like this. Equality can make the richest continent in resources to be also the world leader in true peace and justice, with all its spheres of leadership and development administered well. Many long to see this seal of freedom's approval of Africa in place. The founding fathers of the Organization of African Unity (OAU) longed to see a free Africa with dignity, respect and glowing prosperity in all its future endeavours. This would be a memorial to the many people who sacrificed their lives so that the fruits of freedom should come to every home of the continent. Only when true justice prevails will many celebrate and taste the freedom, which has thus far been untapped for many years.

The wars disrupt the bridges and roads of peace and the progress of development. Greedy evil policy makers are indirect perpetrators or dictators behind the ruthless wars on the continent. The solutions cannot only come from those sitting in parliament and the many who are trying to manage the malfunctioning organs of societies. These folks can only do so much. Arrogance is not willing to bring justice to the situations and so it simple enlarges the wide slippery road of injustice. We can narrow it with wisdom to have better life for all. Inherited unfair policies and trends of irregular wealth distribution are the chief promoters of inequality among the people. Big budgets meant for rates and taxes for rich suburbs and small budgets for black townships are a sign of biased government management systems. Old-fashioned ways are failing and haunting people today. Blacks in Africa have to have a sense of belonging in their countries in order to contribute with a right attitude and make a positive impact. I have often seen townships using tractors to pick refuse while suburbs have great trucks picking around their areas. That is how it was back in the apartheid-era days and still is today. Something is wrong here and correction is necessary. Women's poor representation in government leadership and society is another big matter of concern.

Imprisoned mentality

The world needs to develop a non-sexist, non-racist and "non-people playing victim" attitude as this latter is a common phenomenon among the black majority of Africa. The acceptance and tolerance of races, ethnic groups and gender equality is still an issue of debate around the nations of the world. Civil wars caused by tribal hatred, resenting each other and not respecting each other are the worst sins among our people. Religious conflicts are becoming a cancer among many nations. The recent film from the USA about Mohammed has caused a big problem from the Muslim world. The United States ambassador and other Americans killed in Libya is a sign of an intolerant world. The Rwanda genocides were tribally instigated and carried out. The African history and pattern of leadership that was based on chieftainship rather than democracy has instilled a mentality that whenever talent comes from outside one's own chief's family, most people will rebel and make the countries ungovernable. It is very difficult to change people from what they have been learning for years. The problem is that such people have been learning to look down at other tribes and regard themselves as superior. And you cannot accept what you regard as inferior to rule over you. The gospel of this kind of leadership has been propagating a wrong example of politics all over Africa and the world for ages.

Even the bride's price for the so-called royal families is way beyond reasonable or affordable means. In fact, these kinds of people rule others by traditions of superiority of class. Land and resources are controlled under the same leadership style. Regarding other tribes as inferior and keeping them away from these self-declared royal society groups is the order of the day. Their children are taught not to mix with other tribes and intermarriages are discouraged with other lesser people or tribes. In a democratic society, this mentality has ruined nations and communities, as many will accept only leadership based on traditional basis. It is very difficult to unlearn what one has learnt. There is absolute no validity to this kind of leadership.

Many tribal political parties are trying to win over people who understand democratic rights and the new leadership processes of this day and age. The folly of trying to hold on to a province or state to advance minority desires while not tolerating other people is the number one enemy of democratic liberty in Africa and the world. The fear of the unknown has gripped the minds of these societies, as the teaching was wrong from the start. We see it in political parties of this nature when leaders are murdered if choose to differ. Firstly, it is the wrong teaching they received but even worse is that they continued to believe that lie. The second factor is the fear of receiving the same treatment they gave others. It is a sad thing to be fearful and not believing in other races and tribes or people. When you consider everything doomed in the hands of others, it simply means you might be too arrogant to understand true leadership.

Once people do away with the two problems of looking down upon others and not believing in equality, real free and fair leadership will have its course and all people will experience it. When Zimbabwe declared a government of national unity in 1987, many Ndebele people who did not migrate in their political minds felt betrayed by ZAPU (PF) leader and party president, Joshua Nkomo. The cry was, "stay with us," being only one tribe party people until die losers, as long as only comprised of one tribe and language people, it is okay. That is why some went on to try to start ZAPU 2000 political party, even when the respected founding fathers had long closed the ZAPU party chapter. If a leader makes a mistake, many in government would rather criticize and use it to rebel and start new parties that only cause more damage than good. Leadership is about teamwork; stop pointing fingers and correct any wrongs you see so you will be part of the solution for your nation. A rebellious spirit is proud and always finds a way to air its arrogance whenever the opportunity comes. It is not change of leadership that Africa needs, but strong positive policies with effective implementation and good governance, which meet 21st century challenges and demands. Africans lack understanding if they believe freedom comes by voting the right man in office.

What about when women play major roles in leadership? Queens have led the nations in times past. Was the teaching different and groomed better? Yes! I suppose they were accepted and tolerated as any other members of society. Given the necessary support and respect, women can dispel all gender inequality myths. It is a foolish mentality that says women can only receive decisions from men and cannot initiate. Men have been labelling them weak from the beginning. We continue to see one tribe, one gender and one race raised up above another. This is a sign of a confused, intolerant mindset with no fair leadership processes. Unless you free yourself from the mental bondage you find yourself in, no one else can.

The curse of this generation is not believing in others and having a false perception about itself with interests based on its own agendas. Boys' upbringing was better than girls'. In some African states girls do not go to school, as their duty is to be lifetime house cleaners, and baby breeding machines. Men toss them from one type of abuse to another. Look at how many women in Africa walk long distances to fetch firewood and water around African villages. It is as if they are men's slaves. In most parts of Africa, men marry more than one wife not because of love but because they have use of them. Men pay for every one of them and finally own the castle and them. So they become modern slave teams for men who hide behind cultural practices.

If men's mentality changed, we would begin to see them beat the water and electricity problems of underdeveloped countries. The fact is that men live like kings while women suffer physical and emotional abuse as if they were second-class citizens. That will make development go very slowly on the continent if it is not stopped. If men could just put themselves in those women's shoes, they would think soberly and consider things from a better perspective in life. Some men are intimidated when women are paid more than they are or are paid the same. Old habits die-hard, what men learnt remain wanting revalidation by all people in order to bring justice in our malfunctioning societies of our nations.

On the other hand, if Africa can involve women with talent in leadership and let them lead with the full support of men who will not sabotage them, I believe Africa can quickly heal and prosper. The abuse of women is the stigma of not respecting women and considering them lesser-minded beings who are inferior to men. That is why sometimes some feel women rights are much of exaggeration propagation. I am not talking about being irresponsible here but about empowering women to empower their children and all people in return. Much potential strength lies in this group of lionesses that have been coming to take their place in societies and nations but for too long have been denied a chance. The 21st century could be the right time for them to step up and take a stand for the cause of freedom.

The nations have been neglecting women for too long and that has caused a weakness in modern society that lives on in the old society's failures and culture. This is what has killed confidence in African children; the boys love their sisters but begin to believe they are less important when they see them raised differently, growing up to be given in marriage prematurely by the same parents. How can they say girls do not matter? May we begin to see women and men as our Creator sees them!

Can the developing world ever hope to build a society that is non-racial and non-sexist? Many blacks on the continent have come to believe they are inferior to whites and will never live prosperously as the whites do. If a white is the boss or a work colleague, blacks react differently in his or her presence. When a white man comes into a room where blacks are, you will see the atmosphere change immediately. A black man will work better for a white person, even if underpaid than for his own. A majority of blacks resent their own people when they prosper, that mentality indirectly undermines their prosperity and freedom as a whole. Black employers also like practising greedy tactics against their own by paying them poorly—another obstacle towards the empowerment of African citizens.

Many black employers often take advantage of their own black people as governments do with African civil servants by not paying them good salaries. A white employer will pay a black person with the same qualifications and service position as a white a third of what the white person receives. All this is hidden in the name of a confidential salary package. It seems it is black empowerment versus sophisticated white tactics, which never allow level scales for both groups up to now, all over Africa. Where is this generation going? With all it has, it could do much better if, determined to leave the past behind and focus on truth in the future, it moved toward true reconciliation and social cohesion.

One day, when I went to pick up a relative's child from a multiracial preschool, she told me a white boy had told some white kids not to play with her because she was black. Now, she was the only Black there because her father is a well-to-do black businessman. I said to her, next time you tell that boy that you are black and that your father is rich. In my heart, I pondered the question, "South Africa, what have you taught your children?" When it is time for workshop groups in African universities, most white students tend to stand aloof from their black peers. They argue that they feel better and more comfortable with their own. Some of them will not go to Universities where you find many blacks. Neither do those kinds of universities admit many black students. This is what has kept education unaffordable all over Africa. It could be because of funds or back room policies that continue to discriminate against people. Money always seems to be the issue and many black students drop out as tuition fees keep rising and become unaffordable.

It happened again that I was driving with the same child and this time her daddy was with us. She asked her father to buy her some sweets, chocolate, chips and her favourite juice drink from the garage kiosk. The father answered that he had no money. The girl said angrily, "Please buy me, Daddy, I know you are rich." The father stopped the car immediately and got her what she wanted. At the same time, he asked her why she could not ask her mother to buy her those things; she said her mom has no money. Now, the mother worked and was well paid but she always answered the child by saying she had no money. This child was just four years old. We must be careful what we teach our children as the generations to come will inherit those teachings.

Most times her mother would tell her she had no money but advised her to ask from her father whom she said had lots of money. Now she knew what her father was worth and what I had said about her father the other day. Her father was not carrying money but swiped a card with a R20 balance to buy her the things she wanted. To her it was impossible for her father to be broke. Children learn from parents and it is those teachings that continue to surface throughout their lifetime. White people would agree that the slavery of blacks was wrong, as well as all the mistreatment that was directed to black people by it. Some whites, however, still enforce the same mistreatment in sophisticated ways in order always have an upper hand in everything. In this state of affairs, true reconciliation is not achieving its purpose.

If not careful, you will even fear when you are not supposed to fear. I have never seen the shadow of a dog biting someone. The last obstacle of many minds is insecurity and poverty. This has caused more harm than good in our societies and countries. Many leaders and people in management positions do not believe they have made it there, but instead their minds are enslaved to painful memories of poverty in the past. When a black child leaves a village to taste city life, they never want to go back to the village; as if they fear planting themselves there again. When people taste what is better, indeed, good becomes the enemy of best. But if the same people had power to develop those rural villages, they would love staying there and not need to put up shacks around cities while searching for jobs that never come by.

I will never forget when I was in a remote village in Malawi near Mzuzu how an old retired teacher spoke with me for hours about how people leave for South Africa and never come back. Indeed, life was a nightmare in this place. People struggle to get water, food and firewood and almost no basic human need is easily obtainable here. Africa's virgin land needs to be developed, and explorations carried out by native companies. Right now much of the land lies barren and wasted; someone has to pick up the bits and pieces and build for the generations to come. The generations to come will have to learn the history of a racial divide that only resulted in cheating the poor masses and thereafter left them to die in poverty without remedy. Freedom is in peaceful minds. Africa's identification with poverty is an enslaving yoke that needs to be dealt with by the strong, not the faint-hearted.

Some people when they got into parliament divorced the beautiful youth wives or husbands because they thought they could not have a chance to have the best, as poverty or culture was the defining factor in the time of their marriage decisions. Good character and behaviour is important. The HIV and AIDS infection rate is still high on the African continent and people must start loving life rather than trying to escape their poor self-image through drugs and sexual indulgence. Extra-marital affairs have denied families the peace of mind and prosperity they deserve. When people begin to feel unfulfilled, with a bad self-image, it makes them find no fulfilment in life at all. Rehabilitation centres are full of people with an attention-seeking syndrome, filled with fear of sliding back into poverty.

On the other hand, some people seem not to believe that prosperity is part of their life gift from the Creator. God has destined all people and races to have a meaningful life, and to enjoy true prosperity. The kind of people that do everything hurriedly, with the fear of losing everything have strayed. A wrong mentality is one that claims people live once on this earth. I do not believe in this nonsensical idea, which robs people of a sense of belonging and responsibility. This mentality is entertained among foolish societies. The only result you get here is fraud and many other things that are wrong. You build your life carefully. True success is not about material wealth alone though capital is one of the prerequisites of success. One needs to be prosperous in order to achieve fulfilment in life. Doing what you love doing the most is fulfilling, as this is part of your purpose for living on earth. In the end, this is what brings prosperity.

People will go and enslave themselves with loads of credits because they have government tender businesses going on. After a short while, the banks repossess all assets and the end result is the rehab centre or suicide being committed. They never budgeted for the future hard times because of a wrong mentality that goes with a tormenting fear. Politicians or ministers charged with fraud against state organs and many other corruption shenanigans are a sign of people without a servant's heart. It is as if they are hungry hunters, late to put their hands into the food bowl that has everything finished and no more left. It affects their performance and interests in serving people and companies or organisations.

Relax; you are just a human being and not God. Get your ego right. You are special and unique, just as are all other people. Nothing is inferior or superior about you. You are the best you you can be, being yourself, so stop worrying about your race colour. Your purpose in this life needed exactly that colour; fulfilment and happiness will come to you if you accept yourself as your Creator coded you. Success without stress and anxiety is imminent all your days on earth if only you know yourself. You will leave a true heritage to your children, which is to be just themselves and confident of themselves regardless of race or colour boundaries. What happened in the past is history and we can only use it to draw conclusions of how far we have come and have to go. Let history be our reference map for shaping our future lives.

The true forgiveness of nations does not base relationships on aid donations or trade relationships but on how much they repair their bridges of peace and justice towards each other. This remains the beacon and treasure of their freedom and justice. So stop letting anything stand on your way as if it is your god. I dream of a developing world where all races will come together to live side by side, and rebuild their moral foundations out of love for each other and a shared appreciation of the need for each other in life. We all can pick each other up and rise from where we have fallen. Let the world admit the truth that most of the old people did not teach the latter generations of the world truth. Using the name of God was only to get other people to give up their land and live with only the Bible in their hands, being told their riches are in heaven. This is the worst kind of deception; God has given people more than just a bible.

The old tactics used before made it difficult to know the truth and enter into the true grace of God as the bible teaches. Many foreigners introduced religion to Africa as a means to tame the children of the soil and blind them while looting and cheating went on. Using God's name to bring fear to others or declaring that God is the leader and all must follow is another very common error witnessed among illiterate societies led by only a few educated people. Many groups used their religion to enslave blacks with a wrong image of God. It was their religion because God is not the designer of religion nor is He religious! It is time for the black man to find the real God and His truth and teach it to other ethnic groups who seem not to understand or know God. How could the religious messengers miss the teaching and practising of justice and truth, which are God's heartbeat? Some of these people even lied about God and used His name to gain riches and cheat blacks in Africa.

Many South African black criminals will steal or harm other ethnic groups without a sense of guilt. They believe every white person owes them and is rich at the expense of their fathers and mothers. Even now, you still find a mentality that says the white folks are the only remaining enemy of black people's freedom. Rarely and in very few places can whites go unguarded in many of our African townships and ghettos. Whites have become a perennial prey of criminals in poor townships and many whites in turn manipulate blacks with poor salaries. The poor and rich criminals alike will leave townships for places where other races live in order to work, steal, rob and commit worst crimes because they have a feeling that it does not matter when it is against another group of people. The mentality that thinks all whites are rich has made this group of black folks play the victim too long and more than necessary.

The racial divide has taught people of African countries they are not equal and will not be able to live side by side with "superior" groups who, in the past, were favoured by the governments' systems. An injury to one is an injury to all, is a one-race slogan in Africa. This mentality has stood on our way too long and has indeed become like a god to many of our people. The lie of the racist folks is that they are better than blacks are and continue to teach their children this lie. When their children come short in class and blacks take the lead, these children become surprised because it proves their parents wrong.

The most perceived superior folks have been trying to protect the lie of teaching their children false things. Separating their children from blacks, lest the children find out about the lie is a strategy practised and haunting many whites today. To say they are the same with blacks, is an astonishing revelation to racist parents. Colour is simply a code of the earth suit of different peoples and races that God chose to clothe them with. Now if a black child accepts the saying that he or she is less than other ethnic people groups, it becomes a most damaging mentality. That same black child will then be a slave to a system designed to lower blacks to submit and serve the white supremacy ideology, which is tantamount to the robbery of other people's dignity and respect. Most blacks today in Africa are suffering from the dangerous philosophy that they are lesser people than other colours. Freedom has to be in the minds of people, not just verbally announced and written on documents.

A slave mentality is the worst state of mind one can have. Slaves eat anything and never get enough, at the same time they queue for everything. Slaves can never have ownership of anything but only serve under the master's instruction. And this mutual understanding exists between the slave and its master. The slave serves the master with all he has, from wife to children. The children of the slave are groomed to serve the master even if not paid, they are automatically enslaved under the system. It is a mentality instilled in them. The master always teaches his children how to master and pin down the slave. No man can be free if he still walks with a slave mentality in the twenty first century. Everyone need to own their own destiny, own a home and control the economy in order for their children to break free from economic oppression.

The mentality of rushing to steal and embezzle funds in our government departments shows that the people still have a slave mentality. They still think and work with an attitude that says steal everything for yourself. "Let the rest starve and die it does not matter," is a slave mentality since slaves can never help anyone or be responsible as nothing is theirs. "No place to sleep and nothing to wear but somehow something might come my way, even if not good, I will take it," is the slave's attitude. Nothing much to live for in life but fighting to keep breath in the body is a normal slave outlook.

Jails are overcrowded and large budgets are required to keep those inmates alive. Some African blacks find it easy to live in jail because everything is free. Many released prisoners do not stay outside long but slide back into prison. Why is this so? Should you have to die with great potential still untapped within you? You are an achiever by nature not by colour, tribe or language. You might have focused your energy in doing what is not right. Now with the same power and focus, determination and dedication, drive your life to fulfilment! All things are possible for you in life. Would you not be proud to succeed without stealing or cheating because you have chosen to work and do something good with your life?

The children of the African continent and developing world should not necessarily stick to bookish norms or culture to develop their economies, as there are many flaws with the taught knowledge of one race or even culture. Africa will have to dig deep and devise better methods of dealing with their situations than just relying on one race of people's suggestions that always come at a hefty price. Educational institutions need research for better developments in the future rather than just spoon-feeding the old poisonous doctrine from one group of people. Suggestions from African people are mostly turned down because of a mentality that says Africans are not capable of even thinking. That is not the truth but is a mentality that is still promoted all over the world. We must be able to separate senseless cultures from the true think tanks of Africa and of the developing world. The cry of my heart is to see the developing world's children understand that they are a special people whom God made with a special purpose. God planted Africans on a rich continent that all other nations envy and foreigners from other continents have always fought to get a share of it. Blacks will have to teach the other ethnic groups about the true living God since what they received from many of these groups was something that looked like religion but in reality was a snare trapping blacks into low self-esteem and poverty.

Liberation and freedom is something in the state of mind if already declared among people. This kind of independence is not enough if it is accompanied by economic liberalisation. Why do most blacks work hard only when there is a different colour boss around them? Every time Africa tries to do without a certain colour, many cry 'foul'. The reason they do that maybe because they have grown used to poor salaries, which they admit is better than nothing. The fear of failure is great in the minds of blacks who regard moving forward without the recommendation of a man of another colour risky. The talent of creativity is limited to only one colour. That kind of teaching made other races proud and happy when it was used as a tool of manipulation against other people. Many African blacks are taught and are convinced in their minds that there are no inventors and great scientists among their own people; they must free themselves from this warped mentality. In such a racially divided world, to show the world what God has put in others will take not only education but heart and courage. I believe it is now just a matter of time before we see great wonders of God among African blacks. It will be a blessing when all people break free of the mentality that says they are less than other colours of people and that they are nothing.

No one should be tormented by jealousy when fellow human beings succeed. Give others a fair chance and opportunity to make it in life! Stop blaming your background and country leaders but work together to achieve a society we all want. Begin to seek help and break all limitations in your life! I have noticed that some criminals who leave crime and do not return to jail are constructive people we have never recognized. In other words, they needed a platform to start from; it is not that they were destined to be criminals. The false ideology of associating success with one colour is backward and need not be the order of the day in the lives of people. Just and balanced economic practices will heal our nations from high levels of crime and poverty.

People do not need to turn to crime in order to provide for themselves. The old way of doing things makes most people uncomfortable and it needs to be destroyed from its foundation to the top of its roof peak. All people deserve good on this earth and we need not waste time tolerating lies that keep us wandering on this earth without a purpose for living. A reconciled mentality has a sense of responsibility and justice for all people.

Fear of the unknown must be overcome and an inferiority complex no more an obstacle among us as a people. By building together, we can achieve the future we all desire.

Take it to heart

Feared are those in power, envied are the rich, but only a man of character can be trusted. When your gift or talent takes you where your character cannot keep you, you fail or crash. Now is the time to make the world a better place to live for all people. If resolutions do not start from the top, revolution will start from the bottom. The world is trying to control the masses through a few rich, who want to own the continents and bully the world into what they want. Pushing the masses away should not be the slogan now; it is high time that things change. Wars are born out of weak leadership that has direction. Chaos becomes the order of the day in this situation.

You do not vote for a leader because you are of the same tribe or come from the same village or town. People need to understand that modern leadership goes beyond race, tribe, and colour. A leader has to have a right heart of integrity to work through issues that need justice. The skill to serve people brilliantly without seeing their colours will pave the way to real freedom. Leadership is a relative link that has to show everyone the right way to progress. Those who lead must be able to see further and pave the way forward rather than just dress smart and enjoy the luxury salary packages. The main cause of the recession that the world saw was a lack of integrity in both governments and private sector management.

Integrity is the essence of life. Faithfulness is its cornerstone. The misappropriation of funds is a major problem with our civil servant generation. It seems everyone is late and so all are hurrying to make it through—whichever way it takes. The African nations have been subjected to debt not through their own choice but through the will of the rich nations that brought Africa into debt. Debt cancellation comes very late if it does come to African states. Pawning countries has been the game of the day, and compound interests have caused many underdeveloped nations to suffer without remedy.

Many times that borrowed money is swindled away by the leaders in governments, while the private sector seeks after stock exchange fraud—corruption is rife within this huge industry. More investment fraud has been unveiled in the twenty first century than in any other era. These cases involved billions of dollars all over the world. The people who lost out were those trying to earn a genuine living through both off shore investment markets and local. The shrewd beneficiaries were unscrupulous business directors and financial advisers who took advantage of those who invested in their companies at their own risk. Most countries are doing very little through their governments to bring the perpetrators to book. Are not governments supposed to stop lawlessness? It seemed many devious business persons enjoyed the pleasures of sin that ripped off people. Government officials and politicians who have huge unnecessary hotel budgets at the expense of poor people's tax money are a worrisome matter. The shopping sprees of many political leaders at government expense would shock their citizens if brought to public knowledge.

The greatest blessing of all is not when one is sworn into office or occupies a high office but when one does good work and succeeds in getting the blessing down to others. Many leaders of today have been unruly too long. Many of them never resign voluntarily and enter into retirement. It results in either forceful removal or unending wars leaving many dead because the masses have spoken against those leaders who enrich themselves at the expense of the people. The fruits of freedom promised by many government administrations today, end by the final vote of thanks from the leaders to those who put them in office – the masses who have voted them in. This poor quality leadership with its unfounded bases of governance is taking advantage of the less fortunate people. The developing world has yet to produce a credible leadership with a sound management system that is worth having.

Corruption has crippled and brought the developing world into disrepute with the world. Music piracy and movie cloning has enriched the dodgy leaders both in government and the private sector. Drugs have become the daily bread of the poor developing world as high profile syndicates enjoy links with police and governments' leadership, who are really secret criminals. This has become an issue of urgency on the African continent. Many African men and women are languishing in foreign jails after being caught working for these highly sophisticated syndicates that deal in drugs. These criminal syndicates are robbing communities of their wealth, peace and dignity.

The drug pushing issue is mostly blamed on black foreign nationals but it is not true that they are the only ones responsible here. The locals use foreign nationals as a scapegoat. We all need to rally together and build our nations with pride. Our first step will be to change anything that impedes our progress toward a bright future – one that is without fear but rather prosperity and peace. The truth remains; if revealed it will bring healing on African soil and in the developing world. And this truth means staying away from drugs.

If it means dismantling policies that have always been on our way, let us do so for the sake of promoting real freedom and peace. Illegal mining in Africa is escalating and this calls for new policies and change in this corrupt industry. People die while mining illegally and some criminal syndicates are using mafia-style tactics to keep legal mines' staff from blowing the whistle, as they even use those legal mines too. African governments need a strong policing unit on minerals and ores control to stop these problems and wars from going on. This would stop illegal jets from flying through African airspace to loot diamonds and ores. Africa will need economic liberalization, good management and the elimination of apartheid's ill-treating policies. A good leader is not the only thing an African country needs. He can be young or old and sleeping in office but that will mean nothing if all is in place on the government policy side. Good candidates in office alone also will not count since it is about teamwork leadership. This is why many do not understand why it seems like developing governments are always failing and cannot function properly.

A new style of leadership must be adopted that removes all residues of apartheid. Africans cannot run government ministries without authority. Old policies that have always protected the old constitutional idealists of post apartheid era are ruling developing countries. If there is anything that can make investors cry 'foul', it is the changing of constitutions to fairly give out services and distribute wealth equally among all people. The investors want nothing to do with the poor and the marginalized. That is why even the system designed by the former puppet workers neglects the poor. The puppet masters are able to bribe government departments and so that they never move from their policies of racial divide. They do it in the name of favourable policies and good investment opportunities. Such policies inevitably favour the rich and neglect the rest of the world. For Africa and the developing world to succeed in creating a healthy prosperous future for their people, there is a need to start afresh and redraft constitutions and policies with justice. Of course, it will affect investors' confidence but this is the only way to go. They will understand it better later, and history will vindicate those leaders who pave the way for this revolution.

The failure of this expected change has discouraged many brilliant sons and daughters of the soil because it leaves them with nothing but broken dreams about the freedom declared because of poor policy makers who fail the people. The dream of a free, prosperous developing world is dawning where we will have respect for each other and live side by side in peace. Senseless wars will be outmoded. A just society requires giving all who live in our countries necessary protection and peace. Also, those who enter our borders should be welcomed warmly and equally in order to enjoy their stay. The 2008 credit crunch saw more homes and assets repossessed in Africa and the developing world than elsewhere in the world. First world countries had a way of cushioning their citizens. Many rising stars or so-called "black diamonds" in my country have sunk down and some have "jumped ship" to search for greener pastures elsewhere in the world. There is no proper empowering as long as the symbols and instruments of capitalist influences are in place. Proper development and empowerment is building on a solid non-risk credit platform that minimizes economic collapses and tender bribe corruption.

More working and business class people own little—they pawn everything to the banks for collateral. This makes people lifelong slaves of their hidden master's interests; even their children will have to pay those compound interests, as they toil with the challenges of their own generation. Salaries are not from hand to mouth now but are from hand to creditors. Many workers and students of the developing world go to work or school with empty stomachs. Rich foreign nationals and locals are able to push off the masses from owning property and land because of the high price. Education has become unaffordable in colleges and universities. Africa needs a swift government intervention in all its spheres of ministry in order to fast track good service delivery. Monitoring watchdogs could help keep an eye on key areas of development.

It is time now for an African child to hate the AK 47 rifle and rather love pen and paper, which will lead to proper planning and development of good leadership skills. Let us use the soil to grow food for the nations of the world. Let developing countries create jobs for themselves and end queues of job seeking hungry people who are dying of malnutrition. A recent article published in South Africa showed that 30 trainee vacancies attracted 10 000 people, who stood in long queues without success. This shows the desperate plight of jobless people and that the nation is sitting on a time bomb. Why are our hard-trained nurses, doctors, teachers and many other professions leaving the continent to take employment in other continents? In many cases, they end up working worse jobs than they had in their respective countries. Why have we not cared for our own prized professionals so that they left our countries? It is like a married couple that does not sit down and resolve issues but chooses divorce. Then, after divorce, they discover they need each other desperately, but the unwillingness to compromise lands them in a love desert and a life of regret. Our governments have taken advantage of their people as much as the postcolonial powers did. The salaries paid to the civil servants in developing nations would be an insult in developed countries. The civil servants must moonlight in order to make ends meet and this in turn has made them render poor quality service to the people. Trade unions negotiate salary increases that are even below the inflation target, which seems confusing.

Africa must use those power-sharing governments – not just decorate them with a few women who stand to portray right demographic standards – but also to move forward together to develop all people. The hardest thing to do is to try to grow economies at the expense of the poor masses. Who drives the leadership to force the masses to dance to this tune? It seems the trends are similar to the oppressors', the only difference being that now the oppressor is black or of local origin. The rich greedy exploit the developing world's governments, as they know how to make them listen and neglect the masses' needs. You might argue that the colonial era was very bad compared to the new independent developing world and I would say yes, to a certain extent. Statistics have shown that the death figures of the liberation wars were less than recent civil war numbers. Whites are making more money in Africa now, than at any other time of history. Though there is some change among a few Blacks, the majority have gone poorer and this tells me something is wrong here.

Genocides, civil and religious wars, including hunger, led by poor health and bad morals fuelling HIV and AIDS have left us with more diseases and dead than at any other time. Africa leads in resource richness and it is the richest resource continent in the world. But the ores will only benefit its people when well managed. The continent that has been winning the trophy of poverty repeatedly for years now is Africa. We have a multitude of orphans because of wars, starvation, sickness and disease. The future of many children in Africa is bleak. Africa needs to address its issue of poverty with new vigour in order to bring answers for some of its self-imposed yokes of slavery. The curse of the continent is to fail to keep and manage such a rich heritage of resources on the planet. The future of Africans and the developing world is in their hands and I believe the true change is yet to come.

Until Africans accept that Africa is theirs to have and keep, they will never share it with each other well. God was thinking about the sons and daughters of Africa regardless of their colour when He gave its borders and marvellous beauty to them. This is a rainbow continent with all colours of people. But false religion with its evil workers has lied to people. God is not so evil as to destroy men in order that His influences might dominate. Africans need to know what is of God and what is not. Illiteracy makes the developing world's people easy prey for evil people.

Children used for cheap labour and in wars by evil warlords and strategists have caused concern all over the world. An arrogant philosophy needs to die among the people of the developing world. I wish many developing world children could rise up for an urgent cause, which is to liberate millions of minds trapped in war zones and to resolve disputes peacefully on the earth. No one has the right to kill a person in order to acquire diamonds, gold and other precious ores. Human blood is not cheap. We have the power to be free from the oppression that stands on our way as if it was our god. Let us remember the golden rule: "DO TO OTHERS WHAT YOU WOULD LIKE THEM TO DO TO YOU." The developing world needs to develop leaders who can put right all governing policies and laws. If need be, consider changing constitutions and legislations without fear or apology in favour of development of infrastructure and human capital. Freedom's fruits must reach all people on the earth. All people need to partake of a free democratic environment, where embracing and cherishing human rights is the standard course of action.

Study and add value to your nation without feeling embarrassed or that you are a liability! You were not born to watch others succeed and you being just a face in the crowd, destroyed by the struggles of life. For such a time as this, you are to captain your life's "ship" to its destination. The fact that you haven't had privilege as others did does not mean you cannot excel above them all! I tell you that the time has come to outshine other nations and races, especially when many have failed and incurred big losses that led the whole world into a recession. Africa and the developing world need to forgive their former enemies and not be accusatory even now to those who are failing it. It does not matter what happened and how dismally we failed; success is a guarantee if we do things well. We should fight tooth and nail this enemy of underdevelopment in Africa and the developing states, and its poverty. Good strategic planning can map out better ways of winning this battle against underdevelopment and poverty.

It is imperative to know we can achieve a prosperous future even when covered with scars. We must never lose out because of concentrating on foolish wars. Our focused efforts will address fundamental issues like housing, global warming, poverty, sickness and disease, illiteracy and joblessness. Military equipment like the AK 47 are to be our farming hoes and implements. In South Africa, a jeweller bought all illegal imports of firearms from the government and makes jewellery out of the lot. Peace gives birth to good governance, and good governance brings prosperity to all people. Access of basic needs for people is essential. The pillars of economic development lie on basic needs like water, electricity and communication. The government must closely monitor the high port tariffs that hamper growth. We all hope and pray that Africa and the developing world will meet the deadlines of development as stipulated with United Nations bodies.

Character frees people

In every society and community, something drives people. It could be tradition mingled with customs, which form a lifestyle of a particular tribe or society. This could be, at the end of the day, a culture of that very sect of people. The end result of this driving force is the same teaching abiding from generation to generation. In this teaching are various mannerisms that form the basis of lifestyle behaviour and order. The focus of this order in life is to dwell with each other in harmony. Every tribe and tongue has its own culture. There is good and bad (if not evil) in almost every culture. The philosophy of culture has two platforms it rests its foundations on. The first seeks to do well to humankind and please people with good morals, and the second seeks to reverence a higher authority such as a king.

The latter scenario overrides the will of the people and focuses attention on the kingdom of the higher office on the land or community. It has little interest in the things of others, as many times it disregards what people think in order to please its makers. That is why it is always opposed to democracy. People are always shocked in South Africa when the winter circumcision death toll takes dozens to the grave. The philosophy of the culture is weird at times; a real man has to survive the butchering of his flesh in circumcision during the extreme cold of winter. Ignorant about modern methods and lacking in expertise, bogus initiation schools make their way into this lucrative market. Police close illegal initiation schools all the time and leaders are arrested for murder as young men die because of pain from poor surgery operations.

Someone is male as a matter of birth but to be a man is a matter of choice. Dozens of males die every year in African initiation schools trying to be men, as culture depicts manhood. When culture surfaces, it often reveals the core values of that tribe, people or nation. Over many centuries, different cultures have been handed down to later generations bloodlines. In recent generations, as modern civilization took its toll, and even currently many people are breaking away from the grip of culture. Culture is so strong that even nations' laws and judicial systems rest on its shoulders. Those that went before us paved the way for deducing law from culture, and its implementation is from culture and cultural values. The prime focus of culture was to instil order in the lives and hearts of people. There are things that are taboo in every culture, as a means to prevent the worst evils among people. However, even this is not a real antidote to many problems of today.

The whole process of understanding culture comes from learning it from a young age through parents in homes. That is why it leaves such a strong mental and psychological effect in people's minds. Culture has remained strong in third world countries because where there is little education and reasoning, change takes place slowly. First world countries have developed systems that work best for everyone as much research has been devoted to free people in the times they live in. Identifying things that people need is easy and the "excess baggage" people do not want to put up with today.

Sometimes cultures have deep secrets that are practised by those who belong in them. There seems to be a longing to revere a higher power among cultures. You hear people attached to the culture argue that they received it like that and that is the reason they practise it. The longing is born out of a desperation to find a better more fulfilling lifestyle. Now, you will see a certain form of worship among African cultures in the name of ancestral powers who supposedly give great assistance in the lives of the living. Who say the dead who made that culture and then taught it to others have the power to bless those who are alive.

Most cultures have no place in modern societies, as they are backward and lack sense among other people who examine them. Ignorance reigns in most cultures as people do things not knowing why they have to do them. In a Zulu or African culture, a young man or person is not supposed to look an elder person in the eye. Why was this said to be disrespectful? We could speculate that child abuse was rampant in the days when that culture came into effect. Anything could be imagined but we are still in the dark as even today none of the elders can answer the question. Perhaps only those who made it had the understanding of what purpose it served among their tribe or people. It may well have been simple prejudice against young people. I have seen university and college graduates who still fall into this cultural trap and come out confused, saying it is their culture.

Herbal healers of old had a way of helping and serving their communities with the knowledge of many herbs. When modern science came, it proved to work better as it did away with senseless overdoses and the side effects of many herbs, which people would consume in order to get healing. This is civilization at its best that many still resist in the developing world today as they have little understanding concerning such matters. I sometimes think some people have been so much cheating themselves that they cannot believe in modern medicines, as they think it is white men's idea to put away their traditions. In many instances, these herbal doctors are more expensive than modern doctors are and tend to deliver worse results.

Using goats, sheep and cattle as a form of payment is still common among such people. Some African states have allowed these herbal doctors to take medical aid card payments and issue letters of check up and diagnosed or treated diseases. It is part of the democratic process as the continent's traditions try to align with the modern health industry. This ancient industry deals in raw bush herbs, which they dry up or consume while still fresh. Certain animal skins and meats are also part of this ancient culture of healing. The study of this ancient science with its different beliefs of cultures is fascinating.

You will see herbal doctors sending out pamphlets with claims that they cure all sicknesses, even HIV and AIDS. They are from all four corners of Africa, the queues are long in their offices but it is a false advertisement that draws people to what they have believed in for centuries. Many black people are illiterate and even if not HIV positive, ignorance about the disease makes them go to some herbal doctor charlatans who take their money through false pretence. There is a need to transform culture, as it is often times not keeping up with modern civilization's changes and challenges. The belief is, if it was taught and used by those who have gone before, it should still be given high priority even if not much can come of it now. That is the basis for the cultural mindset.

I get heartbroken every time when I see culture used manipulate others by those societies who uphold it. I will mention a few cultural boundaries I know and can identify with among many more that remain a sensitive issue among people of our continent. A woman must stay one full month in the house with the baby after having given birth without leaving the house. Perhaps in the days that custom was put in place, temperatures were extremely cold and windy, quickly killing children less than a month old who go outside. Also, people will dance, stir up dust, sneeze because of that dust and say, "makhosi." It means ancestors have come and touched that person or those people, which is not true but simply there is too much dust affecting the dancers. This is what many cultures celebrate on heritage day on this side of the world.

Virgin young women must parade almost naked before the king and young men in order for the African king to touch and feel the figure until he gets one he chooses and thereafter all other men can choose their own. Polygamy is common among men of this kind of culture. It humiliates women and makes them symbols of exploitation in the name of "This is how our forefathers did," and so people will continue doing it that way. The grievous sin of African cultures was injustices of men toward women, which continue to this day. There is very little that an African average woman can do to break away from this prison of cultural injustices. Surely, I would not like to see my daughter parading naked to try her luck with an old man who has many wives already.

There are times when culture makes no sense but just brain washes people. The fact that the grandparents practised that culture does not necessarily mean it is right to follow it now. It is a shame to see how young men are injured and sometimes die through bogus initiation schools in the name of being circumcised men, which culture refers to as real manhood. People are accepted as men only if they stay and endure a cold winter away from home almost naked the whole time during the healing process and ritual practices which can take months. Some of these young men even drop out of school and go for these initiation school classes, put above normal education. This is what the parent generation regards as manhood among many black cultures. In true essence, cutting off the foreskin does not make one a man. Hospital circumcision is not usually acceptable, as father figures perceive it to be for weak, sissy men. Most African cultures treat men as kings and the women as slaves. Violence against women is rife among African black communities, and it is the number one cause of divorce today since most women are beginning to understand their rights. A man trained by culture does not believe that a woman can suggest something or disagree with a man.

The moment a woman disagrees with a man, she is accused of infidelity and even gets assaulted by the man who thinks this is the way to put her back to her place of submission and being less than man is. And when a man has several mistresses, a black African woman must risk contracting HIV OR AIDS in silence lest a beating or ridicule by society ensue. Most of them get HIV and AIDS after protesting with several confrontations, which fall on deaf ears and in vain with their men. Until death, a cultured man is proud of his decaying culture that lost good moral values or never had them at all. There is the pride of one gender lifted above another. The curse of this culture is the spread of HIV and AIDS, which has contributed to the increase of orphans on the continent.

Most African cultures regard women as children. That is why the bride's price has little meaning today. Why has it gone so expensive? Is it serving its original purpose, or is it just a business transaction where women are sold to men they did not choose or love? At times negotiations are between parents only. Culture only allows the so-called royal families to rule others even with an iron fist at times. Others cannot rule the royal families as they regard that inferior. That is why most political parties are comprised by one tribe of people on the continent of Africa and in other third world countries where culture still has a strong grip.

All this is just a strong mentality instilled in royal families' minds from their youth, which says they are better than others are. In order to get a point across with an African king, you will have to say to the king that he is king and you are nothing and praise him as you abase yourself. You will then see smiles all over the king's face and the wrong kind of pride taking over. With him, all people are nothing and the royals are the only worthy people. HIV and AIDS infection rates are high because of cultural traditions that fuel ignorance among the people of Africa. Men of Africa can bring a halt to the HIV epidemic if only they can grasp the purpose of manhood on the continent and stop behaving and walking around with lustful hearts that are never satisfied or fulfilling a purpose in life.

A couple took an infant to an herbalist who took some dry herb leaves and burnt them on fire. The smell permeated the atmosphere and was very strong; the child swung over that smoke for hours. The diagnosis was that the child had an attack from the powers of witchcraft that had caused her influenza or sneezing. You can see such flaws of research and assumptions had no basis in fact. It could have been that the child picked up a flu bug or infection. The next day the child was much worse and the herbalist could not be of much help. The parents took the child to hospital where an x-ray showed the baby lungs had been affected adversely by the smoke, putting the child's life in danger. Eventually, the child passed away in hospital. Culture accompanies its beliefs that make up the base of its foundation and is not the answer to most people's problems today. Culture is a strong form of manipulation for some leaders as it takes advantage of the ignorance of people.

Where people are well-educated the grip of culture breaks off and there is usually true freedom. In many black societies, children are not respected and therefore do not matter. That is why many children have to continually look after cattle in the bush until the government intervenes with policies that protect children and encourage them to go to school. Some Africans discourage children from going to school as they argue that education is meaningless in their culture. There has to be a culture of educating people, as change is hard to come by without education, which instils proper reasoning in people. The hard thing is to unlearn what you have learnt. Underdevelopment is the pain of Africa that needs to be taken seriously and used as a wakeup call, to value and evaluate much needed change and human capital development requirements among nations. When people do away with cultures that have left them behind and not allowed them to break free from inferior past ways of life, a constant learning of new ways and means of modern civilization survival will become a wonderful experience for such communities.

Culture remains wanting change, and organs of justice and truth need to be in place with it. Why has it lacked the fundamental cornerstones of peace? Was the design of many cultures out of fear and favour? That is its main problem—that it has most times not stayed abreast of modern civilization, as it is our elders' life philosophy inherited through the elders' teachings and lifestyles. Can a man or woman build character based on culture's questionable values? No, it doesn't seem possible. We will need something more here.

We are going to explore all our society's pillars of character on this chapter. Why do religious people pervert religion's values? Religion and culture are synonymous. Both are manmade ways to equip humankind with tools for a well-mannered and disciplined life. From the beginning of time, we have never heard that God made culture or religion. It is interesting to see how men articulate culture and religion. I said before that some cultures have forms of worship too. Now I want to dwell on religion without the spirit and life of God. It tears down nations and people to preserve its interests of power. The religion discoverers have always put the rules and laws of religion around a high force centre named god or leader.

It adapts culture, customs and traditions and incorporates them together in reverence of a main god or statue if not a created or existing thing. It serves the interests of those who started it and captures the imagination of those that come into it through teaching or channels of their elderly people. Simple is its definition, now let us move right along. Most religions in the world have gods and dedicated places of worship designated. The places are connected with the leaders' birth and death or any other significant events that may be ordained as special for services or annual events of a religion. Often a greed for power and a selfish nature, together with ignorance about God are found in men who initiated a religion. And the founder of the religion is often the worshipped person. The danger is the confusion and damages that religion without life and the spirit of God does to people's minds. Religion adheres to its own teachings and accepts no others even if they are right. If it does not come from the religion or philosophy's originator, it is not welcome. Many times good religious people neglect truth without fully considering it.

Religion runs parallel with cultural values. Both have a strong hold and dire consequences in the minds of those who live and practise each of them. Most people become guilty of not doing, practising religion or culture at one time or another, as these often become part of their lives. That is why culture or religion teaches people to dress in certain attires for various occasions or in everyday life. Sometimes they will dress in their ancestors' style of skin wear and certain grass or animal skin types used as bangles around the arms. It reminds the people how their grandparents lived and felt in those attires before modern civilisation. Now religion teaches the way of dressing and meditation or dancing for a god or gods. Most cultures do away with meditation but worship ancestors by killing animals for meat simply because the people love to eat lots of meat and drink beer with much dancing on most of their celebrations. Life is a celebration around material stuff most times here with little or no emphasis on righteousness and holiness. Even the slaughtering of animals is in certain ways, and most cultured people do not like city life. Why is it so? Perhaps it is because their ancestors never designed that lifestyle.

Religion is a fabricated idea to try to reach God. Ancestral worship tries to use the dead to speak to God on behalf of the living. The only difference between the two is that religion sometimes goes via the dead too but mostly it performs its rituals through one man who leads them as one who has studied religion in order to perform it before people. Exhaustive cultural materials and ways of conducting ritual performances are passed down to all those who belong to it. Long dignified clothes are mainly the order of the dress code. Religion tries hard to focus its attention to a higher source, which can be seen or unseen. The fact of the matter is that the source referred to as god is the most adored. Some religions are born out of hurt and resent certain peoples as culture does. Many times if you are not of that religion or culture, you do not count to those people.

Religion offers little justice and truth as culture does in most times. I know religions that say the reason God made women was for the pleasure of men. This agrees one hundred percent with many cultures that prey on women. Religion teaches you cannot cheat your religious mate but anyone outside your religion you are free to cheat. Religion will put a few good works in practice before men but in reality, the intentions may be evil. It pins masses down by putting the fear of a higher force in their hearts and that higher force is said to be above all. This keeps the followers on track as they only listen to their blind leaders. Both religion and culture use many resources to do and advance their cause, whether it is good or bad works. Large traditional celebrations that manipulate women and the less fortunate are common here. Cows are good things if used for good causes. Billions of dollars have been used to finance corrupt religious deals and wars. Even apartheid governments were religious, as their evil works explicitly proved them to be without justice and love for others.

The fact of the matter is neither culture nor religion can help people develop character. I never met anyone excited and all smiles saying, "God said dress this style or that and celebrate with much meat, then, you will be His child." Both of the above are self gratifying and have within them hidden agendas to bring people under subjection so that the propaganda continues for men's pleasure only, not for others or God. When you study the heart of the true living God, you will realize the folly of churches that backed apartheid during the colonial era, who were simply evil people without life and the spirit of God. That has made even African leaders confused when it comes to church and religions as they know not the truth and neither understand God. Many leaders see religion as a way of pinning people down for financial gains under false pretence. Yet, all people must look to God to receive a change of heart by new birth, which is only in God and according to His instruction in His explicitly given way.

The South African apartheid Parliament prayed 24/7 but produced the same bad works every day. The prayers offered by leaders who had no understanding of God was evil and even those who did prayers were only interested in the money and food offered there. All seemed right and great in the eyes of religion and its masters, but it was vanity before God. Does God allow any of us to degrade a man because of the colour of skin? The religious church never accepted Blacks within its church walls. Some came up with theories that blacks had no soul to believe in God. The country never had a true church as it all boiled down to looting resources in the name of God and abusing blacks. The country's economy grew at the expense of poor blacks. Now is the time for a true church to shine and pave the way to heal the nation.

The church of the apartheid regime reverenced its masters who started it more than the Holy God it professed to represent. That is why even God is never religious because it would make His world too small if men would design it for Him. All men are created equal and I believe if they can be right in their hearts, God will cloth them with a garment of righteousness. There should be no flaws with true worship and reverence of the living God. It gives people liberty and peace including love for God and one another. This means we cannot hate, cheat, hurt or murder others if joined to our lovely Creator. In sum, then, nothing that has no justice, truth, peace and love for all people is of God.

Choosing culture, religion or church is personal but choosing God is not optional since we need character in our lives.

Only our creator can save us from all the struggles and folly of trying to perfect ourselves without justice. If we accept His divine nature and love, we can have a new meaning for life and zest for creating a better world for everyone to live in. Men have lied and confused people's minds but God never does that and will always make us understand the right way of living. His ways are truth and justice to all wanting true life and to abide by it. God brought us the gospel—the good news of justice and truth that brings love, fulfilment and success to people from all walks of life. This came with a heavenly gift package for all humankind to choose and forever be free to live with God. Here it is God reaching out to humankind not vice versa!

"Manners make a man," is a cultural saying embraced by many. Perhaps this is true. People are said to be what they eat. Maybe the person that said that was right. And I say that you are also a product of the teachings you have received. If you have character, will you allow others to sell their bodies for a living without feeling sorry for them and give them your hand to help them do something better with their lives? Would you not care when your mother or sister sells her body to make a living? Character goes beyond mere lust for gain. You begin to measure everything by the golden rule which is to do unto others what you would like them to do for you. Life is simply God's planned purpose on earth with seasons of sowing and reaping. We reap everything we sow in our lives.

Character can save all people from doomed lives and the misery that the world has plunged into. Religion or culture cannot give a person character. There is a difference between obeying God your Creator and using Him to fulfil the deceitful pleasures of life. I believe strongly and am fully persuaded that heaven and hell are in fact real places that separate people according to God's word. Faith in God through His (only) Son Jesus Christ—not culture or religion—gives salvation that saves from eternal death received from the (only) living God and is mankind's only solution to sin and eternal condemnation. No other name on earth can save a person but Jesus. Anything outside Christ is only religion associated with the philosophies of men. To me the Bible not only makes sense, but is true and therefore I choose to abide by it, as I believe it is God's word. You might ask why I believe the bible is true. If all things have owners on this earth, then someone owns all. It makes sense to me to believe in God so that when I leave this world I may go to heaven. I know it is impossible for God to lie. Character cannot just fall from the sky; otherwise, it would be a false pretence of character. That is a main source of frauds and evil in our generation today. Without God infusing His nature in us, no leader can have true character.

All things work together if one is led by faith in the awesome God, who is supreme over all. This is the only way I find fulfilment and He teaches me to uphold justice, truth, peace and love to all people. God is inclusive not exclusive. The hope of a lifetime with my holy heavenly Father is the anchor and pillar of my lifestyle of worship. I then live to please Him, not lusts or other people or things. Anything else that man tries to do to reach God always leads him to a vicious circle of confusion. Every time God gives humankind His truth it sets people free, as this is not religion but a divine union of God and humankind. God is interested in putting His nature and life in His people so that they may live like Him. And this brings freedom and peace rather than wars, violence and confusion. To me it makes sense to worship the true living God. The worship of the true living God equips all people with love, freedom and power to live peaceful lives regardless of colour, race or culture. Colour, race and culture dim during true worship of God and love blends all worshippers with the colour of God's spirit. I am sharing profound truths here. If you do not know Jesus just find out about Him; this man is the love of God to the world. You can receive Him as your Lord and saviour if you want true life.

I usually say that the bottom line is being with God by faith now on earth before getting to heaven. Faith is my vehicle to the unseen glorious expected end of my hope in God. This is my personal choice that makes me focus on doing well never being sorry at the end nor finding myself thrown into hell by God because of disobedience to His sacrifice for humankind's sins (Jesus). Have I been to heaven? No, I just take the promises of God, instructed from His word, by faith I believe and hope in Him, walking my journey in His truth every day towards the goal of my destiny. My understanding and love for life led me to make this choice without fear, and not just through logic. That is why I can only say it is my choice of faith-by-faith. I can confidently confess I believe in God through His son Jesus Christ who died for me on the cross of Calvary. Oh, yes, I love Jesus! God is the one who gives me my identity and character through Christ.

I sat down and looked at every culture and religion and nothing made sense to me except that Jesus is Lord of Lords and king of kings. I made my choice based on truths without flaws. True freedom for humanity is God's heartbeat for life in the instructive love letter called Bible. Nothing all my parents and ancestors taught me could match this overwhelming truth of life of given freely to anyone who chooses to trust God unswervingly. With all the abuses of culture and religion I went through, I finally rested on the day I received Jesus into my life and, thank God, the truth dawned on me. All other forms of worship lacked the fundamental truths of God's love and justice, which are the supports of peace and freedom for all people. Religion and culture tend to lift one race above another, one tribe above another, and one gender above another.

Religion and culture remain wanting and short of the glory which is the nature of God. I say lacking in glory because when justice, truth, peace and love come together it is glorious and can save people from many evils of life. These four elements, together with accepting Christ the author of life become what I call salvation for humankind. All people from all walks of life are safe in this truth and can dwell in peace and freedom. Above all, it comes with a true blessing for all humanity and makes all striving to cease. These are universal truths of life concerning faith in Christ although I cannot dwell on them now.

Now, you can still have character without having made a choice to go to heaven. Unless your talent is exposed to an environment where it can develop and flourish, it may lie dormant forever. The truth is that your potential cannot be fully maximized unless the Living God touches your life with His. Unless God shares with you His divine nature, you will always fall back into man's failures because culture and religion can be great snares. People are not robots but beings with free choice, a will and emotions. Their souls and spirits make them know what is right according to their Creator's will and the choice comes when one obeys or disobeys their Maker's still, small voice inside them. Knowing good and bad is innate in all people. That is why the bible says God has put eternity in the hearts of all people. My spirit tells me there is a God without me trying to figure it out. I just need to find the right way to be with Him.

There is a feeling of an expectation of goodness that people feel the Creator wants to see from them. That is why religion tries to emphasize holiness among people and culture too has some good to teach people. Concerning all these matters, there must be some truth hidden that, when it becomes clear in the people's minds and hearts, brings a new dawn to people's hearts and lives. It would be good for human flesh to discover the heritage of justice from their Maker rather than culture or vain religions. What I can only say is that religion and culture remain wanting. They cannot bring true salvation to our dying and morally decaying world. We have to quit trying to justify our choices without love and justice in life. We have to rely on truth that makes sense rather than be led into a bottomless pit by cunning ideologies that are foolish and backward.

Integrity is the essence of life. Faithfulness is its cornerstone, I often say. If education, prosperity or success takes you where your character cannot keep you, you will crash and be doomed to dismal failure. Character is not always the basis for religion or culture, because the two can often contain hidden intentions and agendas as I mentioned before. Character is right ego in a person, which overflows with the same measure of good ego towards others in life. If you have character, you will also have principles in place rather than just being tossed back and forth by winds of teachings. Character is a deep longing to bring fairness and justification to all areas of our life without hurting others or ourselves. Without principles in place, you cannot be successful. Who has to teach you principles? Most principles monitor our will from deep inside and govern our outward demeanour. Their intention is to do good to all people with love and peace. When making laws and rules, leaders sat down and looked at how the Creator made people's behavioural patterns to align with human rights and democracy. The main role that law plays in our lives is to encourage good character in all people.

Stealing is not right and therefore anyone who steals faces the wrath of the law. Generations gone-by put the law in place and today we learn about those laws and uphold them because we believe they are good for our society even when we amend some at times. Some evil laws that had no character have been amended or eradicated. They could not be justified as they enslaved other people and served its cruel makers' interests. The purpose of the justice system is to administer law and to prosecute without fear nor favour the wrong doers. Thus, character is good, just behaviour, which does not offend others or take advantage the weak. Character is a fruit of self-discipline that goes along with authenticity – a justification that comes from inside the human heart and is manifested in a life. Character has nothing to do with who is watching you. One of the pillars of character is honesty. To have honesty, you must start with being honest to yourself and then to others, otherwise it is just lip service. It must come from you without fear and with authenticity – a true spirit of love for life, others and even nature. Character requires a lifestyle of constant evaluation of oneself and one's values towards others.

When a man says to his creditor "The Cheque is on the mail" when he knows well he has not sent it, he has just lied, but above all he has no character to understand that this will affect the only business asset he has, which is his reputation. It may not be noticeable at first but in the end, the fruits will show. Character sows the right seed and reaps the right harvest. Having no character may be the reason a business closes down – not because the owner has no knowledge or skill to run it – but for lack of good character. Anyone who lacks character is as dangerous as a loose lion in the zoo. Character educates and matures people to live well and make the world a better place.

Let us talk about infidelity among married couples today. It is not that the partner does not love the other one but has allowed lust to take over their heart and control it. Character could have gone out with the wind a long time ago. Today this dilemma has cost families the lives of their mothers and fathers. The spread of HIV and AIDS is a result of lack of character among men and women within different cultures, religions or church affiliations. What has contributed to such a high rate of family breakdown currently? The high rate of divorce is another matter of concern among our communities today. Have prosperity and civilization spoiled us as people? Maybe cars and cell phones have made it too easy to keep in touch with nonsense issues and connections today. However, those gadgets are not meant for evil but for good.

Racism is a culture with no moral basis of character among those who practise it today. Its evil effects have haunted millions around the world and are still doing the same today. Those that started it lacked character and those who are still enforcing it have followed suit. A teenage boy drops out of school and battles to keep a job after that. He then becomes fed up with his poor lifestyle, and goes and joins himself to a bank-robbing gang. After a year, his colleagues get shot by police at the robbery scene and he surrenders with some of his gang members there. In court, he gets a few life sentences. The boy and his peers lacked the most important ingredient of life and that was their problem. For a while, he was rich with proceeds of corruption until he reaped the fruits of his work. People without character live and die unfulfilled in life.

If a woman is beautiful, does she have to sell her beauty? No, it will be beauty with no brains if she does that. Disgusting debates of legalizing prostitution all over the world are a matter of concern in our morally decaying societies today. Let us look at the moral fibres of our societies. Even the government leaders lack character when they begin to push for such issues of to be legalised. It creates a situation of drug abusers, which empowers drug dealers who in turn prey on the weak and helpless prostitutes. The pimps stand to gain, not the sex workers. Again, even the job itself lacks character and sanity and has very little to offer in terms of job security to those who practise it.

Let us talk about the notorious fraudsters we have seen in recent times. A greedy attitude and proud intentions led these people to a fall. They gathered for themselves false riches with money swindled from state or society organisations. It did not matter to them how it would affect others or its investors but self-gratifying motives led to these disasters. Mines and companies, mistreating workers and leaving them in hazardous health conditions without any compensation, lacked business ethics and character. The owners of such companies were also evil and lacked integrity and character. Do our leaders have character? Surely if leaders had character, there would be no fraud and money misappropriations that are accompanied by sex scandals within our government departments today, leading to heavy fines, expulsions and jail sentence terms.

Many musicians, sportsmen and women today fall because they lack character and get involved in extra-marital affairs that expose them to shame and regrets. When they are caught with their pants down, they say in apology to their fans that they had a wrong ego when they prospered. This was just a lack of focus, discipline and fulfilment, which boils down to a character crisis. This cancer afflicts all people in all spheres of life. The choice remains simple; we can resist our temptations if we have character. Not having character is simply neglecting what is right in order to satisfy our wrong ego. In other words, you suddenly become a cowardly person before those who had highly esteemed your integrity.

Most inmates in prison today had one common problem. They continually travelled the slippery road of having no character. Surely, many of them could have avoided that road long ago but chose not to. The making of law is in such a way that, when found guilty, it means you have been proven to lack the standards of character that a citizen should have and respect. That is why people who offend others so grievously are called criminals. They knew what was right but chose not to do it. It means that in them are no more good morals but bad only. The correctional service plays a role in bringing back character among such men and women by putting them away from societies. Many of them have become dangerous or can put societies at risk if allowed to live among them.

People appreciate the parole system in the new justice administration very much. The only problem is that the society seems not to serve well in helping to rehabilitate ex-convicts. The institution of correctional services must instil character in the minds of inmates. With the help of other role players and organizations, the bad character of individuals in Africa and the world can be patched up. Scarcity of jobs and resources for people will need to be addressed in order to stop crime. Many crimes are committed because of the poverty and lack found in our societies today. Do the service delivery services of our nations have fair platforms of wealth distribution? It is a shame to note that many African states have allowed tender business corruption to get out of hand. Companies are now relying on tenders and the governments are just building tendering states. The future of these companies is bleak as the governments continue to have great budget deficits. Therefore, the process only enriches a few rich who in turn are doomed to fail eventually.

I looked at South Africa's hottest debates, even among the ruling party alliances and saw the urgency for an immediate change in the tender awarding system. The youth league has proposed the nationalization of mines as a solution to the country's joblessness. Agriculture, land and black emerging farmers getting a fair chance are other issues of debate today in the country. Indeed all the above issues are important areas that need urgent attention. The giving of tenders to a corrupt few has widened the gap between the poor and the rich. It does not benefit all the intended stakeholders of the government's targeted beneficiaries, but rather spends precious resources on unintended recipients.

There is no doubt that Blacks deserve good land and empowerment when it comes to breaking new ground on long protected industries. Why has land gone so expensive recently? Farmland has become the most contested commodity among African citizens. When most people looked at the future of South Africa, they noted the problems ahead, despite its encouraging economic growth among other nations of Africa. South Africa never owed any credit to the International Monetary Fund or the World Bank when it became independent. Only in recent years when the major project of hosting the FIFA world cup loomed, did it borrow funds. Things were not easy even during the building of the stadiums and it is still not easy as we cannot yet tell when we are going to breakthrough to a safer financial status. The government had a severe budget deficit in 2010 as a wave of recession took many industries into a nosedive and even closure at the end.

The focus now is on paying back the monies and creating conducive sources of revenue within the country. Most business leaders are thinking deep and would have to dig deep to keep their companies above waters. If the companies are retrenching people every day and closing down, it makes sense to say that the government finance departments will collect only little into their coffers. That is the worrying problem with many politicians, as they feel the government will fail the people if it is not well focused and quickly resorts to a better means of turning the economy around.

How the mining industry is empowering people remains a serious question. Has the industry dealt with this issue well before? By all appearances, it seems like it has used the poor workers and discarded them by the wayside, as this has been the practice of this rich industry on the land and around Africa. The pathetic salaries paid to the poor illiterate miners with little job security in the industry are distressing facts.

Many people still believe governments have to get into some businesses and manage them to benefit the people on the continent. Some people think the mining industry is one profitable business that governments need to explore. If the African governments could take over the mines, they could most probably give people better job security as well. Additionally, mine production would guarantee easy repayment for World Bank or IMF loans even if the economies are struggling in the future. The whole idea is not to burden people with high taxes in order to raise money and meet the deadlines of development in the countries. Management and the financing of mines by governments is a question of concern in the debate. The struggling parastatal divisions' poor monitoring mechanism is failing nations on the continent. There is no enough financial injection to spare for them. Further government spending cuts are expected as the years ahead are clouded with speculations of drought and the suffering of masses on the continent. In addition, global warming or climate change might take a toll and the future remains uncertain. It seems nations will leave no stone unturned. The only alternative to nationalization or government interference to bring a transitional process that is just and fair, is if the industry can move away from its ruthless culture of abusing workers and bullying the governments of the developing world. If the mining industry can begin to focus on creating sustainable jobs and people empowerment, it might survive the storm of harsh taxes or the upheaval of nationalisation and get approval from the public for a change. Its transformation process in the right direction could be the answer to its survival. Mining industry leaders will need to have character.

When the South African government made the Kruger gold coin years back, it had most mines under its control and it was truly a rich government with a majority of poor people. Much generated revenue went to the government and this is the hoped for results if nationalization takes place now. There is a great need for equality in people empowerment as South Africa is now a democratic country. The mine companies' C-Level or brass management is notorious and will need to have an attitude change and restore character within their organisations. The many strikes that we have seen are a sign that it could be possible to see even more harsh strikes, as times seem to get tough for both private and government sector workers. No one wants to lose. Everyone wants to know how to gain. The nationalisation of mines can work very well if the governments have money to fund these mining projects and to make them benefit the poor. Issues of concern remain in mines' management, funding, and eliminating corruption and crime in this ruthless industry.

There is no doubt about the theory working as all things are possible if only the governments are willing to inject capital into the mines' take-over processes. There will be a need for a wisely planned approach to mining transformation and management. Here is where the test of time on the government's part comes. Government maturity, strength and power depends on its ability to solve the impulse of nationalisation of mines or tax reforms when the time comes to deal with this issue directly and squarely. There is no doubt that after meeting the United Nations millennium goals and deadlines, developing countries will be able to tell when they can accomplish certain other projects. Let us not promote the ideas of the few lying in ambush to corrupt good concepts for their gain and benefit. I pray that the nation will not lack character in such challenging times as these. Even though President Jacob Zuma told the nation that the government was not looking at the nationalisation of mines issue—as it was not part of the country or party policy—a recent policy conference touched on this issue and the feeling is the government's stance on this subject is evolving. The ruling party leadership could not dissuade the party from thinking about solutions that can bring much needed change to the industry and workers empowerment. Many avenues and proposals are on the table and introducing new tax reform policies in the near future is on the cards.

Moreover, the South African Federal Reserve Bank shareholders wanted the government to buy the bank. What was at stake for this elite group of people? The old government system that lacked character has caused problems today. It is good to close every door to these problems before it is too late and we live to regret the works of a generation of leaders gone by, who were without character. The unjust means of running governments and organizations without character are haunting our generation and could harm generations to come if not dealt with well. Some think they have the right to get all, as it has been others' right to have all before, while still others think others owe them everything. This sick world situation needs character in order to bring justice to day-to-day operations within our nations and societies.

Unjust mineral ore management, which amounts to looting, is criminal. Rebel leaders in the developing world are criminals that lack character. Buyers of illegal minerals and ores are perpetrators of many civil wars on the African continent. The ruthless rich sponsor the wars indirectly, as the ores are given priority above people's lives here. Is there truth and integrity among men and women of this type? I think not. On numerous occasions, people die in unnecessary wars around the world. Masses of people lose their homes and precious possessions through the wars. Does it mean the law is not there? No, it is a matter of having no integrity management system in place. The reason the developing world needs powerful management by politicians is to make sure good policies are put in place and upheld through good implementation processes. The day African people learn to say no to bad and yes to good, will be a healing day for the continent.

You need character in your life more than anything else. If you have character, you can go far in life. Even if you do not reach a pinnacle point, you can still live blessed. You can retire happily and finish your career with fulfilment. Even sport at the professional level can have meaning until retirement. People who abuse alcohol and drugs lack character. Stop drinking excessively and focus on leaving an indelible legacy! Greediness for riches and pride are arch-enemies of character. Those who committed big frauds and were not needy, but rather greedy for riches, we see have been lured to the snare of jail.

Character does not compete, as we always come across different offers in various times of our lives. Ours is to be able to choose to say yes to good and no to bad. The bribes paid in our court justice system today have made people neither fear the law nor respect it. A sugared pill ruins nations and promote corruption. White-collar fraud is ruining countries. From the top leadership to the least officer, character is an essential ingredient if we are serious about living in peace. Sound policies and laws are nothing if people have no character. It will be just as if the laws never existed and they will not be able to better the lives of ordinary people who look up to the ruling government of the day. Leaders have to learn to take responsibility and be accountable at all times and on all levels.

Let us as a people learn to love what builds us rather than what destroys us. Life without character is empty and meaningless. People have to embrace character in order to overcome poverty, lack, sickness and disease. As we make goals, we can meet all our deadlines if we pursue them with good character. The problem is, every time Africa had goals in place, donors gave money, but the money disappeared into the pockets of a few corrupt leaders. The culture of having no character among our leaders must stop. A character crisis is responsible for the underdevelopment of people in many areas of life.

All people, regardless of where we find them, remain the products of their will and characters. Some have sacrificed their freedom and even their lives to defend justice. The abolition of slavery was accomplished by men and women who stood up to stop it; some even went to the point of dying for this cause of freedom. It seems that once in every generation there is a revolution to overcome evil. I believe people are never free from things which mistreat them until they understand the power within that stems from true personal freedom and joy. Character allows us to live together without being harmful to each other, allowing peace and harmony to rule over the emotions and feelings of our insecurity, and letting go of hurts and fears of being on an equal platform in life.

The mentality of enslaving others by taking resources and prosperity away from them has been and always will be wrong. Working in some companies around Africa is just legalized slavery, leaving people with no choice but to try to earn a living and not die. This not only hurts the people but also these companies practice such ruthless, immoral. Hungry, grumbling people cannot perform best at work. In addition, business owners who pay people poor wages and practise dishonest ways are not genuine business people but ruthless capitalists.

In the twenty first century, human resources have shifted from just managing structures and assets to managing people because this is the most important lifeline of any business. Companies that care more about resources and material stuff than the work force lack character and are opportunists who aim at maximum profits in whichever way. All of us have a responsibility to have character and administer justice with all our power and all we have, at all expense, in all times.

Something unites us as a people

The African continent is great and very rich in all mineral ores, but still lags behind when it comes to development and management. Let us look at the core issues of this cause. The history of Africa's colonization is true and it does not help ignoring it if the continent is to move forward in this twenty first century. Strong world nations took over the continent for a long time and they all exploited it in the same way though they even resented each other in their same white skin colours. It is a mistake to just look at those that had the last grip on the continent and miss the role of those who left earlier as Africa was beginning to gain independence. The countries of Africa have a unique pattern of development. The countries that achieved independence first were not yet well developed and you can easily distinguish them from those that received their freedom later.

Where the grip was strong to the later end, the countries look great and strive to own the great infrastructure developments and have a better life for the middle class people. What haunts those who got independence earlier are the inherited residual policies that were followed by sanctions whenever the leaders tried to break free from them. The handover of the countries to the founding fathers of the developing world nations did not come without strings attached. This made development progress and programmes slow, as most times these countries were outside the world common wealth and did not benefit from being member states of such institutions. Instead, that made them slaves of a "closed circuit" surveillance by super powers. Anything that the super powers did not like about these countries meant that sanctions were to be the order of the day. Though time has passed the same problem persists in Africa and in other developing states of the world today.

The countries with young democracies look better. The white men are not a problem hindering development and growth in Africa and many other developing countries. The superpowers' seeds of unfair control over developing world economies are what has been the problem. The colonial powers sowed a seed and their children enjoyed an inheritance to their children's children. Those with an upper hand over the economies have always been the non-African, who were beneficiaries of the past governments' segregation system. This was a controlling grip that none was willing to let go of to practise fairness. Unless Africans control the economy, Africa is not free and its sons and daughters will never be free. Africa is declared free but in reality is not yet free and liberated from the former oppressors' hands. Where did it go wrong?

The tailor-designed governance style for developing world leadership by colonial masters is a root cause of many problems around the world. The continent's division by the languages of the so-called super powers is interesting to note as it plays a big role in political influence to date. Some countries of Africa had to adopt foreign languages as their own. I was driving in Tete, Mozambique and not everyone I met could speak his or her mother tongue but only Portuguese. This showed me how sharp were the instruments of colonial times. Africans were better tools if they spoke their masters' language well. It tended to make them feel their language was inferior and that they were nothing.

The amazing thing is that those same people, men and women that spoke Portuguese so fluently could not write it or spell their names. If they went to school, it was an education designed to make them effective in serving whites. It was the same in the French, Germany, British, Spanish, Italian, Dutch and Arab colonies. The colonial masters developed the education system, handing it down to the developing world and those it oppressed. The rest of the Blacks worked under the supervision of a white man who was helped by a black man to ease communication at work places if the majority of workers were black. Blacks being lowly paid if not outright enslaved by the colonial masters' dogmatic ways, was the order of the day. During World War 2, many African soldiers went to fight alongside their colonial masters. This was not willingly but by force.

Some African heroes died in the war while a few remained to tell the pain of their ordeal. The colonial masters had many characteristics in common. The fertile land went into the hands of the whites and all mineral ores were automatically under their authority, which would continue from generation to generation. The riches of the African nations were continually transferred to the hands of whites only. That is the best way to describe colonialism and the apartheid system.

As long as you were a white person, you could enjoy the privileges of your colour while blacks were your servants. Whites took all the fertile land and blacks were relegated to native reserves that were large barren landscapes where soil erosion is prevalent. There was nothing much blacks could do but go back to begging from the men and women who had now taken all things for themselves. The system had a lot of flaws and injustices. Countries suffered even after independence as signed agreements at the hand-over of countries often went unfulfilled. The conditions were never easy and are still not easy to adopt. Wealth distribution was not just and the system never allowed it to be just even after the developing states attained independence. Trade was commonly done directly with colonial countries as those sons and daughters had strong bonds with their parent countries of origin. The import and export industry was reserved for those types of people who made money their god.

The whites built rich suburbs where a few blacks have joined them today. The settlement of people was according to their races. The blacks were the ones to suffer more than other races. Blacks got few subsidies for housing and education. Neither were rates and tax budgets in these various settlements fair. The old apartheid way transformed the economy into a complex capitalist society rather than keeping it simple. It meant that all other people had to use money to live even when they never had it. If they did not have money, then it meant they were to suffer hunger or die. As a result, many settled for low-paying jobs or cheap Labour. The dignity and heritage of the developing world's children were under enemy control.

African people have been always been great subsistence farmers by nature and their rich soils produced abundant harvests. The colonial masters made sure that blacks do not get land to farm nor have decent homes. They also deprived them of good education. These two tools of the colonial masters worked wonders in producing illiteracy and poverty on the continent and the world. It made many developing world people think they could not study agriculture and farm as other races do. The mind has been in prison so long that, even when the prison doors are open, many black folks cannot go out, as they fear failure and would rather stay by the comfort zone. The way the system works is to make the rich richer and richest, and the poor poorer until poorest.

The banks were using the same system of racial management, which makes it hard now to break free from its past ways of operation. The banking sector always saw the black market as being a risk. The banks saw the black market through of apartheid glasses. White folks enjoyed life from security to security and it gave them wonderful lifestyles on the continent.

Black children went from poverty to poverty so much that even today, they are still trying to come up from this era of deliberated deeds by white racists but it is very difficult. A large percentage of blacks in African states live in rural places where life is unbearable. These people can hardly afford to buy anything; many are jobless folks who end up putting up squatter camps around big cities. The impact of continuous droughts as global warming prevails and their soil being of the worst quality makes it difficult for them to survive on their homeland communities. They have no money to live by cities, and no one is willing to take up their cause or plight. The governments of Africa have burdens that are not easy to bear. Governments are for the people but have difficulty serving the same people well.

I am also of the opinion that the developing world is not so corrupt but the inherited system makes it corrupt. Surely, other races should share the countries' wealth with blacks rather than export the African wealth to their nations of origin in the name of trade relations. True black empowerment has to be the driving force of the African governments. Empowerment must be accomplished quickly before governments run out of options, as future challenges look even greater than today's problems. The fear of banks take over by Africans for a total overhaul has made many rich folks prevent Africans from getting involved in such businesses or sectors.

The cry of African children is to participate in certain industries in their nations. The insurance industry is one of them and is not explored nor tapped fully. Africa needs a new insurance program that will serve its entire people. Financial security is a great need all over the world now. It will be fair if the rich soils of the continent go first to its people and secondly to foreigners. The expensive services of banks must be updated. A complete balanced overhaul and a fair banking sector is what the developing world needs. It will need a system that addresses the problems of our generation and empowers all people with equal opportunities. The banks must align with the governments' goals of building an equal platform for all people in terms of development.

Land and property is big business in Africa but only a few rich own houses and land. These two items are an acceptable form of security to banks, since the two fixed properties are a form of collateral. Banks also recognize insurance policies of surrendered value as security or collateral. But the majority of people in Africa cannot taste the fruits of financial freedom because they cannot afford to participate in these things to build their financial security. They often do not even have a savings account in place. They will remain beggars until their problems are addressed, if ever they will be.

The whites had developed Africa with blacks and never allowed blacks to enjoy the fruit of their work as whites did. When black people fought against the system the whites claimed to own a lot of things and that made it hard to have a fair hand-over of countries to black leadership. The whites wanted control of what they claimed was theirs. This was not done in truth and transparency, but rather the schemed ways of keeping a tight grip on the land, ores and many industries have been in place for a long time. This gave them an upper hand in controlling the economies. I looked in my country South Africa and saw something that is wrong. Most universities are privately owned and the few rich Federal Reserve Bank shareholders who had voting rights controlled even the reserve bank. The new reserve bank governor had to correct many flaws with the central bank including limiting the control of the rich shareholders and taking away their voting rights.

The tertiary education fees are expensive and continually increase year by year above the inflation rate. Some of these universities are teaching students in the Afrikaner language and have no regard for students who cannot speak the language. When exams come, they are both in Afrikaner and English. The black students receive teaching in the Afrikaner language and have to write the exams in English. This means the English students then battle much more in this state of confusion. The real truth is that these institutions were never intending to educate blacks nor English speaking folks but Afrikaner whites only. Change seems hard to come by even when the country has good people in office.

Now in Africa we have a few emerging black farmers who are having difficulty getting market access for their sugar cane and crops. These farmers of sugar cane cannot bring their harvests into the refineries of their countries easily. Horticulture and animal rearing is a matter of debate among blacks. Most black farmers' crops have difficulty reaching good markets within their own countries in Africa. The whites have established the markets and therefore mostly only white farmers have access to those markets. This is ruining black farmers' production all over Africa. Blacks also do not want to start what is their own since they do not believe much in themselves and others of their same colour. This curse has exposed the black man to abuses from other races.

In addition to giving education and sharing land resources with blacks, there must be a fair chance given to all the poor regardless of race. It reminds me of a story of one sailor who said, "All my father left me I have squandered as all men usually do." The developing countries cannot afford to build up the weak by pulling down the giants. The capitalist economy has empowered a few whites even above their own white race at times. Many whites are also living below the bread line in Africa and around the world now. They will also need to have a chance to participate in the economic mainstream. Away with the mentality that says all whites owe blacks, or are rich.

Some whites need to remember that blacks own Africa and all that is within its borders. The message has to be loud and clear: Africa must never be a looting zone for the rich or those with hidden agendas. The mineral ores of Africa must benefit the economies of Africa and its people first before going abroad. Africa must fight wars as being one since most of its wars are justice cold wars now. Ruthless wars stop when countries' borders close so that no ammunition can get in. All economic sectors have to put to the test the initial plan of the African Union organisation in order to bring justice to all Africa nations. The continent must leave no stone unturned; a determination to move forward must drive the nations. Africa has wasted time in solving its problems and that has put the continent into the predicament it is in right now.

As long as some have unfair power over others, the dividing walls will not fall nor come to end. The African governments have to invest in their own people and start believing in their own all the way. As long as the majority of African people are under the bread line, progress will be only a farfetched dream. The change of policies and constitutions must have watchdogs that closely monitor and, if necessary, dismantle the grips of harmful post apartheid ways. When you look at the countries that achieved independence long ago, you will see that real progress is only beginning now.

During the early years of independence, African states were dismantling the policies of minority rule, which drew sanctions to many former colony countries as the corrupt elements rallied behind a few and instigated wars in the name of dictatorship and bad governance. Civil wars are often a result of this propaganda. When economic liberalization achieves its goal on the continent, we will see true growth in both the development of economies and in the populations at large. True economic growth is never at the expense of the poor. The buying power of Africa is large if its entire people play a role in the economy mainstream. The potential of the continent is awesome when I look at it. Most Africans walk with a poverty mentality that cannot make them see beyond their pain. When their healing comes, they will celebrate with jubilation a new dawn of a continent of peace and prosperity.

Some may think I am referring to life in heaven. No, I mean right here on this earth. If the enemy of freedom is abusing legislated laws of men, putting a yoke on the necks of people, then this generation has no alternative except to break the yoke and be free. I feel it is time for the child of Africa to think and work hard to come out of poverty. Remember the greatest blessing is when all win not just the few. Village people need to turn their communities into cities and create jobs right there rather than flocking to urban centres where there is little or nothing to offer the jobless and illiterate crowds. African farming methods need to change in order to provide better food security in countries.

Livestock and fields are not for show but wealth lies right there. Black men need to real farm and sell his animals yearly, if there are crops they will need to harvest and sell them. Regardless of past unfair ways of protecting markets, the world will now need food and it will not matter which colour produces it. It will be a matter of, "Give us food please!" Africa needs to take advantage of the times we live in now. The world earnestly needs food and the market structure will change, so that the colour of the people producing the food will no longer matter. When real problems affect real people, who seek real solutions for their problems, the sought-after answer, in all its truth, will be immediately applied.

The twenty first century is a time for correcting humankind's mistakes and building on a solid foundation of truth and justice rather than racial division. True reconciliation is nothing other than admitting our wrongs and moving away from them, by forsaking evil practices against other races or people. Let us always use the golden rule of life, "Do unto others what you would like them to do for you."

All people want to have someone to listen to them and hear their deepest concerns. The deep longing of every soul is to know other people care enough to listen when he is in trouble or needing someone to speak to or hear them. The question that all people have for each other is, "Do I matter to you?" Accepting people equally and loving them is a goal we must all strive for. Once people know the truth about this question, they begin to feel free and fulfilled regardless of the mistakes they have made. Next time you see a white person, let them be your friend, and this also applies for the white about a black person. Some African states have very few whites now but they occupy business class in planes to those countries. Airfares are unnecessarily expensive on the continent and that makes travelling and doing business in Africa costly.

Many whites have interests in many African states, which blacks manage and run. Globalisation forces us to have free markets and work with the world. Africa has been losing out on great revenue, as it could not tap into a broader world market share because of its traditional manner of operation. The nations of Africa should not allow other nations to dump their goods on their countries. Some still believe Africa is a continent with no trade boundaries. What cannot sell well in other continents will always sell well in Africa, is a philosophy of the world. That is why some African countries are blaming others for dumping their cheap quality clothing in their countries. Most African states do not regulate or control import-clothing quality, which is not the case with most first world countries. Introducing anti-dumping duties in some African countries is not an answer to this problem, however.

Some Asian countries have exported cheap clothing that people wear once only. We now call that kind of clothing, "Asian disposables." The piracy of brand clothing is high also from Asia to Africa and this includes pirated music too. Drugs are reaching African shores every day and substance abuse is rife on African soil. World criminals take advantage of Africa. It could be because of its security measures that are lax or not in place.

The bottom line is we can stand together as a people and live life in harmony regardless of colour, race tribe and gender. Prosperity and peace must come to all people all over the world. Cowards do not say anything against the wrong going on in the world today. If we do not confront our problems head on today, they will haunt us tomorrow and be a snare to the generations to come. The unforgivable sin of this generation is to run away from truth, which alone can set it. Some argue that we should leave the past alone. But what will we do when the past keeps on surfacing in our generation and seems to blaze through to future generations because we do not confront it head on? We will have to take a stand and correct it in order to move on. Those that think digging up the past justifies the present are dead wrong. This generation must understand the role of the past in our lives today. Otherwise, we will produce two kinds of people from this subject if we are not careful: those who just want to hide behind the finger and enjoy the past by enforcing its inherited style of life, and those who come to power and use it as an excuse not to give masses good service delivery. That kind of politics is soon going to pass away. Whenever the past is brought to light with its evil intentions, the beneficiaries of that evil historic background cry 'foul' and are quick to say it is past. But this fails to recognize the dire modern day consequences of the issue—an unbalanced distribution of wealth.

The world needs a new just code of ethics

A justice cold war has overtaken us without notice and has forced us to provide answers to the many sensitive issues of tribal, racial, and economic divisions we find ourselves in. The matter of injustice highlights and affects many issues, which Africa and the world need to look at squarely and begin to tackle in order to pave a fair way forward in the twenty first century. If we can defeat racism, we will have come close to achieving our goal of a peaceful world. Let us get off many hands that are on the cake. I believe all people know that poverty, disease, corruption and wars are disturbing our pillars of freedom. The world needs just, innovative ways of tackling the blight of major world problems.

Two obvious pillars of future development will be to empower the poor to benefit from the economies and in turn plough back into their countries' economic streams. This will increase our buying power and at the same time answer many problems of our hampered development strategies. We should not move with a only few participants in our formal economies but all people must contribute. It is a big challenge but its future fruits would turn around the world economies from being just for a few to the hands of all people. Even strikes that bring our economies to a halt will be outdated and no one will take advantage of anyone or prevent them from getting involved in the economic mainstream.

World leaders have to roll up their sleeves and fight to break the unfair past ways of governing African nations. All legalized corruption harms societies and will need to be uprooted. Many previous governments have allowed an evil, rich style of running countries to guide them. Its motto was making money at the expense of the poor. And it labelled the less fortunate with a seal, dooming them and their generations to come to a vicious circle of poverty, as it never afforded to others a fair chance to live in true economic freedom. Now this had nothing to do with colour, though delivered from colour racism, and snared more and more people in the trap of failure, as the pit, which was dug first for weak and helpless blacks, now drew even the so-called strong whites into its trap.

This became a culture of eliminating people from being productive in the formal economies of their nations. As unproductive numbers of people increased, those jobless figures became a problem too. A high crime rate was born out of all these injustices directed to masses. They were left out in the cold, having to watch life pass by. These people have no medical aid, homes or education and neither can they earn a living without other people's help. The world leadership system gave birth to this segment of society through its ruthless greedy empowerment of the few that neglected others. This system made the world a difficult place to live, rather than making it a better place for all people to live in.

The world problems today challenge all people to change their manner from "Business as usual" to improving the self-image of all people. This will help to bring all people to be part of a solution that creates a world we dream of and want to have. We note with regret the many past injustices and those present within our world today. The most important thing is to bring answers to strategic questions in our history and modern day lives. Correct solutions will help us eliminate many social ills and lead us to a future with a better world for all. The world will need to guide some people concerning how they are supposed to see themselves before others. Leadership systems must articulate and instil a mind in all races that all people are valuable and precious. All people must be encouraged to play a role in their economies in order to have the lives they want. Above all, a spirit of truth and reconciliation with past injustices must be addressed, that will bring liberty and peace. This will drive out insecurity, and do away with the stigma of our shaky past filled with greed, war and segregation. Facts and history have consequences in our lives, but what matters now is that the future of the people be in their own hands.

T he world faces a few giants and that would require its undivided attention and focus in order to adequately deal with all that is happening around it. Some nations have made headlines more than others even when not everything said about them is good! The world's economies have grown, mostly at the expense of the poor. Many rich nations have been seen indirectly taking over third world countries and many other developing nations that have cheap labour. Many of the world's clothing brands are relocating to Asia and Africa because labour is still cheap in the two continents. But even if labour is cheap here, it does not justify the squalid working conditions that workers have to put up with. The brand owners should do more than just advertise and make sure they get the maximum profit from every side of the world. There is absolutely no respect for the poor. Even if it is said to be business, in real essence there is no fairness here.

The two continents produce little of their own. The reason being there is a lack of creative skill with the majority of people of the two continents. Now, some Asian and African countries are advancing rapidly but still lack long-lasting development goals that will empower their entire people. This is especially true with the former colonized states of two continents by different masters but with the same results. India has a huge population; coming very close to China yet Japan and China are international powerhouses of export while India struggles most of its people being unemployed and in poverty. Women have very little say in India and are suffer much due to the culture and religion. Religion says God made women for the pleasure of men. Rarely do women find their way through the school gates except to be given in marriage at very young ages of about twelve. Girls are treated the same way in most African states and that leaves them out of the economic mainstream. Divorce has left a lot of women stranded and in poverty, as they often remain poor and lacking survival skills within these two continents.

Indeed a circle of poverty continues fuelled by cultures that look down upon women and this has continued for many years. Poverty is a disease that begets many other sicknesses in life. When people are poor, they do not eat well nor have a balanced diet of food. The homes they live in are substandard and that always affects people negatively. There is a high mortality rate of infants in most poor countries of the world. We have been seeing climate change in Africa and the world, which has been making the winters colder. The global warming phenomenon has brought change in many spheres of the world. The droughts that accompany these weather conditions are not easy for the poor, as they get no subsidies from governments or elsewhere. Once their seeds are in the ground and do not yield good harvests, they are doomed as that is all they have. The next stop is the hunger zone and that is why development comes so slowly here. Cultures affect development one way or another. As long as opportunities do not reach all people equally, that culture abets poverty and there will always be many poor in nations that continue in that route. The nations of the world need to stand together and fight this number one enemy of health, which is poverty. It causes many wars which increase the poor in the world. This scourge of poverty is often a result of illiteracy.

Most of the old twentieth century leadership styles have little merit and are the cause of the mess the world finds itself in today. The problems have not been confined to the twenty century but are throughout human history. We see the spirit of greed ruling the world. From the slave trade to colonization era, we see the whole world in chaos. A few people started it and forced others under these yokes of bondage for many years until some men and women stood up for freedom, and broke the yoke off people's necks. We constantly see women left on the wayside throughout this era. The rich and greedy had everything so they could care better for their women. The poor could not even get the right to own anything. I will never forget a story when I was in Germany; the newspaper had the first slave trade era story on it dating back to the late 18th century. It showed the first blacks to reach European soil being objects of exhibition in Berlin during the late eighteenth century. The poor are always the weak but that was not the issue with those blacks. They could have been peace-loving people who found themselves in the trap of evil men of their day. Truly many died on those ships and were thrown into the seawaters without any consideration that they were people of equal value with the slave traders.

With time, slavery and colonization were abolished, but their victims continued to suffer the effects of their consequences for longer. After abolishing them, their masters ran in the shadows checking out for new ways to keep an upper hand in everything. Surely, what they owned was theirs and they intended to hold on to it whether in evil ways it mattered not to them. The same groups of slave masters went on to develop new ways of mastering civil societies with an aim to keeping a grip on everything and to determine who gets what. We saw countries gaining independence through bloodshed which showed that freedom does not come cheap. And the policies of the countries that achieved independence did not free people from the painful oppression in their lives. The reason was that the lawmakers were in favour of people of certain skin pigmentation, and offered nothing good to the simple native citizen of the country. The design of this system was done by the so-called educated ones of the day and was evil. Their education was tainted as it only catered to minority groups for the dubious gains involved.

Since then people of different ethnic groups had to fight for survival among each other and achieved nothing as the scarcity of resources took a new toll. The struggle was so strong that it never allowed women to contribute to solving the riddle. Men trying to twist each other's arms and not working together have been the order of the day. That has intensified the culture of not allowing women to participate in mainstream economics nor powerful leadership positions. Men began to think that if they could not get it right, what could lowly women do? While on the other hand the greedy rich had their families with all the tools to work well, be smart, and inherit the earth.

When history visits a generation, that generation will need answers in order to deal with the particular problems that come from past and perplex the living. The twenty first century surrounds us with questions like, "Where have we gone wrong and what makes some people poor while others flourish next door? Has culture overlooked women and children so long that we have bred a group of poor and marginalized people among us without realizing it? Is our world running short of resources? Racism has been a culture of the evil rich who wanted to gain at the expense of other colours without considering them as people worthy of respect and dignity. That is why, even today, the people of Africa do not stand together when it comes to fighting the challenges of our time. The greedy rich are able to use money to divide people.

Some believe that our only real challenge is to force other groups to share land and resources equally. Wealth distribution has never been on a parity for centuries until now. The question of wealth distribution makes African people blame their governments as they have turned them into beggars who can never become free easily. The African father generation had nothing and if they had something, they would have been in parliament, which makes it wrong. Blacks have always felt neglected by their own governments who are trying to be free from their own oppression masters. It is hard for a poor black person to have a decent place to stay around African cities.

Africa's birth rate is beginning to slow down as many countries are introducing effective measures of family planning. The scourge of HIV and AIDS is one of the factors slowing down Africa's population growth. Great resources and much research have been dedicated to the fight of this number one killer disease on the continent and are now yielding fruit. Though these are not the only problems that need to be addressed quickly, it is a positive sign that the continent is on the right footing. Education is slowly reaching the masses though many do not believe in it—predominately countries with a new democracy. Their people do not grasp the opportunity with both hands but feel justice can answer their plight of poverty without them doing anything. This kind of people thinks governments owe them everything—food, clothing and houses without them doing anything. They wait for governments to guide them to things they do not know or otherwise simply become other people's liability.

The fact that people once lost their countries to powerful nations does not mean that they cannot regain their state of independence. Those who think themselves to be superior must adjust and accept other people as equal to them. If we can have that mind, we will see even the state of Israel in peace and its enemies walking shoulder to shoulder with it. It just takes admitting our wrongs, repenting of them, and letting freedom reach us all. Remember the fight is not just about a truth or a cause but a wrong mentality. It is folly for a man to hate another man when he is not able to get what is another man's forcefully. The reason why the other man will not give away his treasure could be that he wants to give it to his children's children. It is wearisome to be unable to tell your offspring you are poor or rich. When true independence prevails with peace among the nations, people reap the choice fruits of freedom. The world is taking shape and those who resist its progress will soon be enemies of the world. People are sick and tired of the lies and corruption that have gone on for ages now. The world feels enough is enough and now almost all people want only the right way of doing things. If they cannot find the right way, they should not twist arms to get things right in their generation.

I began to look at land and economic empowerment issues closely on my continent including my country. South Africa has come on the spotlight lately, with construction, mining and farm workers who are always on the receiving end, striking. The rest of the continent wants land redistribution, and fair wealth distribution of rich resources such as minerals, and equal rights to mining and fair granting of fishery licences. Many Africans are worried about many issues taking place on the African continent. Those things that divide them must never force them to take up arms against each other. Genuine things that need the attention of governments and people should not see people fighting against each other but rather unify them against the enemy, which is after fuelling divisions in order to gain monetary interests. The worst kind of enemy is the one who does not value the lives of other people.

Land redistribution in Zimbabwe is said to be going well even though some Blacks do not believe in their own people who are getting into this new business of farming. The economic recovery is great, as its exports are improving and making a new great turn. Two forces are in the fight here; the mentality of self-pity, and the ignorance of thinking blacks cannot farm. In a country like Zimbabwe, which has hit bottom, it is easy for the country to build up and take a better position on the continent. Most white folks were said to never have bought or owned land in Zimbabwe but to control it through farming leases with the government, staying in the country with no intent of sharing land with blacks but only of sabotaging the government. That was the old man's version when he condoned people driving whites out of their farms after war veterans had rallied behind the land revolution. Whites were accused of seeing blacks as objects of exploitation in that country. The government of the day claimed that the farms most whites refused to share were not under those whites' ownership. Mugabe told the world that it seems his people had run out of patience and he witnessed the riots on television, as did other people in the country and the world. How could both parties concerned here have brought a solution to this problem without the human suffering we saw? Sanctions were never a solution and having them kick in quickly against Zimbabwe was a disaster.

That has always been a problem that made African states rise one moment and fall the next. The colonial entity masters seemed to care a lot about the white minority who promoted the old propaganda that said African people mean nothing and should be the servants of whites always. Whenever black countries tried to confront racism and unfair wealth distribution in their countries the colonial masters intervened with sanctions that kept the racial residues in check. This kind of leadership has led to the rise and fall of African states without remedy while their first world counterparts enjoyed steady economic growth.

The rest of the world considers what these white minority groups are doing wrong in Africa, totally unacceptable. People are sick and tired of not being allowed to be equal with other races or people, nor to use the potential and capabilities deposited in them by their Creator. Some countries still condone harsh treatments from the minority elite, as they are mostly dependant on the white farming minority. The food prices are exorbitant and unjustifiable now all over Africa and the world. Farm workers are still paid very little. There is little or no regard for the empowerment of blacks in the farming industry. One AWB leader in South Africa said blacks who cannot stay and work by the farms must leave if feel cheated or paid less, as they are not compelled to stay by the farms.

The man was on national TV after the death of their leader Eugene Terre'Blanche whose murder was said to be over a wage dispute and later on, the case took a twist. The government of South Africa has tried to get farmers to pay people a minimum wage of R800 to R1200 a month but some are still paying people far less than this. These rich farmers have an association of their own where they discuss peripheral matters and ignore the welfare of their workers who furnish their lavish lifestyles. They will not pay workers for months and not because they do not have the money but because they resent blacks. Nothing could be further from the truth, the industry needs to change with the times; otherwise, it will fail to provide adequate food security for the nation. The stigma of racial hatred is the ultimate enemy of both blacks and whites and must be destroyed in South Africa and the continent.

The white farmers know what apartheid did to our country and to Africa as a whole, and they claim that only their fathers did it. Yet they themselves continue to enforce it through sophisticated ways of economic injustice. The AWB leader who said black farm workers could leave the farms was in denial of the problems of our people and cared little about their wellbeing. It seems he had no regard for blacks and showed no remorse about what white farmers are doing against black workers. Blacks are suffering in most white farms, and taken advantage of as most black farm workers are illiterate, and cannot go anywhere else to earn a living.

Most whites are still in white party politics where the majority of people in those countries is black. Ignorance and lack of understanding of life's realities ruin harmony and peace in such communities. These people fail to understand that it was never right to have enslaved blacks under past governments. They still see a black person as an enemy and, in turn, make blacks see whites as the problem barring them from progress and joy in life. Whites will now and then be on the papers after having assaulted black workers and blacks will also be on the papers having done crimes on whites. Until the heart attitude of both changes, the country and the continent will remain in chaos. Some of the black illiterate poor believe whites owe them tickets to a good life. It is because of the way things have happened and continue to happen.

The two divided groups of people still believe it is revenge when one of them is in pain or injured. The day an injury for one becomes an injury for all, regardless of colour, will be the day Africa is on its way to healing. I have often seen black criminals not regretting having killed a white person and white criminals doing the same. To each of these people, there is nothing wrong if you rob, steal or kill outside your own colour. What makes them enemies is the distorted notion that said whites are better and deserve to be pampered with everything from service to opportunities while blacks are neglected. This group of people has varying characteristics. The whites try so hard to keep blacks working for them by enforcing old schemes and tactics of racism. These sophisticated racial tactics do not allow blacks the time or opportunity to study and better their lives. The secret lies in paying blacks very little lest they study and be like whites if they are paid well. They greatly fear blacks becoming like them in terms of financial and economic status. It seems some whites want a surety from black men that they will serve the white men's children for generations to come. Signs of restlessness show that the black child is tired of this nonsense and wants his true freedom and identity now. When blacks are fed up with not getting their small salaries in time, they fight to the point of bloodshed. In court, blacks commemorate the killers as heroes since they feel this is the only way to instil sense in their enemy's mind.

The majority of whites and blacks are still hurting over sensitive and tangible issues that can be resolved only if both parties are willing to do the right thing. Since the new dawn of a democratic government, dating from 1994 to 2010, South Africa has lost about 3000 white farmers, murdered for unknown reasons. It seems this has continued for a long time and an extra police wing has been assigned to protect the farmers and investigate the killings. Many farmers are trying to do the same thing that suburban rich folks do: they build large walls around their houses and buy maximum security for themselves. Yet still they are at risk from ruthless poor black criminals. People that are just farmers do not need that kind of protection. They are safe as long as they do their duty well and within acceptable norms. Enemies are not usually attracted to a simple farming environment.

White cowards believe they can continue to abuse blacks while black criminals think they will continue preying on whites. The dividing wall is falling slowly with extremists from each side not understanding nor knowing what to do next. People will always know their downfall and fix it if at all they choose to. Why do the nations have to wait so long for the racial divide to fall away in Africa? The problem is that some have and others do not. Those who do not have beg and those who have make policies and laws on how wealth is to be distributed. Many minority groups who live in Africa do not feel they belong there. And many blacks who live in Africa do not feel they are at home here. Both parties have issues that they must deal with in order to overcome their differences and be at peace with each other and even with themselves.

It does not matter how many meetings people schedule to work out strategies of protection and economic empowerment; if there is no justice the plans will frustrate those who devise them, waste resources and kill the desire to live on the land among its people. No one enjoys living in a confused state in which productivity and potential of people is hindered and being in prisons of fear. It is painful to see people looking free but actually entrapped in terrible fears of premature death and failure. Land issues need to be addressed well whether now or in future. Industries that are not environmentally friendly tend to benefit a few, but fuel global warming which is a huge threat on the planet right now. Businesses that promote maximum profit for the owners and ignore the rights of the workers must be discouraged from continuing. It is time for the world to rethink its ways and patterns of doing things. If it means paying better salaries in those continents being taken advantage of, let it be so for the sake of peace and sustained economic growth.

All people have a responsibility to pursue peace in our world and make it a better place to live in. Foreign ethnic groups need to reconcile with Africans of the continent without any strings attached. It is easy for white people to speak well, treat the educated black people well, and even bribe the government labour inspectors in order not to pay workers what they are worth. That has been the continuing trend on the continent for too long now. Doing business with overseas companies was on a racial basis and those groups still have an advantage since most of them are still are rooted in the past. In Africa, some sports are played according to colour and also some industries are not opening up for blacks since the policy makers have been white and have made policies that are difficult to change. The enslaving yokes of apartheid were applied in such a way that a fair opportunity to blacks was never afforded. The young farm boys and girls are supposed to be at school but have to join their mothers and fathers by the big fields in many farms of the continent and the world. When those children are not able to enter into the formal economy stream later the whites say blacks are stupid, which is not true. Let us fight the evil of this generation with justice and truth, which are tools previous generations did not use but ignored.

Young underfed children should not be subjected to child labour because there are no parents or anyone to look after them or defend their rights. What causes poverty in Africa is the system that allows minority groups and rich politicians to enjoy salaries that allow them to provide good education for their children and lavish lifestyles while neglecting the masses. Since almost all African states have become independent, nations have made more and more jobless people because of the system found on the ground. Everyone is working forward but the old system pulls all that work backward unnoticed. Africa could be richer than any other continent if it was given a fair chance and its people were developed better. Corruption has resulted as nations remain in poverty while political leaders who are not even doing a good job enjoy the ride. The moment they get into those offices, they begin to realize that the problem of underdevelopment is bigger than what they think.

The difference between Africa and other continents is that Africa's people have never been empowered well. Empowerment has been for certain groups of people but not for the native indigenous people. At the end of the day, the pillars of empowerment are removed and replaced with things that sabotage people and make it impossible for all Africans to taste freedom. Education is not easily accessible on the continent and bursaries are limited to a few people who suit the sponsoring companies' criteria. Then, eventually they leave for overseas opportunities instead of benefiting their own countries. This continent that waits for people to come invest in it and later employ its people has been not doing well for ages. By not educating its own people, it has denied them an opportunity to be creative as nations and continental people. The healthier the economies, the better and healthier lifestyles the people of those economies have. Even crime decreases when people have the means to earn a living. This does not mean black people will have to forever work for other ethnic groups. That is a lie! But let Africa get rid of everything that has stood on its way to developing goals and strategies for a long time. Those who use child labour must receive severe punishment from our courts. Millions who are unemployed and without formal education must receive a chance to obtain some survival skills so that African states can give their entire people a role in the economic mainstream.

The blessing of all

There are many good men and women out there who, knowing the truth, would love to make it known to many who need it in order to be free. The lie is what many evil people have defended for years and still want upheld: that certain races are better than others. Many blacks who believe whites are their enemy and owe them a better life as they feel they cannot do what whites do hold the other lie. Both groups of people have to drop these notions and move away from that false mentality. Nothing can justify suppressing the truth and upholding wrong priorities. Many people, who have travelled around the world and seen many things in life, disapprove and defy the stigma of poverty being associated with blacks only. Talents and gifts exist among all peoples and races regardless of their skin pigmentation. All people can do something well if you teach them how to do it and give them a chance. The evil of supremacy robbed every opportunity from others and made them look sorry for having breath in themselves. The black man was made to believe that his Creator had made a mistake when he made him and that therefore there is nothing better for him on this planet than to serve other races. All the good possessions of a black man are now transferred into other races' hands since he is the only one not deserving anything.

Blacks have suffered grievously from an inferiority complex, that for too long informed their identity as a people among other races. Everything seems to be unattainable even their very acceptance by other peoples. Most blacks have nothing to lay their hands on in order to have food for them or their children sometimes. The shame of this is that other races have taken control of the land and resources. Everything seems to be under one people, who continually make sure those blacks never get a good education or learn skills. And their children continue to reign on the continent with an upper hand because they use the influence of their fathers. This kind of management of the black continent is what has plunged it into violent civil wars and bloodshed. The people of Africa have remained divided for too long. Some people think the process of liberating Africa has not gone fast enough to yield the necessary results. This is where corruption starts because the rich will then bribe to have their desires met. The African governments seem to always have blessed wealthy whites and blacks cursed with poverty. Nonetheless, we will see the truth prevail, as no man can hide behind the finger forever. There are some white people who love truth: when something is wrong it is wrong. They stand by the truth with strong convictions and this shows us that we are all equal people.

Let us look at a great example of a man who lived such a fulfilling life—a man who never used the gospel to further white influence, but showed the light of God's truth to all whom he came across in his lifetime. "You shall know them by their fruits," is a statement that would summarize the life of this hero. He never acted like many whites who love to announce their faith convictions to the world and then do evil using the name of God as a cover for their sins. It was after his wife had died and he was about to leave this planet after a rich missionary past. Indeed, here was a gospel legend who had works of only love and peace and truth in the service of Christ. I believe that when he got in heaven, he received a great welcome like this: "Good and faithful servant, you have done your work well on earth." The heavenly host most probably gave him a standing ovation as they applauded him before the Lord he served.

If people can talk so favourably about a man, I guess the heavens were also witness to this heroic and selfless life, giving love to many even when gone. Religion or faith faking has often been an easy way for white criminals to penetrate Africa with their wrong motives and influences. Many cruel people still believe oppressing black men in Africa is legitimate. This is what their ancestors taught them and, because of ever- increasing greed, they pay bribes to a corrupt African leadership. And by doing so, they gain access have to ores and resources even at the expense of African people's lives. To such evil people, an African's life is worth nothing and that is how they can take those ores and bring a curse on themselves without even thinking. With racist and greedy folks, it is all about extracting wealth from Africa and even if people are paid next to nothing it is all right with them. The question often asked is, "Where is the diamond or the stuff?" White drug dealers often pose as missionaries and preachers—including Africans—in these syndicates operating from other countries and also within Africa. But our man set a standard that made one think, "If only the gospel was always displayed with such a truthful and powerful life, Africa could have understood it and be at a better position."

This missionary hosted different ethnic groups under his roof for many years. To him all races were his children and he treasured them all during his lifetime as a missionary around the world. A letter he wrote was read at his funeral gathering as many came to pay their last respects. Every man's life at the end must have love and a sense of meaning to life. Surely, this was a rare jewel of a man, who stepped on this planet and the devil shivered. He was one among many who loved truth and preached it and lived it out openly for all to see and follow suit. Such people's lives always point to God's love for humankind. These kinds of people are not only role models but also world changers. Philosophies, religions and cultural values fed from view when the truth brings forward such a great life for the living God. The truth will bless people and, when known and embraced, will free them from all the oppressions of life and cause them to live together in their maker's presence in peace. But some people love to do evil things in secret after telling everyone they are converted and have a religion. Since neither of these things can answer the need for salvation or produce good works worthy of conversion, hiding evil just becomes a norm for these people. It is all done with good lip service.

Death often visits those who are not prepared, but those at peace with the Lord never stumble in fear of this torment or the condemnation that goes with it. This is their opportunity to enter a life of eternal glory filled with joy in the absence of sin and pain forever. Good men and women leave a legacy of joy and peace in many hearts when they are gone. Their joy and fulfilment is in serving the most vulnerable people who cannot give them anything in return. Such people have a servant's heart. On the other hand, it also holds that those who serve others enjoy being served back even better by the same people whom they have served. That is why your parents will talk about how hard it was to take you through school, and that now it is your time to give back. Once a victim, you now become a volunteer and it is how good spreads. The serving spirit is when you do for others what they cannot afford to pay you back for; this kind of serving comes from love for life and others, as it keeps no records of its service deeds. The level of love and peace I saw in this one man was awesome. When we strive to follow in the footsteps of a good man, we will all be wonderful towards each other and our colours will never serve to pin other people down or enslave ourselves.

The letter read:

Dear Joe, my elder son and family.

I wrote this letter in my spirit earlier in my life to you and my family. But today I thought of drawing this treasure out for you. The family has been large and as you know, even the church was my family. When I looked closely at life, I discovered that my immediate family is a makeup of people from all over the world. I brought together nations under my roof and raised them up as my children. I could not have done one bit of work without Christ and His love for me in my life. All glory goes to God. Drawing conclusions in life, I can tell you one thing, that life is fulfilling when you take love and put it in action by serving others. All my days on earth, I have lived to explain the mystery that many people do not understand in this life. I thought if I could only demonstrate the love of God to the world, I would leave a legacy of peace for another generation to come, and it would be passed on to generations as a heritage of love.

Little did I know, I would have to teach justice and peace among different tribes and races. I used to tell you the story of a man with six sons during our family reunions and dinners. Indeed, the father loved his sons so much that he wanted them to succeed together in life. He took six sticks of the same size, placed each one in the hands of his six sons, and told them to break the sticks. All the six boys broke the sticks easily. The father then took the six sticks of the same size, bound them together, and gave them to each of his sons to break and they could not break them. He looked right in their eyes and said, "That is a life lesson I have to teach you. If divided, you easily break and your enemies will destroy you. But in unity none shall be able to break you or come between you." Let this be a life lesson for my family and those who hear it.

You all know that in our family we produced scholars of various professions among both girls and boys. I believe God did this through me to show a token of His love for all humanity. I knew little when I first went into ministry but as I continued, I saw the need to preach truth and live it as a continual example of love in action. This is what separates the children of God from the world. The children of God walk in this world with a focus on getting the blessings of God to all people. Justice, truth, love and peace bring a blessing to all people. Religion has none of these four pillars of salvation for humankind, let alone the blessing of God that comes with them and gives success to all men. Which when translated is freedom for all and to all who find it.

My faith in God has shown you a great example of love and truth regardless of your colours and races. You are of your race for your purpose that is from God. Let no one divide you because of colour. The blood of Christ washes and cleanses all the human race the same. When you came to Christ He qualified you to be my spiritual sons and daughters even when you were not of my flesh. This is what most people on earth fight about as they want to keep others from knowing that they are equally loved and created by God as any other people. Many fools have gone out preaching messages that cannot save man, but rather puff him up in pride and arrogance. I hope you can learn from me: the way I treated you is the same you are supposed to treat others. I might not have been perfect in many things but I implore you to use no other standard than Christ Jesus. Use it not as mere men do, but allow the Lord Jesus to constantly show you the truth that is of God.

I am sorry to say, it is an easy thing for a man to use the name of God for gain or wrong purposes in this life. Seek truth and know it, and you shall be free. The truth does not set any man free, it is the knowing of truth that sets a man free. The fact of the matter is the truth has been there all the time but people have not known it. If people knew the truth, we would have a better world for everyone to live in. Get this in your heart; let the work of truth in love for justice and peace make you continue to love in order to advocate its cause to bring freedom to all people, which is God's will. This has been my reasonable sacrifice of worship to God daily. I taught you the truth and I want you to learn that you count and that all other people count before God. Love them enough to tell them the truth of God and treat them, as you would want to be treated.

I am happy that I have left men and women who can take up the cause of true freedom to all people, no matter where they find themselves or their colour in the world. I wished to see peaceful ambassadors who are not judgmental but model God's will on earth. None has seen God, but His love is manifest in this, that we love one another, and this includes reconciliation and justice. All the problems we see in the world today are the result of evil that man continues to promote. Stand up and abolish it, as there is no need for it to oppress people. I know you will face opposition. When you do, know that this is what separates you from the world. You are of the kingdom of God, the children of light! Anything not pure and holy is not yours but the enemy's. The short cut has become a great temptation in the world today. Do not love positions of influence unless you can advance truth from there. Let it sink into your hearts, that as much as I defended you from doomed lives and instilled hope and peace in your lives, so you should do for others.

THAT YOU MAY CONSIDER HOW TO APPLY THE GOLDEN RULE OF LIFE, WHICH IS, "DO UNTO OTHERS WHAT YOU WOULD LIKE THEM TO DO FOR YOU."

Now I say that all people have suffered injustice at one point or another in their lives. It is a grievous thing and experience when one ethnic group of people becomes a prey of another. How would you feel if your enemy devoured you until you were swallowed alive? The same is the feeling of many who have their rights infringed on by big companies with unfair business tactics around the world. How would you feel if you were to go out of business because of unfair competition? How would you react if you worked your whole life for very little pay? How would you feel if you had no place to call home all your life but lived in the back room of someone's house? How would you feel if you were spitefully used all your life to make other people rich?

How would you feel if your mother and father were killed because of some ores someone wanted from your land? Such shocking injustice that ruins people's lives is the collateral damage as companies aim for maximized profits. I appeal to you not to be perpetrators or victims but part of the solution to change this world mentality. Let us all refuse to enslave others or ourselves by making wrong choices, but rather advocate true freedom with a good faith commitment from our hearts.

Help your children achieve an education and getting a home of their own, and help others achieve the same. Aim to be a good manager of your own life and, when trusted to lead others, do so to the best of your ability and knowledge. Aim to leave a legacy of leadership for generations to come. Always remember that life on this earth is a temporary assignment from God. Time is life, so use it to the best of your ability whenever you get an opportunity to show God to the world. Do not wear religious smiles and have no works of holy faith, as has become the norm of this generation. Do not rest until all have made it, as I did not rest until you all made it. There are lawyers, doctors, engineers and many more professions among you, my children.

Know that education without God is insufficient, but if you know the bible, you are very educated. Practise what you preach and walk before your children with humility and love, as children learn more from what they see you do than what you teach them. I left it all to you and above all give glory to God my Father. Now, pass on to your children the heritage I gave you. It will also be a blessing to your children's children and the generations to come. If you succeed in laying the peaceful foundation of freedom, others will be able to build on it. Remember, God will destroy those who destroy the earth. Even when I am gone, my works preach to all of you and I pray you do the same. Defend the cause of the poor and the weak, the marginalized and the less fortunate. You all know what has brought the world to where it finds itself right now. It is the evil systems of this world. The fight against poverty and lack can only be realised when truth and justice prevail.

I am grateful to many human rights activists who advocate a spirit of unity, equality and peace among the nations. May their work continue until all is completely adequate. The pillars of true freedom are to make the world a better place to live in for all and everything is distinct with clear-cut good goals. Start working towards the mark from this day and we will achieve a world that bears fruits of peace, justice and freedom for all. The cry of the world today is for change of heart attitude towards people, as there seems to be much intolerance.

The letter was then closed and the words sealed by a name and a signature. All the recipients of the letter sat and gazed down with reverence and respect for a man who lived to give others opportunities. The above letter, read on his funeral day left all thinking deeply about life's meaning.

Two of his sons and a daughter spoke to the multitude of mourners who had come to give their last respects to a hero who had a heart larger than life.

Here are the words of the daughter who was adopted from a war-torn country, had studied law, and was practising with a wealthy attorney firm.

She cleared her throat and started reading from a piece of paper, as follows, "I want to thank the family and all who came to gather here today on this special day of a man who has returned to his Creator with something in his hand. Indeed daddy took a gift with him to God. I am a product of his love for others and life. He lived his life with love and peace, which we have seen in his words and deeds. I knew him when I was seven in a war-torn country where I had already lost my mother and father because of war. Little did I know that God had a special man and woman who would later assume the position of parents in my life? They took me in their home and never got tired of doing good for me. They introduced me to a father above all fathers, who is God so that even though he is gone, I have peace and fulfilment in my life. I believe he is at a better place—I know he is at a better place! He took me to school, gave me an opportunity to enter university, and become a law scholar. Whenever I serve others, the fact that we are all gifts to each other in life, humbles me. That is what my daddy taught me and it has always enriched my life. I will forever be grateful to have had him cross my path and pick me up. I have always been daddy's daughter and will always feel the warmth of his spirit with me. I cannot stop thanking God for him and his life of love. He taught me many things in life. His teachings have carried me throughout my life. To all of us who lived around daddy, this is a loss that will take time for us to come to terms with. But we agree and believe his mission on earth has ended in fulfilment. We will indeed miss him greatly."

She sobbed, and tears went down her cheeks. She could not continue but went to sit down.

The younger son took over the microphone, started by greeting the audience, and went straight to the point.

"If I was honest in my life, I would say that the man deserves the award for best daddy in the whole world. He was a legend in his own right. He changed nations and communities, transformed culture and the way the world does things. All this was his tribute of worship to the almighty God that he served all his life. I did not know my real daddy and mother in Africa. In my teenage years, I found myself in the streets of a big city that never had a place for my peers or me. We lived on the streets and begged for food. I say food because we would not beg for a bath and other things since they seemed like luxuries to us. When he took me to a better place, he first cleaned me with the word of life that instilled discipline in my life. As a teenage boy from the street, I would not have made it without his guidance since I had no more dignity or self-respect. I had lost it all, and the hope to live a normal life had been dashed. I saw many of my peers fall by the wayside of life. Some went back to the streets and he would follow them until he made something good out of them. I then realized that there is good in all people, but opportunities are not the same for all people. Today, I can tell you that this street kid has become a successful commercial pilot. I owe it to the man whom I can say without shame is my father and hero regardless of my DNA and colour. My colour is black and the man is white. But he succeeded in teaching me and many of my sisters and brothers who are sitting here today from various ethnic groups that we are all equal before our Creator. Sometimes it is hard to understand that we are all created equal before God. It is because of the distorted thinking of a racially divided world. Without him, I would not be here. Daddy was a man who would take truth, give it to any people, and let them embrace it to live. I believe if we can all unite to make the world a better place for all, it possible to achieve it. He did it and we can go beyond the level he took it. He is gone but his good fruits are beginning to grow. Daddy was nothing other than a gift of God to the world we live in. We must fight tirelessly against racism, tribalism, xenophobia, injustice and wars that have such evil results. All these evils and their dire consequences are mainly born out of a religion without life nor the spirit of God and many other social ills of society are from a tribal or cultural perspective. His life was a lesson of truth about God. Now I say, "Daddy rest in peace." You have been a true example of a father figure in life and a preacher of the good news of God on earth!"

He further asked the family to stay united and to follow suit with good works and Christ's true fruits.

Finally, Joe took the stage to give a few words about his true biological father who was such a hero of life and adored by so many for a true life of righteousness. The following words were from Joe's mouth.

"The man's body lying in that coffin is of my daddy, who is no more in his tent, earthly house, or garment with which he was clothed by God when he visited the earth in the twentieth century. He lived a life of selflessness as you have heard and seen our family today. Daddy was a calm man when you looked at his face but that was not all he was. Daddy was a warring man in spirit. He believed that the kingdom of God was not just religion and a few good works. Daddy's philosophy is what kept him going even when things got tough. To him it was impossible to fail, live in poverty and get sick, as in God, he looked at life differently. That is what drove daddy to work tirelessly towards building nations, wherever he went. All his life, his missionary work provided a witness to the living and the dead. The colour of daddy's skin was white, which he always put off and said the best colour to put on is Christ. His work, life and style of leadership blessed me and all those who walked, worked and lived with him. He never made the life style of Christianity burdensome on people but described it with four simple words: justice, truth, (reconciliation) love, and peace with a heavenly citizenship. He taught many of us how to love others as they are without trying to remake or abase them but treating them with the same dignity and respect we think we deserve. Daddy donated his life to the world through his entire lifetime. I am so humbled to have been a son of a man of his calibre."

Then he moved to the closure of his speech with a vote of thanks for the family. Many other children of this man spoke from all the continents of the earth, but the three above speakers had the most inspiring words. Thus ends the story of what the life of one just man could accomplish. Surely we can all learn what life is and begin doing what we are supposed to. We can build our world into a better place. The greatest blessing of all is not when a few make it but when we all make it.

Hurting voices

Unheard are hungry voices crying behind the scenes. These people are crying for fathers that have left them with mothers who have neither a support system nor a job in place. The mothers are blaming their husbands and boyfriends who have left them with broken promises and dreams and even life-threatening diseases. It seems this is a "first Adam" type of people. When God said, "Why have you eaten from the tree?" Adam blamed it on the woman that God gave him. God had not given the woman instruction not to eat the tree but Adam. When the woman ate the fruit, nothing took place initially until she offered it to Adam to eat. The moment Adam ate something happened. The glory of God left and they discovered they were naked. Since then Adam and all his seed have sinned and come short of the glory of God. The woman blamed the giving in to temptation on the snake. Adam was not tempted but disobeyed God's word that he was to keep. The story of the fall of man is very simple but important for the effect it has on men and women's lives today.

The times we live in require not sissies but men with a strong backbone. Men have to understand the powerful position of responsibility they have on earth, if they are to live in the authority given to them by their Creator. A man's genes and strengths are very different when compared to a woman's. When God made man, he gave him one mission to accomplish, one adventure to live for, and one woman to win. God, the Creator, is a lover of family. Three institutions that God gave to humankind are family, government and church. Whenever man fails to uphold all three well, chaos reigns in the kingdom of man. Man is a shield of God for the woman and children in the family. Men are to love and cherish their wives as long as they live on this earth. In turn, both man and woman help each other achieve their purposes in life. Children are the result of a man and woman's cherished love.

According to God's plan, the man has a higher authority in this family institution. He is to make sure all works together with his wife so that the love may flow down to the children as the Creator intended. The man is the foundation of all the human race. He must uphold justice in the sight of his wife and children, which blesses God and in return allows blessings to flow back to the man. What was God's original plan when He made man and woman? Remember, a woman before God is an equal helpmate to the man. We do not see God saying she is weak. Man called her weak only after temptation came through her, as she did not resist it. God had cushioned her with strength but she did not protect herself. But her man had a responsibility and duty to see that she was always safe. Adam only used Eve as a scapegoat when he could not protect her from the sin and death that only came through him. The woman was a beautiful thing from the day Adam received her. But he failed to find a way to mature the strengths of her beauty.

When man fell, the woman also fell. Today many men have fallen into a playboy lifestyle and the women into whoredom. Men sleep out even when married and refer to it as "fun" and "the joy of living" even when it is irresponsible. Some men impregnate women out of wedlock and claim to have been playing and never intending for a serious relationship. Many men pin down women by claiming they are weak. Women find themselves limited by men's cultural values, having no say in most societies. The pain inflicted on these women goes deeper than we all think. In some countries, men fight over mineral ores, and what those wars do is leave widows and orphans, rather than solve the problem. Rebel soldiers prey on women when the men are gone. Many rapes take place in these war torn countries. Women become victims with their children especially in African states and the developing world. Man has fallen from his position and job description from the family point of view of the Creator. We see even children fighting in unending civil wars in Africa and many parts of the world.

If a man cannot stand up for the truth, it affects his loved ones and seed. The enemy is after the seed of men. I will never forget a story I read about the slave trade of blacks to Europe and America during the eighteenth century. The book stated that in the ship, the rape of women was rife and the perpetrators made sure these women were pregnant before reaching the other side so that upon arrival the price would be more since there was another slave coming. There were no words to describe the evil inflicted on those women and the children born out of this predicament. The actions of some men had no regard for other people. All they did was practise evil at its worst. The affected men and women were rendered powerless by a harsh system that gave them no chance for a better life including their children for generations until the abolition of slavery. Remember, the fall of Adam, affected all the children who were in him, which is all the human race. All the men and women who went into slavery had children born into slavery. It took people of character to abolish slavery, and it will take real men and women to bring HIV and AIDS to a halt, stop poverty and wars, and the joblessness in our generation.

Everywhere you turn, there is a cry for real men to stand up for the cause of freedom for women and children, which will in turn free men too. Until women and children are free, men will never have rest and freedom on this earth. There are two kinds of men, the good and the evil. Evil men are busy trafficking women and children who are not theirs to various parts of the world for various evil uses. Women and children are being introduced into a new slavery, which is the profitable trade of human trafficking. No matter how these poor women and children are used, there is to be gain for the criminal syndicates. Underworld syndicates use women and children as symbols of exploitation. Women and young girls are targets of rape, murder and other scandalous acts including drug trafficking, while young boys are used for cheap labour and endless wars. It is a sick world breeding redundant people and career criminals. Some women who are abused by men in their own countries feel that this is a viable option, as they can get food and clothes by selling their bodies or doing other crimes.

I looked at the divorce rate of our nations in Africa and saw a huge gulf that is burying a generation alive. Women are often left by the wayside in many cultures, and having not gone to school in order to study to earn a living, are at a disadvantage. If ever some get work, it is at bottom-rung jobs that pay them next to nothing. Their men are everything to them until the tragedy of divorce, joblessness or death strikes. Life insurance or cover is scarce in Africa and in the developing world, which leads to poverty after the death of the breadwinner spouse. Undisciplined men are dangerous to societies and communities. Men without discipline can ruin a generation. When women are not equipped to be self-reliant, they turn to men as beggars who often disrespect and abuse them. In African states, women who find their way to divorce courts get more headaches than their peers in the first world nations do. It is a shame to see a rude generation of men abusing women and children! Many men who are supposed to pay child maintenance do not put the money in those bank accounts in time to support those poor women and children. Long queues of stranded women with children on their backs testify to the bleak future of them and their innocent children. The most unfortunate part is that those children never chose to come into this world of suffering. Most of their fathers end up in jails, and graduate as career jailbirds.

The empowerment of women is not doing well in Africa and in most developing countries, since the culture of this part of the world has kept it suppressed until now when our problems are surfacing more and more. The problems we face are bigger than what we think. Unscrupulous businesspersons around the world are ready for a new slavery deal with Africa and the developing world. The war is going to shift now from mineral ores to the trading of women and children trading if men and the governments do not stand up and fight this new oppressor. Wars, sickness and diseases that leave them vulnerable, often make more orphans daily than natural death causes. A large number of young boys and girls are flocking into the streets of big cities and towns of our countries. Here they are exposed to foreign influences as many tourists travel here. You will notice that many of them would rather beg from foreigners than their own people. It is either that the locals do not have much to spare or a mentality that tourists, the majority of whom are white, have more.

The high birth rate of Africa is one of its strengths as other nations are now struggling to find a young work force. Africa could have an upper hand if it developed its people to profit their nations and the world. I looked at a strike of Congo DR workers that was in a French airport and began to speculate on a few things. Many immigrant workers now reside throughout first world countries. These economic migrants range from non-skilled, semi-skilled to skilled labour. Are the salaries going to be the same if African nationals take jobs in first world countries? How is it going to affect the development platforms in Africa? Most of the migrant workers do not have their families with them. They also have to be careful of the same old regime policies working now in the name of overseas contract jobs. The women and children are left behind to bear the brunt and burden of life without their husbands and dads. In first world countries, it is easy for those men to move on with other women. The system must not promote a culture of divorce among people but strengthen marriages. Poverty poses a threat to marriage in Africa and the developing world today.

All over the world, women are decent human beings who love their dignity; in fact, they are a special people. I do not dispute the fact that there are some who look like women but are not. Likewise there are men who look like men but are not. It takes character to be a man or woman. I am not referring to men and women who do not know what they want in life and the reason why they are·on this earth. That is why an adulterous generation continues to spread HIV and AIDS—because it has no moral values in place. Those kinds of people give in to all forms of abusive substances like alcohol and drugs. To them nothing is pure and sacred because there is not even respect for marriage here. That is why people become involved in selling their bodies as sex slaves, including all other sorts of criminal and evil practices. That is not the nature of man or woman according to their Creator's will. There is a longing in every one of us to live and enjoy life as people not as dogs.

There is one missing link that we need to make sure is in place: that justice be administered to all people equally. Let our societies and communities raise girls and boys the same, and allow them the same opportunities in life. This will override the culture of not equipping women in our societies. True women's empowerment must reach all and not just be the window dressing of a few government posts for women. When I looked around during a push to legalize prostitution in the Gauteng province of my country, I saw the blindness of democracy without morals. I went out to interview many different sex workers who thought that their breakthrough was about to come. But it was the same thing you find among men in the prisons of Africa and the developing world. Most of these women had no survival skills in life—no better service to offer their communities than selling their bodies.

Some of these women had very little education or none at all. No company has jobs for such people currently. Technology is advancing and people without education and skills are being left by the wayside daily. Even those who are employed must upgrade their skills frequently; otherwise, they will be left with outdated skills and knowledge in today's jobs and service. A few of these women lacked the discipline to finish their careers and dropped out of school to enjoy the pleasures of sin. In many cases, a father was not there to guide them. Children are like arrows in the hands of a warrior. Someone is responsible, and should have given help to these women when they were in their teen years, but chose not to. The responsibility indeed lies with the fathers here. The majority of these women have children, and have left them with their mothers or grand moms who have very little income to live on. These hungry boys and girls have no hope in life, as they will trip off where their dads and moms tripped off. They go to school hungry, if they go at all. Many of them lose hope and drop out of school to wait for an adult life with nothing to offer them. Boys turn to be career criminals and women into men's slave wives if not prostitutes. Their lives are destined for a world of misfortune. This type of people is dangerous to any society and they fill the overcrowded jails of our continent and the world.

I have been to schools, and around mothers with the difficulties of child support problems. Children with hungry stomachs can hardly concentrate at school. The same boys that never go to school attract the same girls and give them children that they never look after or support. Most of these young men are victims of a fatherless stock with no survival skills. The only way to stop this is to empower women to earn a living and raise children in decent homes. Their lives must not depend on men who abuse them or buy them in order to earn a living. The system that has left women incapable of looking after their children independently is evil and is the cause of many other problems in rural and poor communities. We must do away with cultures that prey on women and make them objects of exploitation. The labelling of women as weak in order to prey on them must stop. Women can build their communities with their children if given a fair chance. The sin of this generation is that it has taken all that others have and own and given it to one race or gender only—the greedy rich. Women and children are also people who deserve respect and dignity in our world.

I feel sorry for the black woman in Africa where many injustices are direct toward her. If her man, who had better opportunities, could not get her a house with her children, how will this be possible for her when she is alone? What has made most men turn their backs on their wives is the hard life in this modern economy. Men leave homelands for cities in search of jobs and, when they get one, it only provides enough for one person to survive and that is the man. The only option most men have is to never set foot at home and see their family, which is better than watching their children die. Watching a family die of hunger is something no normal person can stand. In countries where hunger has been killing a lot of people, you will discover that the men have left those women and children long ago before the worst. It is the weak and the helpless who are left behind to die and those are women and children. That is why I say if governments can intervene and make sure men take their position in society and equip women in the same way as men, people can overcome many problems on this earth. Men work better when their women and families are together with them. They are happy and fulfilled when together as a family.

Women need targeted, dynamic job training that will empower them to alleviate poverty in their communities. They need sustainable job opportunities that will bring real answers for poverty reduction all over Africa and the developing world. In first world countries where women are better equipped, poverty is not that prevalent and many women are self-reliant. In Africa and the developing world where women's empowerment is minimal, denying many women opportunities, the countries are poor and suffer hunger and lack. There is a logic here. When the apartheid era ruled, the people under its yoke lived in poverty throughout their generations until its abolition. The system never allowed people to better their lives and the lack of women's empowerment is playing the same evil role today. Children in the custody of powerless women are doomed to fail like their moms and walk on the road of poverty and lack. If poor women cannot educate their children, those children will not be able to afford to educate their children. They will be trapped forever an underdeveloped world with no means of escape.

Empowering women benefits everyone. This is a wonderful tool we can use to end poverty, lack, sickness and disease. Africa has left an important, powerful group of people behind and these are the women and children. Women are special people in the communities of all people. Children are the future of any people. Poverty and many other problems reign in nations that regard women as second-class citizens. When people do not consider women important, the future of those nations or tribes is marred with senseless wars and economic problems. The future of any people who neglect women and children is dismal and bleak. I have also observed that where the family breaks down there is a lot of women and children abuse, which in turn brings poverty to the people. Now, if poverty reigns, men also will suffer. The failure of apartheid to recognize people as equal is no worse than that of men who do not regard women as their equal. It has left African women outside the main economic stream and the consequences have been suffered by men and women equally.

Africa and developing world have one thing they must do and it is to allow the women of their nations to take their stand. I hope the African Union will educate men on the continent to honour women. The blessing is that a woman, who deserves it, holds the most powerful position of the (AU) organisation. It should not be because she is a woman but because her record of accomplishment and credentials prove she can take Africa's agenda seriously and give direction to the continental leadership crises. The mentality that women are just sex objects must end among men. Women are life-producing beings and without them, there would be no men on the earth. Men are seeds of women; if we destroy the women, also her seed will die with her. We need to be very careful about this because too often the world has disregarded women and the children that God gave them. It is easy for a man to turn his back on his wife and children. But it is a tough thing for a woman to do. A woman will hold on to her children even to death. That is why it is not easy for them to give up on their children, even in the worst calamities. If you see a woman giving up, you can know it usually has not been her will but because of a life-threatening condition.

Not to empower women is a gross miscarriage of justice in Africa and the developing world. Where women are empowered with education and tools to face life, there is less abuse of them and their children. When women are self reliant, it makes life easier for them. In the first world countries, many single women raise their children alone. It is easy for them as most of them work decent jobs, while developing world women cannot make ends meet. Women choose to be alone and independent when there are no real true men. Men abuse developing world women by holding back their money and salaries, but no one can get away with this against first world women. In the developing world, manipulating women still works well since the majority of women are powerless and cannot participate in the formal economic stream. A lack of women's empowerment is sad news and a travesty of justice. Nations with this problem may experience economic growth, but it is never truly healthy.

When I looked at the risk of HIV and AIDS that African women face and how it threatens their lives and the lives of their children, I realized that if the wrong mentality of men changes, we would be able to transform culture and have a better life for all. I repeat, if the wrong mentality of men changes for the good, we will be able to transform culture and the ways of doing things. Women and children often find themselves in all forms of abuse because of the cultural mentality that says they do not matter and are not important. I have seen severe physical and emotional abuse, mostly directed among non-working class women. Men physically assault women terribly, afflicting them with serious bodily injuries and they get away with it. Either the woman will not report the case to the police or if she does report it and the husband or boy friend is arrested, she will, at the end, drop the charges as otherwise she has no source of income. I have seen a lot of them cry and say that, because they cannot support their kids, they would rather have the court drop the charges.

These cruel acts of abusive family criminals, who prey on women in the name of being boyfriends and husbands, have become a common lifestyle among families and society at large. The hostility towards the abuse of children and women has turned to tolerance in our communities making citizens turn a blind eye to the subject. Thus, little is done to provoke the government to be more vocal about this horrible crime. Women have little say in these types of societies. Has our law done enough to protect them? It is not enough to protect women and not empower them to be financially independent. Many women hold on to unfaithful men until serious diseases hit them and kill them. If the same abusive men do not kill them, the diseases will. This culture is still too much embraced on the continent and is the number one reason for women and children's poverty. Recently, Kenya made a law that allows men to marry more wives without consulting their spouses.

Every abused woman should declare this saying, "I will never again be abused by anyone—man or woman." African and developing world women mostly work domestic jobs, which pay very little. Their salaries were never the same as men who did the same domestic work—even during the post apartheid era. Even now, many people who pay a minimum wage abuse illiterate black women who work for them. The injustices of the past made men leave women in rural places for a year or so even when married to them. That created another culture of abuse against women. Many men would have other women to stay with by the mine or city flats while their wives stayed in the rural villages and they only saw them once or twice a year.

This kind of life, introduced by apartheid policy, made it impossible for blacks to have wives by mine hostels. That mentality still rules in many men's minds, both locally and throughout Africa. Even when this became outdated, men loved this way of doing things. Most of them ended up enjoying it and did not want to stand up and correct it, and are still not willing to, since they have adopted it as normal. The lobola or bride's price abuses women unless it is used solely for its purpose—as an appreciation token to the parents that raised up the woman. Once the lobola is paid for a woman, the African man is king and she is a de facto slave many times. That lobola price is usually discussed by the men only; a woman is sometimes forced into a marriage that she does not want or consent to. Many tribes would argue that this is their culture and they found it like that. However, just because we found it like that, does not mean we must continue to practise it, if it is found wanting.

It is time for the African black woman to wipe her tears and think about her next move. Where is the continent going from here? What will be the role and contribution of a twenty first century African queen? These need to be her questions to herself. Go to school and learn, Woman! Start your own business and employ those men who are jobless and loitering around. They might try to talk you out of it and tell you, "You cannot do it; it is impossible!" Leave them behind and take the bull by its horns. It is because they have not made it themselves that they keep telling you, you cannot make it. Start to build your character also! Without character in life, it is difficult to get a breakthrough and people with no character never get to their desired destiny. The sky is the limit but you will need more than guts to move to your prosperity point. Gut feelings will allow you to go up, but will also bring you down quickly because it does not keep you up there but character does. Life is designed with an invisible ceiling. But the sky is the limit for those with character because they can break through that ceiling and remain.

Lack of character is the reason many sports men, women and business people have not truly made it and enjoyed the fruits of their hard-earned prosperity. At one point, everybody cheered them. The next moment, they are down, being a disappointment to their fans or followers. This is a journey for the strong not the faint-hearted. Indeed, people can do things well. From your house or rented apartment, develop strategies that work rather than squandering time in tears and regrets. Do not die watching time go by! Your God-given purpose on earth is bigger than that. Doing nothing about your predicament is the route that fails you and your children. This is what your enemy desires, to destroy you and your children. I pray that you will be healed from the disease of poverty and break the cycle of poverty from your bloodline forever. Refuse to quit; instead, fight with all you have, for your dawn is come and the whole world is waiting for you to take centre stage!

You are not a doormat, woman! You are special and have a unique purpose, and as a creation of God, you are by nature victorious. It is in you to overcome any forces that come against you in this life. The problem is you let people design your world and they always make it too small for you. Do you have an identity crisis? You must stand up, captain, and pilot your ship home; it is indeed your time, woman! True healing in a woman's life will allow her to stop worrying about who hurt her and walked out on her and her children, succeed, and have control of things in her life. That man did not understand life and neither did he know any better in life. Forgive that person or those people, even if you have tried a few different men and it seems they were all the same; cheer yourself up and move on! What they all did was leave you with children that they do not support. Surely, those men did wrong but let us check where **you** went wrong in order for you to heal. You made men your all, which was your first big mistake. Men know they are not all, and neither can they have it all together without the blessing of the Creator. Stop abusing alcohol and drugs, take a bath, be smart, wear your best attire, check yourself on the mirror, and say, "I am going out there to make it!" and you will surely make money and find love. It is all in the state of mind. As a man thinks in his mind, so is he the same reflection of his thought.

Your children need you and one day you will be their only applauded heroine who stands out in the midst of all odds. Men are a weird species when not carefully raised up.

That is why they got you to do weird things for them and paid you nothing. And the worst thing is they do not respect you if you do not respect yourself and have character. Most pimps and drug lords who work with women easily abuse those who do not know who they are. In the back of evil men's minds, women are things that do not matter. If you learn to say yes to good things in life and no to bad, you will be on your way to building great character, being healed and finding fulfilment. Woman, redress yourself with dignity and respect; you have been naked too long and many have seen your nakedness and shame! It does not matter now because you did not know that you are a queen. Start respecting yourself and the children you have. Even if you have no children, it is of paramount importance that you achieve financial freedom in life. Do it the right way and never land in jail or have your foot on the wrong side of the law. If you determine to do right, you will do well and succeed in all your endeavours.

Some African and developing world women have resorted to eating from rubbish bins as some men do. It is very easy to attract men of the same calibre as you. If you are a great woman, you can attract a great man. Teach those men how to work and help the families that they have abandoned years ago. Build your home as a queen's palace for you are indeed a queen if you gain your financial stability. I wish above all that you know yourself first as God knows you. Do not allow an identity crisis to hold you back. You do not need a man in order to be happy in your life. This should not be an excuse to avoid others, of course; we need each other in life. If you think you need a man to be happy in life, you already have a problem because most men do not know who they are and what they need. Someone who hops from one woman to another is dangerous for you. Neither snatch him from someone, as this is a sign of your desperation which will bring you many unnecessary problems in life. Be honest to yourself and then to all people. You cannot take a man who has children, who will ever be crying for their daddy. Their mother is a woman who will ever long for her husband who is now with you. If a man makes his so-called "mistakes", you are not there to correct them for him and give him character; it is something he has to do for himself. Are you not tired of the love-desert circle? Should you be carrying a few groceries once a week or month that give him license to use you? Make this your pledge that it is time to seek justice for your life and for your children and the generations to come. Get out of cliques and clubs that keep you enslaved in a cycle of pain and suffering. Be free, you have nothing to lose when you are without a useless man.

Understand that your attitude determines your altitude. Do not fail yourself nor let your circumstances master you. When you stand on your own two feet financially, your family can begin to play a role in the formal economy. Formal economy role players have learned what I call survival skills and the successful living that goes with financial freedom. People of this class make their own jobs when they cannot find one. Sicknesses, poverty and underdevelopment will be a thing of the past for women who learn self-reliance and economic freedom. Women's empowerment will help change the culture of looking down on women. Malnutrition will be a thing of the past in our societies once all women succeed financially. When true prosperity reaches women, they become independent people with character. Parasites cling on the things they feast on, so men will no longer be your prey and in return will not prey on you. The curse of poverty and disease in Africa and the developing world can only be broken when women and children are respected and given opportunities for development and empowerment. Once they are role players and are able to contribute to the economies of Africa, the black giant will surely rise up and take its stand on the world stage. I dream of an Africa and developing world where justice, truth, peace and love (reconciliation) will abide and prevail throughout all generations. It will surely take some hard work but we can get there! We just need to know how to walk the talk.

Justice delayed is justice denied

All over the world, there are those who love life and justice. When they see what others go through, something deep down in their hearts resonates with them. Some of these people choose to leave great careers and advocate justice and human rights with various groups and governments. The weak and helpless have no one to speak for them and thus are often not heard. All people know the right thing to do but not everyone is willing to do it. That is why revolution seems to take place in almost every generation. There has to be someone who stands up and corrects what no one thought could be corrected. That is why some heroes have not survived these revolutions. These bold men and women had to pay with their lives in order to bring freedom to the many that remain. There is always an opposition to every movement that tries to free people from evil. The quest for freedom gets rid of things that mistreat people so that peace may begin to reign. The forces of opposition, however, maintain that achieving freedom is impossible. They do not want to lose their previously enjoyed gains of corruption and injustice.

These are often powerful men and women who enslave others with money and influence in both the government and private sectors. Freedom is not cheap and neither does it come easy. History has proven that men and women who changed the course of history at the end often themselves become targets of the evil forces. Few good men and women overcome these evil groups of people. Martin Luther King said, "It is not the evil men that bring a generation to distraction, but a few good that are quiet." It took good men and women to abolish slavery and segregation. It will take good men and women to abolish economic segregation and racism. When I read about how Martin Luther King rose up after a woman had refused to stand up in the bus and give a white person a seat in America, I always feel an urgency for the same kind of heart attitude to rise in our generation. Someone has to stand up and stop the nonsense that is going on in our communities today. The struggle for the emancipation of blacks in Africa and elsewhere must be characterized by a tenacity to achieve victory at the end. This is a lesson to this generation that must never be forgotten.

Arrests and the murders of innocent people who merely stood for truth and justice were the order of the day, intended to stop people from getting their freedom. People being tortured and kidnapped by security agencies was common. Heavy prison sentences were part of the pain endured by these heroes of freedom. It was through the hard work and sacrifices of many that freedom came; this generation must cherish democracy and understand the price that was paid. Today a measure of freedom has come to all people. Many who fought for it never saw the fruits of their labour but a few who survived did see it happen. When positive change comes into the world, the opposition of the good tries to mar it with violence and wars. Some men and women dare to change what no one thought could ever be changed or corrected. Why, when the economies of Africa and the world grew, but at the expense of the poor, were many leaders just quiet? That simply added to the problems rather than solve them. The real change has to be economic freedom now.

Africa and the world will yet see a generation of talented leaders standing up for truth amid challenging times. The allowing of truth and justice to flow down to all people equally is rare on the continent and in the world today. The revolution of our day is to see the transformation of racial and economic systems that are unjust and do not serve the people fairly. The pillars of gross injustice that denies many people freedom are being dismantled. The race is on! The world is ready for men and women with gold and guts, people that will tell the truth and allow it to free people from the highest government office to the least person on the grass roots. Wars must cease and whoever has been fuelling them will be found out. Those who are behind these catastrophes will have to face the full wrath of law. The broad slippery pathways travelled by some and leading to evildoing are proof that we need reliable change all over the world. Happy are those men and women who will make the changes of the twenty first century a reality to many. It is a pity to live life thinking you are free, while knowing in your heart you are not. We are yet to see the new world order of economic revolution. Ordinary men and women whose hearts are right, who stand up for truth and justice—not pleasing some people while neglecting others will usher it in. The world is sick and tired of cowards of all colours who have no law and justice that they stand for. Truth knows no colour, nor does justice and the poverty caused by lawlessness. The problems the world is having tell us there is a point where we missed it. Most of us know that point but do not want to talk about it nor confront it.

The challenges of our world today are largely due to the negligence and deliberate acts of a few irresponsible people who have unscrupulous ways of gaining money in the name of business investment. Many companies that worked in South Africa which were led by racist promoters of apartheid did more harm than good. When they pulled out of the country, they left many people sick from hazardous working conditions and never compensated them. These companies mined hazardous ores like asbestos and others. One example is Anglo American gold company against which a lawsuit has been filed for leaving miners suffering with silicosis. The victims approached its London head office. It was about 1200 people and soon went up to 1400 people. The victims did win the first round of the lawsuit compelling the company to carry the blame. More people may be joining their number. This looks like it will be a long fight in the courts and there will probably be more lawsuits of this nature in the future. The damage was not limited to South Africa but also all over the continent.

Steel manufacturing companies had many gas emissions, and electric power stations polluted the air with no precautions taken. Air pollution was not considered a threat to the human race and even when known to be a threat to health and our climate, no one wanted to take responsibility. Moneymaking, when put above the lives of people, is a cause for concern. Today, global warming is menacing the world because of a few people who are more interested in gain than the environmentally friendly operations of their companies. Such men and women have been destroying the earth and therefore should not be treated with sympathy but rather forced out of business if necessary; this will help save the earth from pollution and for the generations to come.

Heavy bribes are being paid for mining rights around the African continent and are another source of concern. The nations of Africa and the developing world need investment in their countries, but the problem is they are stranded and do not know how to lure genuine investors into their countries. The investment incentives of the developing world have many flaws since they tend to give the investors more power and benefits than their own people. Labour departments are toiling behind with unethical policies put in place by people who have very little understanding of job security for the people and sustainable economic development. Many times, the developing world's job market has some of the worst labour policies with incompetent labour broking dealers. It has unwittingly opened up the markets and given the companies more power over its people. Most countries suggest that wage packages be discussed and finalised between employers and employees. This gives evil employers the freedom to manipulate the poor illiterate employees by giving them grossly inadequate wages. The cause of these problems and unsatisfactory policies is that the developing world has many people who have no skill or any job training, let alone qualifications. The past history of the developing world continually dictates the standards of business here. Both government departments and the private sector are in confusion when it comes to salary payments.

Apartheid era governments had hospitals for Whites only and native people only. This went the same for schools and job opportunities—even for toilets! When freedom finally came, the abolition of the system was a victory for the majority native people. Unfortunately some whites, comfortable with the old system used money as a tool to keep the system going strong. The pay for work was not the same and the children of the rich did not attend schools with the children of the poor. The quality of education offered in public schools never matched the standard of private education. This meant that the children of a certain class of people continued to have the upper hand over the poor children. The change of the education system in the developing world has been coming into place very slowly. Rich people can use medical aid to avoid the long queues found in public hospitals. The Home Affairs Departments of our countries including driving licensing stations are always congested. Why are most government departments not equipped to handle the influx of people flocking through their doors?

One example is the Zimbabwe refugees' exodus. I was stunned by the number of people who were queuing day and night around Zimbabwe passport offices and other embassies looking for visas. The reason why the queues were so long was the home affairs did not have the capacity to serve the millions of people who suddenly wanted passports. The country had very little to offer its youth and the working class by then. People wanted to leave the country to look for greener pastures. The neighbouring state, South Africa bore a heavy burden, with illegal Zimbabwean nationals being arrested and deported back almost every day. The Zimbabwean government had run out of paper to make passports and could not afford to buy ink to print the notes of a currency that was badly devalued and had the highest inflation rate in the world. The countries of Africa only accepted Zimbabweans as refugees after most of the damage had been done. Why did they wait so long to give appropriate aid to Zimbabwe? Only those who had the power in their hands at the time can answer this question.

Many bad things that happened to the people of Zimbabwe were the result of negligence by those who had the power to act both locally and internationally. Surely, if Africa had been united and not divided by outside enemies of its freedom, a plan to save Zimbabwe would have been forthcoming much earlier. "An injury to one is an injury to all" was a slogan rehearsed throughout the history of Africa's emancipation and I still believe in the saying's effectiveness today. If the Zimbabwean government had been able to provide more people with passports, it would have reduced their illegal travels into neighbouring states and crime in the region dramatically. I am convinced that if Zimbabwe had been helped earlier, it would not have ended up where it did, and the Southern African region would have been better off. Leaving Zimbabwe without a role in the southern hemisphere of Africa caused other countries to lose billions of dollars in trade revenues. It seems they realized too late that they had left a brother behind and caused themselves suffering in the process. Many scholars of economics watched this but were not able to provide answers for the crisis.

The political unrest in Zimbabwe hurt many people, as it mainly affected the masses while the politicians debated the issues with full stomachs. The instigators of the Zimbabwean crisis were expecting a different result, which was obvious to them and everyone. They wanted to win the government rule by having someone of their own choice rather than the people's. This was not new in Africa's political landscape. The new era of Zimbabwean politics brought a dawn of revolution on the continent though Zimbabwe paid a heavy price in the process. The healing of the Zimbabwean people can only come when they truly understand that they are one people. Two problems surfaced when Zimbabwe had to confront its enemies. There were allegations about injustices on land distribution and black economic empowerment caused by minority white sabotage. A lot of sabotage accompanied by some corruption in the government contributed to the downfall of a glorious and prosperous Zimbabwe, which had respect all over Africa. I say "some" corruption because the Zimbabwean government has done much good since it became independent. The country has much to show for its programs of people development—more than many of its counterparts on the continent. It ranks second for nations with the most educated people on the continent, according to the latest statistics.

When the Zimbabwean revolution was taking place, the war veterans pioneered it as they had the struggle for liberation times. The style of doing things this time was aggressive and uncalled for as it opposed the majority will, according to some sources. Land sharing was a big problem in the country, which had a class of people that refused to believe there was equality between them and the blacks. Wealth was used as the main tool to keep the dividing wall in place, maintaining segregation in the developing world. The rift was between those who have and those who do not. Whoever had wealth was the boss while the masses remained slaves of past unjust settlement postings on barren native reserve lands. Some would argue that Mugabe used that as a tool to stay in power and promote a state of dictatorship but that is not really true. Whether he used it for his and his close allies' personal gain, the land question needed to be addressed with much transparency this time. We see land and black empowerment problems all over Africa and even the most industrialised nation, South Africa, is battling to sort out land issues and alleviate poverty in the country. The mining and land laws made by the old oppressors are hard to get around. Yet they are essential elements of people development and empowerment within the developing world. No developing country has it easy here, it seems. The timing might not have been right but, still, it was true that there was no justice in the country's wealth distribution. It may be that the government had enjoyed corruption for so long that when political pressures threatened it, it held on to power with whatever means it could. In any case, the truth remains that the land needed to get back into its people's hands so that they could share with others—the white minority equitably. If we dispute this fact, then the history of Zimbabwe and many developing countries will remain distorted for generations to come.

Sabotage came from large international financial institutions that fuelled sanctions against Zimbabwe in the name of human rights abuse and illegal land invasions. Not all such accusations against the government of Zimbabwe were true even when people were seen being assaulted on television. The country became ungovernable and its economy was ailing so badly that it needed an immediate solution and turnaround. Mugabe had some good men and women who could have done better but the system pinned them down. Many of his spin doctors grew weary of him and turned against him to contest for the same presidential seat. Everyone had run out of options and Mugabe remained the supposed enemy of Zimbabwe's economy and peace. Who said this and how true was it? If there was a secret that Mugabe's government was no longer willing to cover up, it was most likely the Lancaster house land deal. The lack of fulfilment of this land issue agreement signed at Lancaster house in Britain was, according to the Zimbabwean ruling party, the cause of problems. It seemed clear at first but eventually many flaws and lies surfaced.

It was more of a political game than truth to most Zimbabweans. Did Britain ever honour its commitment to compensate Zimbabwe for its land? Were the claims true that Mugabe's government misused land compensation money? Was it true that white farmers had not paid for the land and had vast unused portions that the government was wanting to use for housing people? The long delay should not have been an excuse to fulfil justice. Has standing for truth made Mugabe and his government a less or more popular leader? Did Britain buy time so that Mugabe and all those leaders who had signed the land deal would die and then the issue would be closed? How were generations to come supposed to cope with this land question? When Joshua Nkomo and his military wing went to fight the government of Mugabe, it was also a question of the land problem. Anyway, we saw a government of national unity formed and everything swept under the carpet until it surfaced again later. The honourable and respected father of Zimbabwe, Joshua Nkomo died and not much was done concerning the land question during his time in government.

The country was then set for difficult political unrest after its independence. The opposition party was said to be stable and prominent but it did not have a well-built base, which could provide it with a mandate. It was more governed by outside influences, which seemed to be a threat to the ruling party. But it was the only hope for many people to hold on to. The policies of the opposition party were clear and its priority was to restore land back to the white farmers, and bring back the rule of law and stability in the region. The opposition party pledged to bring in foreign investment in agriculture and the food processing industry, as well as many other sectors of the economy. All looked fine on paper, but implementation of it remained a major obstacle. The opposition leadership had a split and lost its core strength. What is it that divided the opposition party that could have won elections if it had remained united? A new party opened with a few who had never believed in the original party's policies and manifesto. This brought a major setback and denied the party a chance of winning national elections. Not long afterward, the government banned the opposition party's sponsorship from abroad. Surely, there was a cloud over this whole dealing of party politics, including outside influence.

Was the main opposition leader a tool for the enemies of the Zimbabwean revolution? What was the major cause of the split of the party leadership? Had the party deviated from representing the people to the goal of enriching its leadership and a few of its powerful sponsors? The other faction of the opposition party sided with the Zanu party in most of its political goals and policies. Later on, we saw negotiations begin in order to form a government of national unity, which came after a few election rounds marred with violence and intimidation. The small opposition parties were few but all just seemed to want a piece of the cake. Negotiations were difficult tough and many world leaders arrived to help mediate them. But little progress was made and many believed

Zimbabweans would have to sort out their problems on their own. Some world leaders suggested that the deployment of a United Nations peacekeeping force was the only answer to Zimbabwe's problems.

Eventually, these political manoeuvres were over and fresh negotiations began. The ruling party had no compromising stance on putting a fair land redistribution plan in place. It vowed to continue taking back land from whites for the benefit and justice of its people while the opposition party swore to give the land back to the white farmers. The opposition party claimed to have won the elections verbally, yet the actual results did not support their claims. The situation got tense and all parties were forced to compromise for the sake of the people and the economy of the country. In the end, the opposition party aligned itself with the ruling party policies again. Both parties now agreed on one policy concerning the land issue. They spoke with one voice that the land was for the Zimbabweans and should never be given back to white farmers. They also agreed not to pay compensation to the white farmers who had lost their farms.

A smooth transition to a power-sharing government would have been successful if all had worked together between the two parties. But a problem came when people could not trust the opposition as some thought it was going to take people back under the white regime rather than equip them for economic liberalisation. Maybe that is why it battled to get enough votes to take over the government as the main ruling party. Certain government portfolios were important to both parties. The Home Affairs department and the army and police, together with the justice department must always help in protecting and empowering women and children. Finally, they agreed on certain issues and the time had run out for political games so both groups had no option but to forge a unity government. A shaky unity government was put in place for a short period subject to review after the expiry of its term.

It was interesting to see how the unity government mapped its way forward. Finally, the Zimbabwean government announced it would continue with its power sharing deal, reckoned shaky and with an unpredictable future. The work on the ground had to begin. Ministers were sworn in and the Zimbabwean leadership stood with one voice and declared that they needed to forgive each other and be healed from their past since they had lifted their hands together declaring the unity of the nation. Each leader took the stage and spoke the same words with joy and enthusiasm: the land belonged to Zimbabweans and white farmers would never get the land back or be compensated. What they disagreed on united them at the end. I then remembered the words of a wise political guru of Zimbabwe. I had an opportunity to sit down and talk with this man in early 2000. That was the retired former minister of Home Affairs who had occupied various ministerial positions before his retirement. Enos Nkala came from the Joshua Nkomo party, which after 1987 joined a government of national unity comprised of the ZAPU (PF) and ZANU (PF) party. He is a greatly respected politician of his time, who has gone into farming. I supplied cattle dip to him from South Africa and many other farmers around the nation.

This man shared with me many wonderful things. I laughed, as many of them were funny. He was a man with much wisdom and political insight. He told me that in politics you have weak folks or bootlickers, and also men or women with a backbone who know what they are doing. He also said that in politics you never have a permanent enemy or friend. You can agree today and disagree tomorrow. This has remained with me for years. When I see African governments or states come to power sharing deals, I often notice that what caused them to be enemies has ceased to exist, that is if there are no political tactics of outside influences. Then the philosophy is that go with a perception that says if you cannot beat them, join them and fight from within! It is always wonderful to see peace prevail among the nations of the world. In such instances, the problems seem resolved, and the parties agree on what they never agreed on before. Often there was nothing major to fight over to begin with.

The outside influences that have dominated African states for too long played a role in Zimbabwean politics. Did leaders not understand their political position and the times? What does it take to wake up some leaders' minds from sleep? Has the strategy of leaders been right—was it to serve the people? I will never forget when the Zimbabwean MDC faction opposition leader spoke out with frustration against his main opposition alliance and said, "How many more people have to die because parties cannot agree on one or two ministries?" Home affairs and police were two ministries that caused havoc among the party groups. The question is why and who had interests for gain through these two portfolios? Eventually, all the parties sorted out their differences and signed the deal. You could say there was no real problem among the Zimbabwean leaders because all agreed to work together now. But why could they not have started here rather than hurt the economy and lose so many lives?

Outside influence has contributed to many wrong decisions in African politics, as well as causing senseless wars, hunger and economic downfalls. Some think if the opposition party had not stood in the way when the Zimbabwean land revolution took place, there might have been a quick solution to the problem and perhaps no economic setback as well. What brought Zimbabwe to its knees were the two opposition parties the government faced, and the outside influence that sabotaged the economy. The political influences that backed the opposition parties, aiming for a lion's share at the end, have to take a portion of the blame. Africa does not need strong leaders but sound policies with good management mechanisms in place. If there were no outside influences in the African political landscape, many countries would do better. If the Zimbabwean leadership had stood together as one people, speaking with one voice during the years of its political dilemma they could have come out of the fire unscathed. Now the nation must understand that it will take many years to rebuild their economy. The Zimbabwean leadership failed to understand that the enemy was not their brother or sister and neither was it the white man. The enemy was the evil history that has been ruling for generations and must be dismantled in modern revolutionary style. People need the justice of wealth distribution that will lead to a peaceful nation of prosperity rather than debating on how long the leaders should stay in power.

Africa and the developing world fight dirty wars about the length of terms for leaders in office. That is not enough to justify true good governance and non-corrupt political leadership. In the eyes of the people it is not good to stay too long in power but if a leader is constantly doing good then why not allow him to stay and do more good. The curse of mediocre leadership is criticizing one another rather than supporting each other. Politicians seem to want the presidential seat in African politics more than doing the job they are sworn in office for. That is why there was so much factionalism even among the South African ruling party, the African National Congress. The alarming murder rate of councillors and politicians was a sign of a sick leadership.

Political schism has cost the continent many innocent lives, causing economic woos and downfalls that have made Blacks look as if they do not think well nor learn from their mistakes nor are able to define the future they want for generations to come. The Zimbabwean people went through hell and many of them became victims of the injustices of the country's leadership. The illegal immigrants from Zimbabwe increased to Botswana and South Africa and some died without entering their destination countries. I remember when crocodiles ate some Zimbabweans swept by the Limpopo River into its deep waters. Some of the people who had dreams of reaching "Mzansi" land were found dead in the water. The tragedy happened while they were trying to get to South Africa. When it was aired all over the news, I thought it would serve as a warning for people not to come through illegal means into South Africa but instead it got worse. A Zimbabwean truck carrying mangoes to Botswana also had nine illegal immigrants being smuggled into the country. The men were under the mangoes and the border officers could not see them. On the way to Francis town, the illegal immigrants suffocated and died in that closed truck. This was a terrible tragedy.

On the other hand, those who were coming into South Africa and Botswana seemed to be like the rest of whites who loved their good former workers and gave them jobs though they were illegal in these countries. The white farmers who left Zimbabwe and settled in South Africa had farming businesses in many countries of the continent in addition to Zimbabwe. Farmers loved such people and construction companies used a lot of them, who were skilled, semi-skilled or non-skilled. The South African labour market absorbed most of the Zimbabwean nationals. A lot of them used South Africa as a springboard to get to London, since it is an English speaking country. Canada and North America were reached by a few. Zimbabwe had nothing to offer its people who had to go all over the world seeking asylum. Many of them took jobs outside their professional fields, just to try to earn a living. Teachers and many other professionals were getting into construction work and becoming mortar boys or general hand workers. Zimbabwe was a respected nation in Africa and it is very unfortunate that it could not benefit from its professionals. They could have equipped the nation for a position of great influence on the continent and in the world. Zimbabwe had to start all over again after the shaky government of national unity was formed. Rebuilding a country that was once highly esteemed by the world and now with many challenges ahead is no easy task.

Mass starvation hit Zimbabwe. The prisons ran out of food supplies and medicines so that many inmates suffered and starved to death. Some who had terminal illnesses did not make it through. Cholera killed thousands of people. The water was dirty and the government could not afford to buy chemicals to purify water for its people. Medicines were scarce in the country. The sanctions left the bankrupt government with more orphan children and poor in it than at any time in its history. Without question, the sanctions of the west were wrong-headed. If they were right, they should have targeted President Mugabe, his allies, and inner circle of ministers. Instead, they affected innocent people and denied them their basic necessities. Zimbabweans suffered because they could not take their president out who was the enemy of the west. The Zimbabwean leadership, the opposition parties, and the west all cost that country the heavy price of its people's lives. There is very little validity to the political manoeuvre of sanctions. Sanctions will always hit hard if the economies are built around the countries of the west. Thus, economic liberalization will be the way to go for African states. Africa has been bullied by rich nations for too long, it is time for it to pick up the pieces and rebuild without fear.

Africa must be ready for severe storms, as the HIV and AIDS are so prevalent in the poverty-stricken continent. Many children have one or no parent, who often does not work. The aids treatment plan seems to go very slowly and this contributes to poverty as the many sick people cannot play a role in African economies. The elderly are not properly cared for, as most countries do not have a system in place to feed them or give them pension grants. Africa's blessing is in looking after its women, children and elderly people. The poor and the helpless are also people who deserve respect and dignity among societies. I have often wondered why Africa has so many queues in hospitals and in Home Affairs and other departments as well. The reason is that when people have nothing to do, they are more prone to sickness and the only place they know to go is a government department for a treatment or grant.

Now, if the people were busy at work, they would not have the time to spend on long queues for example, of the driving licence departments. Most of them are school leavers trying to get opportunities in the job markets that are so strict and only absorb a few every year. It is an open door for government officials to start doing favours for others, as the opportunity to secure a driver's licence seems to be scarce. The bribes paid for bookings, because the waiting lists are long and it is hard to get appointment dates, are a matter of concern. Those with money just buy their way up to the last process stage. It is countries' governments which are to blame for the poor service delivery in Africa and the developing world. Road accidents that kill so many every day in the developing world are a result of unqualified drivers on the roads. This is because of all the illegal driving permits and licences on the continent. When I travel around Africa, I am always amazed at how poor the services are. One reason is that whenever an African state tries to get up, the next moment it is down and cannot afford to pay staff or keep qualified professional people and technology. One day up and the next day down is the sad story of the developing world community. That will never take the developing world anywhere. Our border officials are mostly corrupt and it is partly due to the developing world governments' failure to put good management mechanisms in place. The ports of Africa and the developing world have become global drug-docking zones because of poor security controls. Africa and the developing world need a progressive development platform that will achieve stipulated goals for the 21st century.

Loved you not culture

Romantic love between a man and a woman is sweet if both understand each other well. Cultural values can be of one race or tribe and it can even be as widespread as national beliefs and customs. As I said earlier, culture is a heritage of customs and traditional values adhered to by a sect of people, as its beliefs and standards of living life. Culture is taught from one generation to another and, as global civilization spreads its influence, we see culture slowly falling apart. People are constantly modifying culture and if they cannot modify it, often times they move away from it. The elders in a society tend to uphold culture better, desiring to preserve it with its values through all generations. This is the case in many cultural societies, and if not many will not keep culture or respect it. Culture is a stronghold in most people's minds around the world. And then, of course, you will always find people who pervert cultural values, as they would with religion, in order to advance their own evil interests.

Most people who love culture in Africa hold nature in high regard. Elderly people and belief in ancestors have influenced them in upholding cultural values. If those elders married ten or more wives, it most probably would be so with the next generations. Ancestral worship beliefs come from culture and are the way said ancestors worshipped. Instead of going directly to God they believed in going to Him via the dead. Past African generations taught that the dead are next to God and are the only ones who can take requests and prayers to God on behalf of the living. It is necessary to dress in old skin hides and perform rituals if one wants to be welcome in these rituals when addressing the dead and giving god worship. How did the elders find out the dead could talk to God on behalf of the living? All of them claimed to have found it like that and so always lived that way. Culture is used to discipline people as well and it had this focus too.

Culture often conflicts with civilization, religion and the true worship of God. The reason is that culture is not always a standard of truth. It is culture because we found it that way. I often laugh when I see how biased the African culture is when it comes to the worship of ancestors. The truth is a dead man or woman has no authority among the living anymore. Spirit-filled children of God cast so-called ancestral spirits out of people in the name of Jesus because they are actually demons. Surely, a spirit will leave a life when commanded out in Jesus' name and it can never come back if the door is forever closed against such false worship. It is interesting to note this truth: dead ancestors have nothing to do with the takeover of a life claiming to be possessed by ancestors.

Remember satan is the serpent of old. He knows very well that if he tells you he wants to take over your life you will surely resist him. The devil is a spirit who knows all your ancestors and what sins they did or loved to do. Every family has a pattern of problems or way that they commit sins. The devil will take up residence in the lives of men and women in the name of their ancestors. Many people will entertain the devil if he comes in dreams in pictures of their ancestors and speaks out to the living in their faked spirit voices. The devil knows what voice the ancestors had or how they spoke. He will then imitate the ancestor's voice and receive permission to take residence in a life by deception. These are what we call evil spirits; the devil uses this line of attack frequently against African people. I have seen many African healers and magicians turning to Christ and surrendering to the salvation that is from God. I used to wonder why some would repent and not others. Others get to know the truth; it is the knowing of the truth that sets them free. Many African healers are still trying to compete with new medical advances and usually come out with inferior results compared to the modern health profession.

The cultural mentality holds people back with a strong spiritual philosophy that ancestors are guiding the processes of people's lives. This is a lie from hell. The devil is the spirit that controls these men and women who practise works of fortune telling and others. The killing of albinos that goes on every day around Africa is said to be a great business ritual for fortune. Apart from albinos, men, women and children are also sought and killed and their body parts sold for various business charms. Some will say that fortune-tellers can foretell the future or things that happened. Yes, I agree with that to some degree, since satan is a spirit. Because satan is a spirit, he can see things in the spirit realm and tell them as they are through his servants. That should not be a surprise to people as it does happen, but you must understand how limited these operations can be.

When you visit the places where the traditional healers sell their herbal medicines and charms, you will begin to see how unhealthy most of those herbs and skins of snakes and animals are. Most of herbal doctors lack proper understanding of health science. The practice is not viable in modern society as it does not solve today's health problems but often rather makes them worse. Injustice often hides in culture and is welcomed to operate in Africa by some scholars of African descent. They hold culture close to their hearts, claiming it is their heritage of science even when it is backward, hardly bringing answers to our health problems. Some governments continue to pump billions into African healers' researches, trying to find a cure for HIV and AIDS. Those government ministers lack true knowledge and their culture blinds them. Many leaders in Africa use spirit science, believing it will help them stay in power rather than sowing seeds of good leadership to produce the desired results.

African traditional leadership hate debating about their cultural values as many customs are without merit in a modern society. Culture is usually strongest where people are illiterate. Thus, in Africa, where the majority of the masses are uneducated, culture is the order of the day. It becomes the knowledge people are taught to embrace from childhood. Culture often hampers development. A good example is that the land that traditional healers get their herbs from cannot be tampered with in most parts of Africa. The sad part is that some leaders try to transform culture into a civilized practice without changing its main foundations. Cult churches of Africa are then born out of these so-called cultures. Cult Churches have mushroomed all over the continent. Often times, the leaders of these cult churches are like gods over their congregations. Such churches attempt to lure people back to their roots without due consideration of modern developments.

In these kinds of churches, people purchase small parcels that they take home to perform rituals. Africans flock to these kinds of churches that lack God's truth only because they understand the culture well. People disappear, and killing for rituals in the name of serving their god is not uncommon. Many African herbalists, the church founders of these cults, have perverted the values of religion. Most of the churches of this type have uniforms they sell to their members and those who worship there keep deep secrets. The name of Jesus is little used in this kind of organisation claiming to be a church, and neither is the Bible the source of truth. Many black preachers of Africa are turning to the small parcel route to lure people to their churches and gain wealth. The regrettable thing is that most of the followers of those congregations love God but a religion of culture cannot take them to God, as it lacks knowledge of who God is. Religion and culture are used to manipulate people in Africa and in many third world countries. The colonial masters used the gospel to wrongly manipulate the people of the continent many times. They told the black man he did not need prosperity here on earth but in heaven, as they gathered everything for the white settlers and left the black man with just the bible. People perish because of lack of knowledge.

Many of the leaders of these cultural groups have shifted from using herbs and other things to oil from Israel and water from the seas around Israel. The oil sells at a high price as does the seawater, and are said to be able to look after people and protect them. The water is put in little pocket-sized bottles and given to people to keep in their possession wherever they are. There is also other stuff they string around their bodies. When the teaching on salvation is not right, masses of followers become prey to a ruthless leadership of so-called men and women of God. Cult church leaders try to use traditional means to make people comfortable in worshiping God from a cultural perspective. It all might look good but the results are sinful and dead. Who is the master of all this? The god of culture rules in most religions of this type since they lack the glory and holiness of the true living God. An uneducated brain often lacks good reasoning capacity and ability. If Africa is to escape from the culture web, it will have to educate its people. Many people of Africa practise the things of culture out of lack of understanding.

Education expels the darkness in a mind and introduces knowledge, understanding and brainpower, which people can then use to do good things for others. Education is not beneficial until others also benefit from it. Education's truth gives power to live peacefully with all people. Sadly, many men and women trapped in culture and religion often commit themselves to false theories of life.

It is interesting that some people hold to their cultural values even as they claim to be Christians. Some cultures recommend that a man should not find a woman on his own but that he let his parents choose one for him. In the past, the bride price was paid as a token of thanks, unlike today where in most of Africa, it is business. Huge amounts of money are paid for a bride in many cultures today, as this has become good business on the continent. Since joblessness is a defining factor for many men, it is not easy for them to marry now. If they marry, they may marry a woman they never intended since some families accept instalment payments for bride price while others will not. Rich polygamist men are able to pay the price for beautiful women as money plays a major role in African marriages. Many young men and women have resorted to living together in big cities without any commitments because the cultural demands are so high and difficult to meet. If the bride price is not paid in full, the family can take their daughter until the final payment of the outstanding balance has been made. The father generation found it like that and very much kept it that way. You get that answer when you confront many cultural practices and values.

Daughters are valued in different categories within African cultures. If she is a virgin, the price is more and it is also high if she is educated or from a royal family. The two categories determine the price even if only one characteristic is in place. Some African parents will go days without eating if their daughter loses her virginity without the bride price being paid for her. Ordinary women are not too expensive but are also not cheap. In most cultures, only a virgin covers her face with a veil on the wedding day. The cultures are quite strict among most tribes and peoples. Some cultures raise their kids with better teaching as there is good and bad with all cultures. In an African culture, women cook and fetch water from distant places, especially in rural areas. Children and house chores are a woman's responsibility in the house. The majority of black African men would hardly change a baby's nappy but, frowning, would call the woman claiming that it is a woman's job. He will not even dish food for himself. If he comes from somewhere in the middle of the night he will ask for food from the sleeping woman. She knows her duty and wakes up and dishes for him. In many African cultures, a woman will go live with her mother and father-in-law. This has caused many incidents of infidelity as some fathers-in-law prey on these women. Their husbands take in other women, too, after their wives go to the remote rural village places and stay with the new family. When the mothers of Africa were married, they received this treatment; now they treat their daughters-in-law the same way. Today where infidelity is widespread many diseases like HIV and AIDS plague the people and are entrenched in Africa because of the men's way of life.

In most African cultures a woman has to submit not because of love only but because money was paid for her to join the other family. Only when an African man has moved away from culture is a woman treated more like a queen. A fine man I know pondered on the various obstacles of culture without success. This was my friend Thomas, whom I had known from his early teenage years. When he started working, his duties involved travelling around Africa; and we would often meet in various countries. We were on holiday going to Lusaka, Zambia when Thomas met a beautiful young woman who had just finished her Advanced level studies at Chinoyi high school of Zimbabwe. The woman's grandmother was sitting opposite her on a bus while Thomas sat next to her on the same row. When we got to Lusaka, all were in good spirits and Thomas got the holiday address and telephone number of this young woman. He told me he was very interested in having a date with her, so the following day he called her and arranged to meet her by the city. As they met, the date went well and before two weeks of time in Zambia, Thomas was madly in love with this young woman by the name of Fiona. Thomas was a Christian and so was this Fiona.

Time flies when having fun! We had to leave to go back to South Africa but it was a trip that we certainly did not regret taking. Zambia is a place known for its warm-hearted people when it comes to tourism and hospitality ratings. We went back to work and, after a few months passed, we arranged to go to Zimbabwe after a few weeks of preparation. It took us a day to get to Bulawayo where we had friends and relatives in both the Lord and the flesh. We slept over and went to Gweru the following day, continuing to the Gweru rural area and spent a night there with relatives. The following morning, we were to go to Chinoyi to see Fiona. I had thought of visiting the area again to see my old schoolmates after years of absence from the Mashonaland province which I loved so much. We boarded the bus in Gweru at about 10;30 a.m but it delayed leaving for some reason until the afternoon. Buses on this side of the world sometimes do not observe the time of departure but wait until they are full before leaving their cities.

I knew the town and its surrounding residential suburbs and townships well. Our aim was to get to Chinoyi, see Fiona first, and then go to the other side of the township to sleep by my friend's place. That was within the same township where Fiona lived and was very close to the main highway that led to town. The woman who sat next to us in the bus knew Fiona's family very well and she suggested we get off with her by the bus stop and she would get her son at home to take us there. My heart was so happy seeing the province I once worked in as we passed through the large farms of the Mashonaland cities' commercial zones. I wished I could visit the farms and speak to people I knew. I loved those people so much and my heart went out to them. It was about 19.45 when we got off the bus and 20.25 pm when we arrived by Fiona's home.

The young man who helped us locate Fiona's home introduced us to the family as visitors from South Africa. Fiona's brother worked the night shift as a police officer but was home that moment. He chatted with us for a few minutes and then left in a police-marked Land Rover. Fiona's mother was home and she was a good woman with strong roots in Shona culture though she was also a devoted Christian of a Pentecostal church. Her husband worked for Chinoyi caves, a local tourist attraction that was well known in the world. He was not at home that evening since he usually came home only on weekends. If at all it happened for him to at home, we still would not tell how everything was going to be. We only wanted to see Fiona in passing because in African culture it is taboo for a man to see a woman by her home unless some financial obligations have been met. We were not really worried about her parents' response because we were prepared to talk to them with wisdom if they had confronted us for not having obeyed the culture. We told ourselves we would tell her family that she was just our friend.

Fiona's brother did not question us about how we knew his sister and neither did he look concerned. The mother called in two young girls who were in high school and asked them if they knew anything about us from their aunt or had ever heard her mention us at anytime. Fiona had mentioned my name and Thomas' and we had written to her a few times. But our trip was a big surprise! After that, the old woman opened her bedroom door and came out to us by the lounge. She greeted us and immediately got Fiona on the line since she was away visiting her sister in Guruve in the former eastern border high lands, old Spolilo. We spoke to her and she asked us to wait five more days until she returned. But that we could not guarantee and we wished her well as we finished our phone conversation. Then we prepared to say good-bye to her family. We told them of our travelling arrangements and the mother refused to let us leave that night for my friend's place. She prepared food for us and told us that in their culture we could not sleep by her house since she did not know exactly what kind of relationship we had with her daughter. But she arranged a place for us to sleep by her neighbour's house.

In her culture, if you were a son-in-law to be, you would not enter their home without proper arrangements being made for the bride price and all ceremonial activities fulfilled. The following morning the two high school girls brought us back to Fiona's house where we bathed and enjoyed a nice breakfast prepared by Fiona's mother. She left us in the lounge to eat and went into her bedroom, as culture did not permit her to stay and watch us eat. After eating, we gave the girls some money out of appreciation for the treatment they had given us and asked the mother's blessing to go. She came in the lounge and spoke to us and asked whether we were Christians. When she found out we were. She smiled, laughed, and discussed various issues of faith. Finally, she told us she knew God would guide us back to Johannesburg, South Africa. She then made a wonderful prayer for us and we left for Bulawayo and then South Africa. The last time I heard from Fiona she was going to study in England, and after a letter from her sister in America, our communication ended. Later on, I found her through Face book, (technology is now the answer to such issues of friends!) She is a university graduate living and working in America. Thomas eventually lost hope as Fiona faded from the picture of his life due to the long distance between them.

I watched Thomas go from one relationship to another. He grew up in church but did not know how to choose a churchwoman as culture had blinded him. Thomas was a good man who grew up in a village, met the Lord in high school as a teenager, and gave his life to God. In his dating, he always preferred born-again women. A problem that he had was surrounding himself with men who did not know the Lord but were much involved in culture. Since he worked with them and spent most of his time with them they taught him their ways and influenced his life. Thomas only differed from these men by going to church on Sundays. He could not influence them; rather, they influenced him. He was a good young man with sound life principles and faith in God. He abstained from sleeping with women outside marriage, as this was one condition of a holy man for him. His upbringing was good, he loved life, and was always career-oriented. At work, he earned respect and had a nice managerial position. Money gave this young man a good life. Now, he had a friend, a womanizer who liked to go out with him after work and during weekends, though Thomas was faithful to be in church every Sunday.

Thomas grew up like any other village boy and he had a good understanding of life for a young man his age. He wanted so much to find a woman of his own and marry her. Now, he loved walking long distances after work and during weekends as a hobby and means of exercise. When he became close to one of his workmates, who also loved walking his life changed. The name of the workmate was Levy, who was of the Tsonga tribe. He was once married to two wives but one had left because of some financial problems he had. He lived with a girlfriend at his workplace and with his wife in his home village along his mother and their three children. Levy was a bad influence on Thomas and steered him into his own naughty lifestyle ways. On a Thursday, they went out together for their walk, now also hunting for women. This had become their practice for some time as they both neither drank alcohol nor smoked. The friendship of the two men had bonded better now through the nasty habits they enjoyed together.

Thomas would ask every girl he dated whether she was a Christian or not, but Levy just enjoyed one-night stands with any woman. Thomas somehow understood the power of a Christian woman in his life. Levy just took anyone whom he wanted to his house when his girlfriend was away, and in the morning it was over. This man loved using women as he claimed they were a part of his food. It was on a Thursday late afternoon when Thomas saw a beautiful young woman coming to the shop and Levy was gazing at her too. Both men saw her and only one could make a move on her. As the young woman entered the shop, Thomas went behind her, patted her shoulder and asked to speak to her on her way home or outside the shop.

The woman just looked at him and said nothing. On her way out he joined her. They spoke for a short distance, and he returned to where Levy was sitting after having no luck with her. The young woman did not agree to anything he wanted and finally warned him about her uncle whom she claimed to be a strict man who was standing by their house outside. She kept telling Thomas to turn back before her uncle saw him walking with her; so he listened and turned back not having achieved his goal. She did tell him her name was Jennifer and it turned out to be her real name. He took steps he would see her again. He found out where Jennifer went to church and paid a visit to that church's youth meeting. Jenifer was usually there in most services of the young people and so Thomas saw her there for the second time.

Something seemed to be bringing him and Jennifer together. They were both Zimbabwean nationals who had Christian upbringings. Thomas continued to try to get Jennifer to go on a date with him, which she always promised to consider, but never got back to him. Life was difficult on Jennifer's side as she was illegal in the country and had to go and live with some of her country township girls in Berea by the city of Johannesburg. Then she seemed to disappear, Thomas could not see her because, though she worked for a florist company not far from Thomas' work place, she would finish work about an hour before he did and go home.

It was hard for them to meet after work since Jennifer would immediately catch the bus to her residence in Berea, Johannesburg. On one Wednesday, afternoon Thomas again visited the youth group where he had seen Jenifer before. This time, he was without a Bible. He tried to borrow a bible from a woman who worked with Jenifer and she gave him an amplified Bible which belonged to Jenifer. This time she was not there by the meeting. After church, he went with the Bible to his house since he was supposed to give it back to Jennifer. Jennifer wanted her bible badly and could not get it until she met him by the bus stop a month later. That day she had finished late at work because she had to do overtime duty.

They stood for some time talking and eventually walked together to Thomas's place to fetch the bible. The two committed this evening to each other. It was late and Jennifer had to sleep by Thomas's house. They made supper together, ate, and then said good night to each other. In the morning, Jennifer went to work wearing the same pair of jeans and t-shirt, which she had washed and ironed at Thomas's place. This was the beginning of their relationship. Levy saw them and was surprised—he could not believe what his eyes were seeing! After four months, Thomas and Jennifer took their relationship to a new level by coming to live together. Both their parents knew about this and it was a big step for them indeed.

The bride's price was proposed and Jennifer's mother came with a friend from Zimbabwe and arrived at Honeydew where her daughter and new son-in-law to be lived. The bride's price was already prepared, as Thomas had even borrowed money from the company where he worked. When he came home from work, the mother-in-law and her friend were already there. Jennifer introduced Thomas to her mother and her friend as the son-in-law to be, and all was great. The mother of Jennifer was Ndebele and her father was Malawian, of a Tumbuka tribe.

The parents of Jennifer were from two strong tribes that embraced culture but at the same time understood western culture and Christian principles. Thomas did not have to send old people to negotiate (Lobola) the bride price for him but instead his wife-to-be had made things easy for him. After having sat and spoken for some time, Thomas gave

Jennifer a lump sum of money, which she took and went to sit before the two women with him on the side. He had raised half of the requested bride price amount. Jennifer was a very liberal-minded woman who could make anyone laugh at any time. She told the two women that it was time to finish business so they could go since it was getting dark.

(The culture did not allow them to sleep at the in-law's house before all the cultural issues were resolved.) Jennifer counted the money and handed it to the other woman to give to her mother, as this was the cultural procedure. A wedding arrangement discussion took place that very moment; the preparations received a go ahead from Jennifer's family representatives who happened to be her mother and the friend. That night Thomas and Jennifer had gone another step higher with their love. It was because they were both committed believers and wanted to do the right thing even when circumstances and situations were against them. A white wedding day became their dream and all preparations continued well until that day.

Thomas and Jennifer started attending the same church after the announcement of their engagement. A pastor in Thomas' church who specialised in marriage counselling counselled with them. Since they were both Zimbabwean nationals, the wedding had to take place in two countries, requiring a budget for a two-venue wedding! Thomas had to be ready for what he was getting himself into since Jennifer had quit her low-paying job to study social sciences. Thomas bought the Junk Mail Newspaper, and began looking for wedding dress hire and sales. There was an advert on the paper that caught his eye. The wedding dress was new, the owner had brought it from Scotland and the size was exactly Jenifer's size. This looked too good to be true and without wasting anytime, he phoned the seller. The seller gave the price and he offered to come down and look at the dress. When he saw it, he fell in love with it and immediately paid for it and took it away with him. Jennifer loved it very much and had only to change the trail and make it longer. The material for the trail was imported for them and she had her dream dress finally done according to what she wanted.

The bridesmaids gear purchase followed. And Thomas got a lovely suit for himself through a woman who had known about the suit, advertised on the papers for some time. That suit was also unique. His boss' mother who was running a cake business prepared the cake. The four-tier cake was given to Thomas at a discounted price, which he paid for with a Cheque that bounced. His boss had to pay for it and deduct the amount from his salary for a few months. The purchase of the wedding rings was the last thing done, and now all was in place including the food ordered and church people available to do the cooking.

Thomas had some friends who were pastors who loved him very much. The bride's pastor was also a good friend of his by now. The night before the wedding, the bride slept at her pastor's house and the matron of honour was with her. In the morning she put on her makeup and dressed, then was taken to the wedding venue. The company gave a car to Thomas to use during his wedding day with a special driver allocated to drive him. He chose to have the car take him to the church and dress for the wedding there as it was still early. The bride was already at the church with her pastor and the other pastors who were Thomas' friends. I think he was suppose to be the first to get there and dress up, and then wait for the bride. His pastor was a Sotho black man managing other language services in that church, which was comprised of black men and women from the surrounding community of domestic workers including their children. As they understood very little English, they rarely mixed with so-called white people's services.

The pastor claimed that he had only found out that Thomas and Jennifer were staying together that morning when some of his boys he sent to check on Thomas brought him the news. The bride was beautifully dressed, but sitting down and crying while the whole church sat surprised at the allegations that had surfaced against the wedding couple. When Thomas arrived, the new twist of events began to dawn on him. He found that his pastor had not prepared for the wedding and neither did he want to marry them anymore. His intention was to cancel the wedding based on what he called unacceptable courtship standards. Sleeping or staying with a woman before marriage is sin according to God's word. Some churches use this blight of sin against people as a standard to compromise holy living by not allowing forgiveness to take place. Pastors need to be very careful when dealing with matters of this nature, as many of them love to sit on God's seat as judges and make Christianity a culture.

The pastor called off the wedding even before Thomas arrived and that is why the bride was sitting with her bride mates and church folks by that separate room crying. It seemed the pastor had coerced the church leadership to boycott the wedding. Some pastors held a meeting and the wedding was delayed. The problem caused many people to wonder at the whole handling of the wedding saga. All the congregants and guests stayed around the church to see the last moment decision of the pastor. The pastor stuck by his guns, claiming that sleeping together before marriage was unacceptable and for that reason he was calling the wedding off. Thomas knew those principles of discipline very well but took a risk, as Jennifer had no good place to stay. They needed to save for the wedding, so he stayed with her. Some pastors began to debate the overall issue, and then approached the pastor of the church with a new proposal. Two pastors asked to marry Thomas and Jenifer. It seemed as if the church leadership had conspired to let Thomas down at the last minute. But the wedding dream of Tom and Jen was yet to come true again. The new pastors performing the wedding were allowed to use the same facilities. The two pastors indeed brought a lifeline to the wedding quandary.

The resident pastor agreed to let the other pastors marry the couple and did not dress up but watched everything with little participation. So the wedding started late but went well. On the vote of thanks, the bride had few words and chose to sing a song, which was her favourite. She sang it until she cried and we could see how difficult the preparation time until the end had been for her. After the wedding, all the friends and many cars headed to their home. They passed through a slum squatter camp close to their home chanting songs and shouting, as celebrations were at their peak now. Thomas and Jennifer's wedding was the first black wedding in the area for more than six years since the community settled there. Within a month, the wedding moved to Zimbabwe's second capital city Bulawayo where Jenifer was born and her parents lived. The four-tier wedding cake was served in South Africa and the two tiers left were mostly served in Bulawayo. Their wedding held on 1 January 1997 in Bulawayo, was a great success and a sublime moment for them.

The family of the bride came in full number, yet Thomas' family disappointed him. Thomas did not have much money left in Bulawayo. When he went to fetch his parents for the wedding, they had many excuses and finally did not attend. The reason Thomas allowed the wedding to go to Zimbabwe was to celebrate the occasion with his parents as a token of appreciation for them. But his family's culture did not allow him to marry before intense consultations with them because the woman was supposed to live at the village home with the parents after the wedding. Thus, for Thomas, many traditional issues impacted his marriage in the African milieu. But Thomas stood by his principles and made it very clear that he had married Jennifer for himself and not for the family.

He kept his goals straight and did not allow culture to rule him more than the Christian world even when he had failed the test of purity with his South African church. His parents and family claimed to be Christians, yet they were heavily influenced by cultural values. His grandmother, a woman of staunch Ndebele culture asked him on his wedding day whether he was finished with the pleasures of women. In the Ndebele culture, you have to have many different women and live with them until you feel you can choose one and marry. If you do not obey the culture, these communities regard you as rude and arrogant. He hired a taxi to take him to the wedding when he was in Bulawayo; his finances were dwindling but he managed okay.

He asked the driver to take off the taxi sign and drop him with his little family by his wife's home. He arrived at the wedding and everything went well even to the photo shoot—and all day long the programme of the wedding was a success. Many church people volunteered their nice cars for the day to the wedding couple. There was no car problem as all looked great here! His sister and her husband, and his grandmother and uncle attended the wedding. But few of his friends came. He seemed to have lived life as a lone ranger because very few people from his side came. Maybe because he had not invited many people. Or perhaps it was because of his background: he was a village boy having his wedding by the city.

When the holidays were over, Thomas and his wife returned to South Africa. It was time to pay a few debts and enjoy life together and surely, they did. Thomas was instructed in the cultural rules from his in-law family before leaving for Johannesburg. Rule number one, he could not eat in the presence of his wife's parents. Only after a year, could he pay with a goat and give money to the mother-in-law. Then, if she accepted all the terms, she could eat with him at the same table. One also cannot greet with a handshake a mother-in-law or father-in-law in their culture. The rest of their time in Zimbabwe was great and enjoyed by all of them.

His mother-in-law drank beer during the wedding as did his father-in-law. This was part of the celebratory style in their way of life. As I looked at Thomas he seemed to be saying, "Thank God, it is over now!" On the way to South Africa, the two spoke of their future and used the time to plan everything well. It seemed definite that the two would make it because they were devoted Christians living according to wisdom. All their friends gathered with them in their home upon their arrival in the country. The two became a good example of what family is and helped several couples arrange fine weddings because of their insight and love for life. I saw a marriage that was true, and filled with love that seemed fulfilling. And now Jenifer had help from her husband in acquiring legal papers for staying in South Africa.

The two would travel to Zimbabwe anytime they liked, as Thomas did not keep his job for long after their wedding. The company closed down and the company that bought it brought him over to their facility in Pretoria. But the new company did not treat him well and he resigned and started his own business. Thomas made money and excelled in his business endeavours. They had clothing boutiques and additional ventures that traded at an international level. After four years of marriage, most of Jennifer's family members lived abroad because conditions in Zimbabwe were deteriorating rapidly. Jennifer wanted to go to London where her sister was and her sister had offered to pay for their airfares, accommodations and upkeep during their stay. But Thomas did not want to go to London. Such differences of opinion have destroyed many families, and so this marriage, too, was now tested.

Who could have told what would happen next? The couple went for many weeks not talking and their marriage problems grew serious. Jennifer's sister and mother wrote letters telling her to leave Thomas if he did not want to leave South Africa. She showed him the letters, and he asked her what she thought about them. She said she was definitely going to take the opportunity to make money overseas. Thomas was devastated by her decision but there was nothing much he could do as he had only paid half the bride price and still owed the balance. It was now Jennifer's family against him. According to culture their daughter was still theirs and they wanted to send overseas above all else. The marriage went through a strain and was in desperate straits because of this problem.

When the phone rang and it was Jennifer's family, she would always tell them she could not speak if Thomas was in the house. The marriage relationship was now on the rocks. Jennifer was now supposed to leave from South Africa for London. Her sister sent her the money to travel. Now Jennifer had a cousin sister who looked exactly like her in South Africa. She borrowed Jennifer's passport to go to Zimbabwe and seem then flew to London on the same passport without returning it. Later she wrote back from the UK, informing Jennifer that the passport had been lost. So Jennifer had to go to Zimbabwe and sort out her travelling documents first. The couple went through a lot and were no longer on speaking terms. A van came by their home to pick up boxes which Jennifer had filled with house utensils and kitchenware things that she believed belonged to a woman in marriage according to her culture. The things were loaded in the van and a friend asked her to say good-bye to Thomas, but her reply was no and she went away. It was the last day she ever set foot in South Africa. She deserted the marriage just like that! Jenifer went back to her family and country of birth, Zimbabwe, to sort out her documents and then fly to London.

The government of Zimbabwe had introduced new policies and laws concerning foreign nationals with children in the country. And since Jennifer had a Malawian father it was harder for her to obtain a passport in her country of birth. She had to apply for a new original birth certificate and it took time to be issued. She even went to Malawi to try to get the passport since she had gone there a few times with her parents when she was young. But she could not take advantage of her father's Malawian citizenship and all ended up in vain. Thomas had followed her for two months after she left South Africa and gave her money, but still she would not change her mind and come back home. After four years of marriage breakdown Thomas applied for a divorce and the court of South Africa granted it to him. It took a long time for Jennifer's new birth certificate to come, and the conditions for travel to London were no longer relaxed but difficult to attain from Zimbabwe. Finally, she received her passport after about six years. She sent a cell phone message on valentine's day to Thomas, which was followed by a long letter saying nothing could take the place of the time they had spent together. It seems she desperately wanted to get back with him now.

Somehow, she managed to get Thomas' home phone number and found out he was having a child with another woman he now lived with. That triggered a new spat of anger, but it could not get very far as he changed his phone number quickly. She was history to him; yet in her mind, he was her darling again to brand her castle in the air. A year passed and Thomas went inside a bar looking for someone, and unexpectedly saw Jennifer's niece working there. She saw him, called him to her side, and told him that her mother wanted to see him and wanted his contact details. When Thomas wanted to know why after so many years she suddenly wanted to see him she suggested they rather go outside and talk. So they went outside. The young woman started dropping tears, quiet for a moment; then she broke the news to Thomas that Jennifer had passed on.

She never made it to London but died with broken dreams. Thomas was hurt to think she could have passed on short of what God had for her. Did her family have too much influence over her life or was it her choices based on immaturity in marriage life? Her funeral was said to have been attended by parliamentarians and many high profile dignitaries from around the country. Her sister wanted to give Thomas a DVD of the funeral but how was this going to sit with him? No one knows. Before her death, she had played a major role in the HIV and AIDS campaigns in her country of birth. After she was diagnosed with cancer, she sought and went through treatment measures before she died. Sources say that doctors certified her as being healthy and having overcome the cancer. She suffered the penalty of living life without fences, having allowed cultural values to prevail above truth and justice in her marriage life.

Thomas had a problem of choosing women. He did not look within his church where he went. The mother of his child was a young woman who also had a Malawian father married to a Zulu woman who happened to be her mother. When Thomas met her, she was wearing a white blouse and black skirt church uniform; but she seldom attended church. Culture and booze, including partying, dominated her lifestyle. Both her parents were domestic workers for the same white family for about forty years. Her name was Mavis. She was one of those snobbish girls from the white suburbs, who thus had two sets of parents! Since Thomas could identify with both the Malawian and Zulu cultures, it made it easy for him to relate with her family. He was going through a lot of financial hardship and had little communication with Mavis who was also working a full time job. There was no sharing of plans and budgets since this was not marriage, and Mavis' culture believed a man must pay all the bills. Thomas and Mavis lived a life of suffering for about two years together. The electricity was switched off most of the time and they lived in darkness for months. Credits were heavy and unbearable for the two. After living a hard life together, Thomas separated with his girlfriend of four years. She stayed with her parents for a few months and went to look for her own place.

Mavis would not allow Thomas to see their child as she always maintained it was their culture since there was no bride price paid for her. Her friends would fight Thomas away when he tried to see his child. One day, he beat up a certain woman who shared a house with Mavis. As he was coming from the house—refused to see the child by Mavis—she took her shoe off and tried to assault Thomas. He then lost control and started beating her badly. These problems continued for some time. Mavis and her family used refusing to see the child as an opportunity for relationship squabbles with Thomas. Mavis and Thomas knew the child's health was poor and that they needed a closely monitor on her eating habits and lifestyle. Instead, she took the child to stay with her retired father. Her mother was still working and staying at her work place during the week. The child was diagnosed with nephritic syndrome and Thomas was not surprised by this. No one knows what caused this disease. It could have been an alcohol foetal syndrome since Mavis drank alcohol throughout her pregnancy. Thomas had no say on the child since he had not paid anything in terms of a bride's price. When he tried to negotiate payment of damages or a bride price the family always promised that they would come back to him but never did. It was not easy to deal with such people, as they seemed to be buying time as well.

When Mavis' father first met Thomas, he told him his boss would prefer to hold his identity document in case he ran away and left his daughter pregnant. The white man and his wife met Thomas in the house with the old man, who again raised the issue of surrendering the identity document. But the white man said that was between him and

Thomas to sort out. That white man was everything to this man. Somehow that saved Thomas from giving his identity document to Mavis' father. Thomas supported his child throughout and even after his financial storms. He was always a responsible father. Whenever there was a problem between him and Mavis, her father always refused to accept that his daughter was wrong. He always said that in his culture, he could not speak to him and that was all. When the child was sick and spent ten days in hospital Thomas only found out by hearsay, and went to hospital to see his only daughter that was his joy and pride. This was life as usual between Mavis and Thomas; she would not answer his calls for some reason. The child recovered and had to receive further treatment outside the hospital. The relationship of Mavis and Thomas was bonded by money even when they were no longer together. Mavis and her family manipulated Thomas.

When Thomas would phone her trying to find out how the child was doing, she would drop his phone calls and not talk to him. Her mother would put all sorts of strings around the child's body; she claimed that this was part of their culture rituals for ancestors to look after the child. Thomas would cut these strings off and great verbal insults came from his girlfriend's mother whenever she discovered the strings cut off. Thomas believed in God and culture was not his part, let alone inquiring about life's problems from fortune-tellers. But Mavis and her family were devotees of that entire world of darkness. Holding on to small parcels, said to save people from evil, was part of the lifestyle of this family. The woman that looked after the child passed away and her burial was at her homeland area. Thomas went for the funeral and started seeing Mavis again. He started taking the child to school and home again after about two years of not being close to his daughter. In a short time, Mavis and Thomas fell in love again. This time it looked like they were going to be successful in their relationship. Thomas was financially sound now. They proposed to marry and Thomas bought her an engagement ring and a wedding ring. Other shopping was to follow and the bride's price was to be next. But her culture did not allow her to put on the engagement ring without lobola (bride price) being paid. Therefore, she kept the rings with her until such time as she could wear them.

Mavis was still drinking alcohol and that made their relationship a constant battle. Mavis was not reliable. She cheated on Thomas with her drinking friend and a few other men reportedly appeared during their times of difficulty. Once, when Thomas was not sure of the relationship, he stayed away for about two weeks. The day he showed up, Mavis threw the rings at him. That night it was over, and according to Thomas she went on to enjoy the pleasures of sin with other men. This happened after Thomas could not pay the school fees for the child on time. She took the child to a different school and the she was at school for only two months. Meanwhile Thomas changed the province where he lived. Mavis continued to not answer his phone calls nor phone him in connection with their daughter. Neither of these two people were mature enough to adequately look after the child.

In the fourth month, Thomas called again to find out how his daughter was. This time she answered and told him that the child was in hospital. She had spent almost four months in hospital already. Mavis, her grandmother, father, mother and brothers—including relatives and friends—were coming to see her in hospital. Only Thomas did not come because he did not know the child was sick; no one had notified him. It was on a Sunday that Thomas received the news after he had called Mavis and it was a shock to him. Thomas was able to speak to his daughter for the first time after four months without a word with her. Then on Monday morning the child's sickness grew worse. The doctors took her into ICU. Thomas flew to Johannesburg on a Wednesday and found her condition worse. What else could he do except pray that his daughter be well. The girl fought for her life for a week and finally pulled through. It was a devastating situation but Thomas saw the grace of God prevail for his daughter.

He returned to his new province and after two weeks returned to see his daughter and she was much better. Her body looked weak and tired though. Thomas loved her very much. When she opened her eyes after hearing his voice, she jumped up and shouted, "My daddy!" But after that she vomited and he had to clean up the mess on the hospital bed. The two spoke, laughed, and even talked about her birthday bash which was about two months and half away. She was quiet after that and you could tell she was in pain. Her condition was up and down from one moment to the next according to the doctors. She never made it out of the hospital. In the fifth, Thomas received a call from the hospital staff that the little girl had passed on. It was very tough for him to handle the news. He had to make his way from his province to go and bury his daughter. Thomas was a peacemaker by nature. Instead of blaming anyone, he simply thanked his in-law family for everything and blessed them.

On the morning of the burial day, Thomas was surprised to find out that neither he nor his family were scheduled to speak at the funeral. This was a cultural influence, Mavis and her friends told him. He asked to speak a word about his daughter and was scheduled to do so at the end of the programme. Thomas had neither friends nor relatives by his daughter's funeral. He feared to bring people who might start arguments with the other family, and cause unnecessary squabbles. He spoke about a few things: how he loved his daughter and how he named her. He mentioned that their love for each other and friendship was unconditional. He said she was a friend and sister to him and that above all, he received her into his life as a gift from God. "What a gift from God!" he said, as he mentioned that it was hard to raise a child out of wedlock. His apologies went out to both his white and black in-laws who had gathered in the funeral tent. He always believed that if he had known earlier about his daughter being in hospital, he could have done more to save her life. His last consolation was that at least God had allowed him to see his daughter twice before she passed away.

On Sunday morning the family had a meeting with him in their midst. He was told that in Malawi they sit together and cut a bit of hair off as part of their culture. This is a ritual practised in many funerals, Mavis' father said. Therefore, they asked him to allow a bit of his hair to be cut off as well. One person went and cut pieces of hair from all of them. According to Mavis' family culture ritual, the slaughter of a goat followed three months down the line and Mavis would then stop wearing her mourning clothes. But the day of the goat slaughter day came and Thomas was not there because Mavis continued to drop Thomas' calls and they had cut off communication for some time. The goat died still tied up for Mavis ritual cleansing and the family had to buy another one. Thomas began to realize where he was tripping every time he wanted to move on in his life. He always chose women he did not understand or know well. This became his downfall in every relationship.

Will Thomas make it next time around? He seemed to have come close to understanding the lives of various peoples and their cultures. But faith in the true living God and people's cultural traditions do not always go hand in hand. Thomas was not a failure, but a man who loved wholeheartedly and never took disappointments too seriously. He and Mavis were a perfect match though she was weak in faith toward God. She needed to turn around and gain some character by stopping the silly affairs that made her seem loose. Thomas needed to commit and become a man this time around. The main question was, would the two find a common platform to bring them together again since the child that brought them together had passed on? In one way they were sick and tired of each other, yet they still had feelings for one another. Something in them kept the past good memories before them. I watched this with great interest as the future looked great for these young people. Both of them had great potentials in life.

Time is a healer, and only it can tell what happens next. Two years passed and nothing happened in the lives of Thomas and Mavis. There was a soft spot in their hearts for each other it seemed. The love they shared was special regardless of what friends and family said about them being "water and oil." Deep in the hearts of people, lies hidden truths regardless of what teaching people uphold or things they say with their mouths sometimes. Mavis had declared it impossible for her to come together again with Thomas. She wanted nothing to do with this man. And Thomas welcomed her decision as he was sick and tired of this modern woman. She worked in a modern office with a nice profession but seemed to lack the zest to live life in freedom. Mavis loved spending money consulting medium and spirits as her parents had taught her. She even bragged about having had strong Malawian charms (muti) used on her when she was young. She supported all her family's inclinations toward culture and traditions.

Culture is often confused truth about life's realities that dissolve into modern life changes and situations of time. Any fortune-teller who would talk to her about her life she would pay money to. She had two young fortune-teller friends who worked in offices, sniffed powder tobacco and practised traditional rituals along with modern perfumes. The two friends had their own problems yet could not fix them. They both could not get married and the other one was battling to get a child. Mavis would always pay them to sort her problems out by words but not in reality. This is the folly of culture-bound people, as often times they cannot think beyond the dogma of traditional boundaries. Culture has brought murkiness to many people's minds in developing world communities.

Having no money is not a healthy thing for a man. When Thomas looked back on his life, he could trace the hard times when he felt like no one loved him or understood who he is. He never felt free to tell any of the women in his life that he had no money. All his love affairs were ruined by lack of money to sustain living expenses. Some might think that all his women were gold-diggers. If it was only about money, why did both of the women he loved stay with him even in the lowest times of his life? When the lights were off for months neither of those women left Thomas. It was surprising to note that even when he found them, he did not have anything more than a regular job. His one mistake was that he had moved too slowly in acquiring a place of his own and building a house that was his. He bought nice cars and furniture but the townhouse rentals were too high at times for him. And he would not accept help from any of his women since he was a proud oak. Proud oaks do not communicate, which is a recipe for disaster in any relationship.

When Thomas separated with Jennifer, he lost a fortune in terms of household assets. He had to start afresh. His life with Mavis was great and the two had almost everything a rising star or "black diamond" would want to have and own. He bought Mavis a car and had a few other cars for his business. When I looked at his life, I thought now there was no turning back. Land in big cities is not cheap and neither are properties easy to buy with their high bonds every month. That was not just Thomas' problem but it was a snare to many men and women of their age group. Flats and town houses being repossessed and tenants being locked out is all too common during the hard times of city life. Jobs were scarce and businesses were not doing well, and logic dictated that people should have less credits to pay. Thomas never had the discipline to save money. He loved the high life and pleasure even though he was a Christian. If ever he were to be successful, he would have needed to overhaul his lifestyle and overcome the stumbling block that always let him and his peers down.

Thomas had purchased a nice piece of land for cash in a nice area and kept it undeveloped for some time. He is a man who had learnt a lot in his life and wanted very much to succeed. His aim was to completely overcome poverty in his life. What had brought him to his knees could not hold him back now, since he understood the enemy he faced. But if he had had a home paid off and owned by him, he could have relaxed even when he was making little money in his businesses. Thomas was an intelligent businessman who liked travelling as well as home life. Were his priorities wrong from the beginning? Not really. He believed he was going to make it, buy his family a house on bond, and maintain its payments for most of his life. That was the way most young people do and also use combined income if married and both work. But this way, it meant the financial institutions dictated his lifestyle. It took away his freedom to work and live the way he wanted, as it forced him to work full time in order to guarantee the bond payment. Thomas tended to blame apartheid and not do anything to break its yoke, as many young people do today. This way it becomes an excuse for their failures.

But later on Thomas got a breakthrough and had his wishes and dreams come true in his life. He broke ground on his property, digging foundations to build a house. A mansion came out on that property, and it was all cash-built. For the first time in his life, he felt more than just being creditworthy but also a sense of self-worth dawned in him. He was very proud of himself. He had the house filled with nice start-up furniture and a DSTV satellite on top of his roof. He bought two big dogs and built a swimming pool, which was finished later. In his garage he parked his small French car that was about eight years old and was paid for cash. He loved motorbikes and always had one car and one motorbike. The telephone landline installed by his house made it easy for him to work from home when he wished. Thomas started prospering in all areas of his life and became a respected community leader who taught others how to beat poverty.

However, it seemed possible for him to get into a relationship and nurture it to succeed. Men that are self-reliant most times attract good women with character. This time around there is a big surprise that many are waiting to see. Poverty and lack is a number one factor in family breakdown and divorce today. This is interesting to note among many individuals. During the recession, the credit crunch caused many people to go into hiding, letting affairs and relationships fall apart. Are love relationships genuine or just a matter of pleasing the partner with delicacies only? "No supplies, no love" could be the game. Hence, with a chocolate everyday can you save your love? The obligation of the marriage relationship is a love that goes with food and groceries. Maybe that is why many people try it by living together without commitment in case it is not what they want. Marching out of the relationship is then easy since there are no strings attached. Some have done this for a lifetime and die lacking understanding of what love is in their solitary world. Love has a few main fundamental pillars that you need to get right, and if you do you can enjoy a relationship with anyone.

Love is not fear of failure but security in failure. Being secure in love means, you can see the beginning and the end of your lives crystal clear in a peaceful prosperous world, regardless of storms and winds of life being around. You do not need to stress about where to live, what to eat and how you will meet future needs. Love that does not have this security leads to a vicious circle of pain, insecurity, and panic every time you get in a wrong relationship. Insecurity, mistrust and poverty cause people not to relax in life but to toil in fear of failure, poverty and rejection. It is necessary to overcome one's fears and anxieties. Your name needs to come out of the credit bureaus and stay away from credits forever if you can. You may need to even leave your city or home in order to start afresh and position yourself to succeed. Even if you could not enjoy the first few years of your life it does not mean that you are bound to die sad and broke. Banks and companies to make money for themselves and nothing for you use the credit system. Your planning now is your future walk to freedom.

Thomas and Mavis met again after more than two years had passed. They had to plan about their late child's tombstone. Their hearts were healing and fighting had ceased between them since they had not spoken for so long nor seen each other. All they wanted to talk about was getting unfinished business finished. They met in the city of gold, Johannesburg, by a restaurant. After a long chat, the two exchanged addresses and agreed to meet again soon to shop for a tombstone.

Mavis had now allowed Thomas to pick her up by her place. A week had passed and Mavis phoned Thomas about a company she had found on the internet. Thomas picked her up and they were at ease with each other now. Mavis was curious to find out where Thomas lived because even when she had the address, she did not know the place. The company they went to had many tombstones to choose from in both shape and style. It was not easy to choose one but, at last, they did. Thomas paid the full price and refused to accept Mavis' contribution because during the funeral, Thomas had been broke and so Mavis had taken care of the funeral with her parents.

After the delivery arrangements, they left the tombstone company and went to a restaurant. While they were eating, Mavis asked Thomas about exactly where he lived. Thomas tried to explain and she still could not figure out the place. (It was a hideout for the rich.) In the end, Thomas offered to show her his home and then take her back to her place and she accepted. He told her he had built the house by the same plan he had shown her years before when they were together. It was his dream house! She further asked which bank had financed the home and he told her cash built it all. He now hated credits and wanted to rebuild his life for a future he wanted to live. When they arrived at the house, Mavis could not believe her eyes. It was the same house they had planned to build together one day. The same woman who had worked for them in their flat was working for him here. The whole environment portrayed his style and taste. Mavis asked him how he did all this. He replied, "I followed my heartfelt dreams and it is how I live my life now. My failures were never my stopping point but my anchors of learning to correct my wrongs and move forward successfully."

Mavis stayed for a while and chatted to the woman who had once worked for them and who had also kept their deceased child. Thomas took a joy ride on his motorbike for about an hour. When he came back, it was time for dinner dishing. Mavis had enjoyed her favourite channels on TV together with the housekeeper. It looked like the world was a different place now after a long time. Who could tell what was happening in Thomas or Mavis' life? Even what was to follow in their lives was unpredictable. After dinner, Mavis was taken back home by Thomas and Rose (who worked in the house). The three saw life differently that day. A family spirit gripped them and they all felt the little one missing from their midst. Such joy could not be explained by words. Smiles, hugs of love and forgiveness among them spoke volumes. It did not matter anymore what the past was or how it looked. All were happy for each other to have made it. Jealousy was now a thing of the past, even with Mavis.

That evening, Thomas was given photos of their deceased little angel by Mavis. It was to keep as a remembrance of her. Many things were talked about until Thomas and Rose had to leave. The three kept the communication lines open between themselves. The day of placing the tombstone was drawing near and many people were amazed at how things now were between Thomas and Mavis, when compared to their past. It became the news of the town among their friends and those who knew them. Some friends of Mavis who had formerly put their nose into their relationship were denied the chance now. Mavis had asked everyone and even her parents to stay away from her personal affairs and stop advising her so much as if she had no brain. She had discovered that Thomas was not as bad as she thought he was. She stopped drinking and was now attending a Pentecostal church. She had come to understand the difference between being just a lover of church and being a child of God. She gave up all her old connections and even the fortune-teller friends of hers. She seemed to have changed very much and had a new calmness and way of speaking. Could not drinking and having faith in God finally save her? These two changes could counteract the weaknesses in her past life. Was Thomas interested in watching this great life of repentance? Perhaps, but only if he had feelings for her again, would he be watching her closely.

Mavis seemed eager to come closer to Thomas and have another chance to prove him wrong. Thomas was not sure whether to trust Mavis again even though he had feelings for her. What could possibly override all the hurts of their past life together? A fresh start was only possible if they allowed true forgiveness to take place in their lives. Maybe they would have to attend Christian counselling by their churches, and together at one stage, in order to get back together. Things were different now; the two could talk and trust each other better than before. The many problems that stood in their way seemed to be gone now. Could the two forget the past and move together into the future that easily? For now, it seems they had only fallen in love with each other's company. The possibility of a love connection was evident and we could not rule out them loving each other again. The parents of Mavis had also softened towards Thomas. All fighting and anger seemed to be a thing of the past. The two had started to experience a fresh breeze of peace in their lives without outside influence or pressure.

Thomas and Mavis started to know what true friends are and what they are for in life. Many of their former friends used to eat away at their relationship, and were jealous towards them, competing with them. It reminds me of the time my friend from the USA was telling me about a hurtful incident. He said, "Frank, in this world there is no true friend." If friends cannot succeed, they want you not to succeed. If they have made it thus far, they want you only to go that far and not more than them. We often have these types of friends in this world. Get out of the cliques and clubs that try to make your world small!

Many friends are like excess baggage we do not need. Entering our lives, they design our worlds too small and leave us with false pictures of who we are. These types of friends never want you to be yourself. Many of the best things in life come out of us only if we are ourselves. God created life with this element of uniqueness. People's gifts, abilities and talents are never exactly alike. You can drink the same brand of beer, smoke the same cigars, play the same sport, and go to the same church but the flair of individuality will still show up. Only when we break free from bad company can we begin to live again. Break out of the mould and live your life as God gave it to you! Stop trying to attain the same results as them for you are not them! Mavis' healing came when she stopped trying to be everyone's friend or pleaser. It is true that she might lose many things she once had but her life would never be the same again. For once, she had joy for who she was, and this would certainly lead her to fulfilment in life. Fulfilled people are happy people.

The tombstone delivery took place and bringing this chapter to a proper close was the most important thing. All the people who came there saw peace between Thomas and Mavis for the first time in a long while. Most of their friends wanted to know whether they were back together again. The two just said they had decided to make peace and forgive each other as they realized they were not in worse problems than other people were. They had a great memorial celebration of the life of their deceased daughter, who had such a short visit on earth. Both parents spoke powerful words of life among their guests and the guests realized that people can change and mature with time. It seemed that both of them had grown up now and also that they had matured in the Lord. It is a grave mistake to write people off and expect no change in their lives. We all make mistakes and deserve a second chance in life.

The greatest thing was to see how these parents of their late daughter overcame their anger towards each other and also towards families and friends who divided them by taking sides. The tombstone ceremony was really about the rebirth of Mavis and Thomas. Rose sat with tears coming down her cheeks. She told how the two had gone through thick and thin together and that for her it was a miracle to see them in such a spirit of peace and joy. At times it looked like all hell would break loose and destroy all their precious moments, she added. Rose was there when the lights were switched off and when they were locked out of a flat and their belongings thrown out by a ruthless property owner. She could identify with the pain the two had gone through. All was in the past yet memories never just vanish from people's minds. All of us have been hurt at one time or another. It is what we do with our anger more than who angered us that matters. Many people are prisoners of anger and only when they forgive does the prisoner go free. They then realize that the prisoner was the one who could not forgive.

Time moved quickly and Thomas and Mavis were moving towards each other every day it seemed. Soon, the two had come together and fallen in love again. These lovers certainly seemed to have been given a second chance and this time they did not fail. The two ended up marrying and having a lovely life together. Rose continued to work for them and things went from better to best, as she reckons. Thomas and Mavis became parents again after a year and half. It was identical lovely twin boys; they became their pride and joy. After two years, again, Mavis became pregnant and she had a girl this time. It was now a family of identical twins and one cute baby girl. Thomas and Mavis began successful business ventures that are continually booming even though the country took a nosedive into the recession. Their relationship has gone from strength to strength. They have become one flesh and have closed every door that poverty and strife came through. The couple has a family trust—a non-profit organization where they help married couples and homeless parents succeed in life. "Once a victim, you become a volunteer," this saying is true with them. Greetings of great smiles of love for people and life will touch and gladden any soul that comes across this couple.

Uncleanliness makes all of us uncomfortable. If someone has not taken a bath for days, he or she will smell and not even want to mix with other people. In such a state, one might lack confidence or self-worth. Every marriage and relationship will be tested in this life. Couples must be very careful of matchmakers who like what they see it even if it is not good for the person in that relationship. Being financially sound will help your relationship but is not the answer for many of relationship's storms. Loving life enough to die for what you believe in, and loving your partner the same can save a marriage or relationship. Two things that ruin a relationship quickly are infidelity and lack of communication, which is equal to lies and arrogance. With sexual health risks escalating every day, people cannot afford changing partners like dogs.

Human beings have been always unique in their choices and tastes. Work through your relationship and you will succeed in getting what you want. Help your partner to build a life you both want. Thomas and Mavis have been through it all but one truth they both accepted: through all the heartbreak, they stopped blaming each other. They fought over everything and still, they did not put a hand on each other. It shows their deep-seated respect for each other. They respected each other's private lives even though Mavis put Thomas' dirty laundry on the line a few times for her friends to see. She was not Thomas, and every time she was stressing or hurting, she would share things with people who in turn used that against her and Thomas. I still believe she did not have any good friends, but neither did she know any better in life.

Rather marry a man or woman with dark pages in their life than someone who pretends to be a saint when all they display is foul play. You can find two kinds of people among men and women. Among men, there are those who love a lavish lifestyle with a few women who finance it for them. On the other side, women who love men with fat wallets, nice cars, and houses to let them be "freeloaders in life." Love based on these factors, that have made people to be showpieces because of their beauty, gadgets and possessions, cannot last. It is all about, what is in it for me? This sabotages relationships, when many do not get what they want they turn to someone else. Realise that most people earn a living through running businesses—or working full time jobs. This generation is a confused one; it spends its money trying to please men or women.

Many credits owed on bankcards and other cards by people today are debts from jewellery and other material stuffs that went to those who claimed to love them. That is why they drop each other so quickly and, if jilted, they stress and worry because it is as much an investment collapse as a relationship ending. People no longer keep commitments but want an easy escape in everything. Holding down five girl friends because you have enough money to do it is foolish and it is the same folly when women do this with men. Indeed, if all people correctly used their finances for themselves and for their families only we would easily solve the credit crunch. There would be no peer pressure on young people to go on shopping sprees trying to look great for friends and others.

You cannot love a stranger that easily unless you are loose and without character. There is no such thing as love at first sight. You can meet someone and feel drawn to him or her. That simply means you are attracted to the person, but you do not love them yet. If you think you love them right then, it is probably lust rather than love. You can only love someone after you have known him or her better. In other words if you love someone at first sight and tomorrow you meet them by the robot selling their body, you will have to love them still. If not, then it was not real love at first sight. You will still have to date the person to make sure what you felt is true about them not how genuine it felt. It could be a true love feeling but is it right to give it to that person?

People who lie about their personal status do not want to accept reality. When you do not have money, you cannot pay rent for the apartment or flat that you might be living in. If you continue to live in it, you will have to go out in arrears, not having paid. Now if you live at your parents' home or with a relative, you do not have to lie about it or even the fact of losing your job and being unemployed. If someone looks down on you because you do not have a job, such a person knows nothing about life. Life treats men and women the same. If you can learn to overcome pride, you will be on your way to many benefits in life. That is a truth you need to know, and once you know it, it sets you free. Remember, it is the "knowing" of the truth that sets you free, not just the truth. The truth has been there all the time but many people are still not free because they do not know it. Do you accept that you are a mere human being and not something puffed up? Certainly, you are not a god. If you agree with me on this, we can move forward systematically now.

If you are a human being, you have human limitations. You will fail in some things in life. You may lose your job but that doesn't mean you have lost your life. You may be homeless at times. If you do not keep your act together and have character, you might even get a prison sentence. You could become poor even though working your budget well, as this could be the result of poor financial planning. You could contract HIV and AIDS if you sleep with different sexual partners who practise unprotected sex. You may have nothing to eat at times. Extreme winters may come and find you without a jersey or enough blankets if you do not earn money to buy these things. You can become divorced when you had almost everything and thought you had arrived. Unpredictable weather can come and destroy your home if you do not have insurance. Everything is in the state of your mind: no human being is immune to life's storms, but also it is possible to attain everything in this life. The police officers and women charged of crimes and jailed, that is not the end. Your colleagues might have arrested you but realise you are just a human being. The powers of living fully blessed continually come back and set us on board. There are always opportunities to live up to our maximum potential in life. Some people may serve a prison sentence or pay a fine. Rich or poor, there is always something to keep us down on our knees before our Creator. You might get sick and lose your job or home. You can become pregnant out of wedlock, but that does not make you an evil person. Someone else is about to blow it too and become a culprit, so don't be too hard at yourself. Accept reality.

If you have lost your job, concentrate on getting another and do not spend precious time devising ways to lie about it. In addition, if you cannot find a job, think of ways to work for yourself. Statistics show that seventy percent of curriculum vitae applications in our country are not true but lies. The reason is that people are putting their energy into what is bad rather than good. Some people even lie about their own children. They lie and say they have no child in order to get a man who says he does not want a woman with a child. Your mistake, woman, is that you have become a condition-suited person instead of having your own standards met. That man could be right concerning what he wants. Maybe he is divorced and paying maintenance for a number of children. So it would be a great inconvenience for him to feed an extra mouth. That was simply being honest with you. But you do not ask him why he wants a woman without a child but make your own assumption.

Lift your standards for the man you want and say "Bye" to him and interview the next one on the queue! There is a candidate for all of us, as long as we live in honesty and truth. You cannot kill your child for it is God's product. Just be your real self at all times. Truth is the power to get right and organized for the best things in life. Stop trying to fit into everyone else's mould. Break out of that mould, and be the person you want to be. People will use money and other things to keep you in miry pits if you are not careful. You are not a doormat but someone special who has visited the earth for a while. You must do something worthwhile with your life before you leave. Leave a lasting legacy of integrity for your generations to come. Let people know you were here on earth' leaving behind great works of truth in your life museum for them to view, in addition to your tombstone!

Embrace love and truth and they will save you from all other troubles. Learn to make a living on your own and do not rely on other people to meet your financial obligations. Anyone who assumes this role, apart from your parents is apt to abuse or enslave you. Your financial independence is a key that ushers you into freedom of life, though money is not everything. People who love to lie about themselves are usually those who refuse to do anything for themselves. Today you meet many university dropouts who sell their bodies on the streets during the night in our big cities. Some of them speak polished English and can sell themselves with confidence to any man. The folly of African men today is to think that when you speak good English you are educated and must be working a high-class job. That is why women can prey on men so easily sometimes. Male tertiary graduate dropouts also know what modern women want. They just portray the image and proceed to hook up with women of their dreams. But these relationships do not last very long, and sometimes cause a lot of harm through the transmission of sexually transmitted diseases.

These people's lifestyle is not stable and they do this to a number of people as the aim is not real love, but usually money and material things. They do not care whether the other person is married or not. As long as you can give them what they want, you are a suitable candidate for the job. It is truth in a love relationship that makes people commit themselves to each other not lies. When people are in a relationship and also have other love affairs, it means they cannot trust what they have and are not seeking truth and reality in their life. It is something both partners need to address and deal with. All insecurities must be rooted out of a relationship, otherwise it is good for nothing. It is not good to stay in a relationship too long without the right commitment being put in place, which should lead to marriage. Many people move away from living with one woman or man and go and get married to another person. It shows that something is wrong with the one marrying and the one left behind. You would be smarter to stay single until the right dove comes along rather than playing the harlot with men. And men must remove the polygamous spirit from their minds in order to solve the scourge of infidelity and sexually transmitted diseases. One partner for each person and we will bring HIV and AIDS to a halt.

How can we overcome the temptation of extra-marital affairs and sexual promiscuity that are engulfing our generation today? Temptation is a spiritual problem that we overcome by the spiritual armour of honesty. Your heart and spirit need the power to say "no" to wrong and "yes" to right. No man can do this in his natural strength. Your life is spiritual since you are a spiritual being in a body. The answer to defeating temptation is to be a new-thinking person. Let the Creator come in you and live His life within you. All evil lusts will fly out the window if you are serious about the change that God instils in every soul who calls Him Father. I know of nothing else that can change a person, set him free and make him right. Those who have accepted life from God can defeat temptation if they abide by God's law of life. Let me talk about the right way of dating. When you see someone, and would like them to be part of your life it is customary to ask them for a date.

Asking for a date means, "I want to know you better because I like you, but I am not sure whether you are the right one to walk life's journey with me." After you know their hobbies, likes and dislikes, you can then tell them about your feelings towards them. This stage will continue until you talk about committing in a love relationship, and that eventually leads to the courtship stage. By now you know exactly where the other person wants to land in life. You understand exactly where God is taking them and you only enter their life to make it easier for them to get where they are going. You do not enter into the relationship to take but to give. You should not seek a woman because she drives a nice car. The same goes for women who see men as the source of meeting their needs. Be a blessing in someone's life. Three institutions God initiated for man to keep are family, government and church. If we want to succeed in any of these institutions, we must involve Him and He will show us how to manage them. That is why I emphasize that relationships are built on truth, not lies, because God is truth.

I will never forget some teaching I heard from one lecturer at college. He was teaching about sexuality in the biblical context. He said, before you can date someone, you have to feel a strong feeling that will rock your nerves and turn you on for that person. This, he said, is a sign to tell you that the person is for you. Then you can tell the person that you have feelings for them. To me, that is a simple case of lust. He went on to say that if you live long enough on this earth, there will be forty women who will come in the same manner your wife came. They will rock your nerves and turn you on and if you do not stand the temptation, you will divorce or take on extra marital affairs. I do not agree with this, and do not think God brings confusion.

One must realize that temptation brings a counterfeit of reality. If you are married to a beautiful blonde woman with a gorgeous figure, you will usually be attracted to those kinds of women. Sometimes it could be someone with your spouse's personality who attracts you. If you are married to a medium or stout woman the same rule applies. This applies to women, also. Many women are attracted to men who look like their first boyfriends or men they married. I say "first boyfriend" for women because he seems like the better choice, as many times married men leave their bodies unattended. Men and women can either choose to ignore thoughts of lust or give in and fulfil the act of infidelity. The devil doesn't tempt you with something new or something you do not know. Otherwise, you would be innocent and not look at or give heed to it. The devil takes the original and makes a counterfeit of it. A counterfeit of your partner is not your partner. So get out from that chain of the fool who wanders all over without knowledge of relationship truth.

One nation, one continent, one world, one goal

The long awaited day came. Everyone on the African soil seemed restless, and even more so the players from the nations of the world. The greatest tournament in the world was on African soil for the first time. The opening was a great moment of celebration even though the guest of honour the then president of USA Barak Obama was not there. An oil spill at home kept the president busy. If he had come, the whole world would have heard a word from a man who has commanded respect for his stand in the political world. It was the hosting country against Mexico in the FIFA World Cup opening. Spectators from all over the globe had taken their seats in the best stadium in the land. More people listened on radios and some glued their eyes on TV screens at home or at other places of comfort, including huge screens which were set up all over the country for people to watch. The match finished with a draw, with each side's fans warmly applauding their team's performance.

The joy of the South African nation was that all the world cup stadiums and venues were completed within the agreed period, even though discrepancies on financial expenditures and transparency marred the work continually during construction. In 2010, studies showed that South Africa had the biggest poverty gap in the world. A shocking 69% of the population relied on grants, 29% employed with the majority paid less than R3500, 00 a month. Projected statistics suggest that 60% of students at school now will not find jobs in their field of study in their lifetime if unemployment and poor economic growth continue. Technology has taken many jobs away from people. Eight hours a week guaranteed for each person might be a way to curve the problem of unemployment. In the USA, the equivalent of R3500, 00 would be a salary bracket of starvation. Such a pathetic salary, paid to the construction workforce, miners and other job sectors like farming will never transform the economy.

During the 2010 World Cup period, new developments continually surprised everyone within our borders and outside. The Minister of Home Affairs instructed all ports of entry into the Republic of South Africa, including airlines to no longer accept six-month temporary travelling documents. This restriction was attributed to FIFA security fears although they denied it. The move came as a blow to many small business traders and temporary immigrant workers who were severely affected. The complete moral drive after the World Cup will forever live in the memory about how the organized work of the African state looked.

 Many flags flew in the air, waved by many people; everything seemed to say: "It is Africa's time!" Could the people of Africa now be one, and rebuild their continent with pride? Had the tournament instilled a different mind and spirit among these nations? The apartheid mentality still grips the continent especially among the large percentage of illiterates. Many were not even able to understand the world cup processes, let alone benefiting from its presence on their own soil. The hope of a new dawn shone as FIFA launched its One Goal campaign. Racism, tribalism and xenophobia had no place during the events of the tournament. Some traditions and abusive customs of tribes remained unshaken though there was much opportunity for discussion here. The greatest challenge will be to keep up the standard of good work and implement the One Goal dream on the continent and in the world.

Some international visitors hired bodyguards and paid as much as R2000-R4000 a day. These were people who perceived South Africa to be a high-risk country, with a reported average of 50 Killings per day (2009). Newer (2011) statistics suggested a drop in these numbers to 43 murders a day. But these visitors chose to be safe rather than sorry. Recent 2012 statistics of 20 children being murdered every week in the country was shocking news. A few other sad incidents took place but the country discovered its potential to respond well to such problems. The corruption trial of the former police commissioner was finalized during this period. The cop boss was found guilty of a few charges and received a jail sentence of fifteen years that he appealed against and lost. He entered prison with life-threatening diseases that kept him in prison hospitals most of the time.

The world had waited to see the South African court in action as it judged such a high-ranking official. A new hope and light were shed upon the country's justice system. Nonetheless, the case dragged on for whatever reasons. But at last, the South African judge assured the nation and the world of a new commitment to justice without fear nor favour as he pronounced his verdict against the commissioner. The case was unique in its aim to uproot corruption and crime from among even top government officials. This judgment has sent a strong warning to all who participate in corrupt deals within the civil service family including its top ranks.

Another unforgettable and disturbing case was in the spotlight during the same period. This case never stopped to surprise the country and the world. It is how DR. Death – Dr. Wouter Basson – continued to practise medicine even though the acts of his past should have condemned him. Finally, after many years, the Health professionals' council of South Africa (HPCSA) has pressed to prosecute the doctor of misconduct and unethical conduct pertaining to human rights. He was still practising as a cardiologist in Cape Town. The HPCSA probe saw Dr. Wouter Basson struck from the medical roll after he was found guilty. Will the outcome of this case bring justice to all those who were affected by this doctor and his allies?

Advanced Passenger Processing (APP) managed to prevent Bara Bravas hooligans from entering into South Africa including many others from around the world who had silly intentions. Cargo containing fake Bafana Bafana jerseys were constantly being confiscated at ports of entry by police and boarder control officials as culprits tried to make money during the World Cup. The nation was buying its team's jersey. Other African states lacked exposure and outlet points seemed very limited for their jerseys. The question for many locals was whether the national team was going to bring the trophy home. Overseas teams were enthusiastic and many of their supporters enjoyed the stay and the tournament in South Africa. A spirit of unity seemed to reign among Africans dating back to 2004 when South Africa had won the bid to host the World Cup. The thought that echoed in almost every child of the soil was, "This is Africa's time!" Shakkira, the Colombian-born USA-based singer livened things up with the song "Waka Waka" on the opening day celebration. Many other singers also saluted the country and continent for being able to have the tournament done well.

Jerome Demon from Athlone was the only South African referee who had a chance to officiate at the World Cup. He grew up in a harsh Cape flats environment. He dared to break out of the mould of violence and crime and travel a different path. It was not easy to qualify as an official said. He had already officiated in three African Cup of Nations tournaments. Indeed the officiating skills of African referees have been improving continually, despite criticism.

Since the soccer World Cup is a FIFA tournament, people should know more about it than just its president and game. FIFA stands for Football International Federation Association. Here is the history of this huge organisation called FIFA, which spins billions of dollars through this prestigious tournament. In 1930, 13 teams originally participated in Uruguay. FIFA was founded in Paris, France and is now based in Switzerland. It is tasked with organizing global tournaments of football for all different age groups, as well as constantly assessing the rules of the game. The (IFAB) International Football Association Board runs FIFA and FIFA has a large representation with them. IFAB is made up of the so-called founding associations of international football, i.e. England's Football Association, The Scottish Football Association of Wales (SFA).The Football Association of Wales (FAW) and Northern Ireland's Irish Football Association (IFA), as well as FIFA.

FIFA is also responsible for ensuring that the national associations toe the line and remain independent of government or other influences. FIFA is said to have netted R26 billion rands from the World Cup. The money would have come from sponsorships, ticket sales and travel packages. There is also (UEFA), the Union of European Football Association. FIFA's voting processes are said to have never been fair and the corruption will probably worsen as time goes on. The problem is that certain parties through their own interests have not considered the healthy will of the organization. FIFA always maintains that the tournament is theirs and that the nations that host it are just privileged. Then FIFA president Sepp Blatter spoke the same words about South Africa.

United Nations leaders like Secretary Ban Ki-moon and others, including the President of South Africa, addressed leaders at the Constitutional Hill in Johannesburg. Africa must achieve its millennium goals with every child being able to go to school being at the top of the agenda. Poverty reduction programmes, better shelter, and other essential services, also topped the agenda. This One Goal summit took place and was welcomed by the world, especially in Africa where education is so urgently needed. On the opening of the World Cup, during the bash night a video clip was shown on television of two girls. It showed two girls of the same age growing up in different environments. One grew up in poverty and picked food by rubbish bins and dump areas. She was trying to make ends meet all during her childhood. She didn't go to school and experienced the vicious circle of failure and pain in the miserable life of poverty. Meanwhile the other one went from one blessing to another. She went to school and became very secure in life as a professional nurse. Poverty is an obstacle that forces innocent masses to live a life of pain, living with hunger and malnutrition.

Many people and visitors to the country noted some unforgettable dates that June. The dates 10 and 11 saw the opening game of the host country against Mexico, which ended up with a draw. Excitement was high among South Africans as they pinned their hopes on their national team in the opening match. On national youth day however, they were met with disappointment as, on the 16th of June, the squad played poorly against Uruguay, losing three goals to nil.

The Youth day was characterized by loud complaints of inequality from both the white and black youth. The white youth said they felt treated as second-class citizens. The black youth argued that the white youth still benefitted from apartheid-era privileges and were in good shape economically. Whites control the economy in the country. As long as poverty is synonymous with being black, freedom will be meaningless to the black youth. Debates about poverty were heated during the day and later everyone settled down to watch the game. To alleviate the problem of inequality in South Africa, the country has been more willing to change its land and mining laws and to offer young job seekers subsidies. The masses seem to be running out of patience with the old apartheid laws that rule them even though their architects are long gone.

Moreover, the World Cup tournament united our nation behind the national team. The national team boys trotted out on the ground as the kick off whistle blew. But the spirit and performance of the squad was not convincing when it played against Uruguay. Some players had to leave the field on red cards because of the unruly behaviour they displayed. Surely, no team would attempt to face a giant like Uruguay in an indeterminate state or with a few men down. The dread of defeat gripped the whole nation who could only hope the team would collect more points as they moved through the stage matches. France was weak this time around, defeated by South Africa 2-1. But still it could not help much as the points were too few the team to progress beyond this stage. After the 2-1 win for the local squad, France went packing and South Africa exited the tournament dismally as well.

Many African teams went out of the tournament early, including overseas giants like Italy—who were defending champions—France, England, Mexico, Serbia, Korea Republic and Greece. It impressed the continent's people to see one African country progress to the quarterfinals as its players displayed a great talent for football. This was the Black Stars, the Ghana team. Ghana gave it their all and seemed hungrier than ever. They went as far as the quarterfinals where Uruguay stopped them after a hard evening of sweat in extra time. Africa's support and jubilation for the Ghana team was seen everywhere, as it was their only team left in the tournament. During the last 30 seconds of added time Ghana was impressive, desperately looking for a goal and they surprised Uruguay by securing a penalty kick. The Uruguay player prevented a goal by punching it out of the net. This was right at thirty seconds to go during extra time. Ghana and the African continent were celebrating and the excitement was felt all over the stadium and in the country where people were watching the match. The hopes of what others call the Dark Continent were alive as people pinned their hopes on one country and one man, who took on the penalty kick. Surely, Africa would make an indelible mark in history if that penalty added to a goal.

The most trusted and experienced player was to take the penalty kick. The spectators by the stadium and the media believed that this was the time for Ghana to bring the goods home. The man who took that penalty kick on behalf of Ghana missed. This dashed many people's hopes that Ghana would win this game, as the Uruguay side was not an easy team to defeat. The two teams now had to go for penalty kicks and whoever lost here would be out. This was a tough competition and Uruguay took the lead as the Black Stars fell behind, struggling to score penalty goals. This was finally the last team of Africa to exit the tournament and Uruguay and its supporters went into celebration mode as they overcame Ghana. It brought sorrow and tears to Ghana and its fellow African countries to witness such a sensational game filled with so many surprises. Everyone consoled themselves with the thought that, when the World Cup came around again in four years, they would do better. The country where the tournament was to take place, Brazil, has won the title more times than any other nation.

Germany played very well in most of their games as the players displayed high quality soccer against their opponents. The disappointing loss of Germany to Spain in the semi-finals, however, showed a lack of quality and enthusiasm and little impact on the field. That gave Spain an upper hand as they beat the Germans 1-0 and booked their place for the World Cup final. The country had never won the world cup before. On the other hand, Netherlands took on Uruguay, who bowed down to them with a painful defeat. The competition was getting very tough now. Germany and Uruguay had to contest for third place on 10 July 2010. The German team came back with their usual skill and talent, thrashing Uruguay. All had gone as predicted by most soccer commentators.

The day of the final game, awaited with great anticipation and excitement, finally came. Thoughts and words of Africa's success in hosting the FIFA World Cup never left many hearts and mouths. The final game was to drive it home. This challenged the reputation of the people of Africa and their way of doing things. Some had not believed Africa could successfully host a big event like World Cup. Yet many African kids and people never got a glimpse of what was happening on their own soil. Poverty and illiteracy did not allow them an opportunity. Yet port, if employed without corruption, can be a powerful force to curb lack of discipline, racism, illiteracy, and poverty.

The game between Spain and the Netherlands was the final game of the FIFA World Cup, 2010. The United Nations and FIFA pioneered the wishes of the world nations and many government organisations at large were talking hope. The day before the final game was played, people were filled with hope for the continent and for the world as One Goal was officially launched here and welcomed by almost all nations. The One Goal summit, which convened before the last day of the Cup; topped the agenda. Spain and Netherlands were at loggerheads—the day to bring home the goods had come for either side! Their supporters did not want to take "no" for an answer concerning who would win the world's top football match.

This was one of the more unforgettable world cups. FIFA applauded it and made quite a substantial amount of money on it. South Africa received nine out of ten success ratings by FIFA. Its critics have raised concerns about the hidden agendas of the board and are concerned about the legitimacy of FIFA's practices. Instability in leadership has been an issue with many of its members since its inception. The two final teams went out on the football pitch with great fighting spirit that made the spectators and their nations proud. For the entire ninety minutes, both teams were goalless which forced the game into extra time. Thirty minutes added time saw Spain scoring within the last five minutes until the final whistle of added time. It was as if the whole stadium exploded with jubilation as supporters got what they wanted. And indeed, after five more minutes, Spain was crowned and declared the 2010 FIFA World Cup champion. Spain has dominated the major football tournaments since their uplifting of the cup. The country broke history by taking the EURO cup twice soon after winning the World Cup. The next world cups might see them leading the world again, as their consistently high football standards show an exciting momentum.

Can South Africa live up to its promises of a non-racial society with no xenophobic attacks against their fellow African nationals? If the country holds on the FIFA ratings well, surely it will be leading by example. The country witnessed new xenophobic attacks on foreigners by locals, which broke out soon after the World Cup. Criminals took advantage and began threatening black foreign business people, especially those in ghettos and townships. Fortunately, business looting had to stop because of the police's early interventions in calming the situation. Nevertheless, foreign black businesses in the Eastern Cape were highly affected and many foreigners were packing and leaving for their countries of origin. Most of these people were Zimbabwean nationals who were asylum seekers. Farmers claimed that they worked harder than locals whom they accused of being lazy. The question is, "Were these farmers not former Zimbabwean employers who attracted Zimbabweans because of their desperation and need for survival or they were genuine employers?" We all hope that farm production will not fall short in the coming years. The future of the country's reconciliation with other ethnic groups and nations is difficult for many African foreign nationals to understand. The social ills found among the societies of the country include a strenuous attitude towards African states' goals and the way forward to development. Nonetheless, the future of South Africa depends on working together with the continent, especially the southern countries block. Afro-phobia attacks must stop, and we hope to see peace reigning among locals and foreigners. The government must work hard to end these ruthless attacks. The preying on of Black African foreign business owners every time protests ensue is brainwashing many black communities.

The continent of Africa will never understand the times it is in if it does not sort out its problems with respect and dignity. Economically and developmentally, the continent needs a face-lift. South Africa, the economic engine of the continent, is marred by many problems, which are housing, illiteracy, joblessness, corruption and land distribution for the poor. Many citizens questioned the mining rights bill, especially the black youth, who wanted the government to nationalise the mines. The squabbles over mines with foreign investors are endless, as the industry seems to stand on one leg. The biggest ore mine in the Northern Cape came into the spotlight for maladministration and dodgy ownership shareholding. Civil servants strikes and the masses who had run out of patience with the government regarding poor wages and poor service delivery (which seems to be a tradition of third world countries) nearly spoiled the 2010 World Cup season. The nation was plunged into panic strikes and demonstrations escalated to a new level. South Africa, as one of the economic engines of the continent, has always had a strong influence and impact on the continent.

More than a year after the world cup, will South Africa avert the worst strikes ever to test its young democracy? The xenophobia of the illiterate masses, who are told by black hooligans that foreigners take their jobs, is also a big threat. The core leadership of the government has been tried and tested; its wisdom in executing good service delivery is crucial. Black foreigners suffered the injustices of xenophobia, including malicious damage to their property, and loss of life. They became targets of elite crime syndicates that preyed strictly on foreign nationals. Zimbabweans seemed to have been the most affected people, but lately that has changed as most Zimbabweans work rather than own businesses. Thousands of foreigners left the country before the final game of the world cup. Heartless local groups had warned them of xenophobic attacks after the world cup. Many who survived the first scourge of xenophobic attacks in 2008, now turned to leave the beloved land of promise and dreams. Even the strong police and government pledge to fight the problem could not stop foreigners from fleeing for their lives and going back to their countries of origin.

After the world cup, the vuvuzelas ceased to sound and real people began to get their hands dirty in some things. Firstly, the nation had to unite and say no to xenophobia as great testing challenges lie on the road ahead. Implementing One-Goal and averting the civil servants' strikes that shook the nation's economy would certainly not be easy. The image of the country was good so far, but could be tarnished overnight by criminal activities that continued to loom. The failure to reason together as fellow African brothers and sisters has been a long-standing problem on the continent. People misled by a philosophy that Blacks are second-class citizens will always use weapons or wars to kill and destroy their own people. The solution to civil wars and the unfair distribution of wealth in Africa that rob the masses of good life and peace remain a continent agenda. The healing of African nations depends on a new dispensation of quality leadership that will not bow to corruption through senseless excuses of financial challenges of the day. Millions of dispersed Africans around the world will have to see stability and peace before they return to their countries of origin. Africa must conceive and bring forth new political and economic reforms in its individual countries.

American novelist Wallace Stegner said that, "Home is a notion that only nations of the homeless fully appreciate and only the uprooted comprehend." Anybody who has suffered as an outsider, or felt that they do not have a home in this world, would agree. When voices emerge, seemingly out of isolation, but brave enough to stand vulnerable in the face of judgement – others, too will join to take a stand. The plight of the desolate millions of uprooted people around the world poses a dangerous threat of people being sold into modern-day slavery. World Refugee Day on Sunday 20th of June 2010, saw about 40 million people around the world recognized under the year's theme, "Home". Only a few countries teach these people skills or empower them to build their lives. People do not choose to be refugees and each one of them has the potential to succeed if given an opportunity. If governments would treat refugees with dignity and respect, rather than exploiting them, the human trafficking syndicates that prey on these poor, innocent souls could be shut down. Refusing to treat refugees well and paying them slave wages should not be allowed. And any treatment of people as lesser beings must be exposed in order to free people from all abuse and trafficking.

Africa still faces a huge challenge in dealing with human trafficking, especially against women and children. Since the FIFA World Cup was on African soil, it provided many blessings for the future but also called for stricter measures in dealing with sophisticated new human trafficking that may surface. The governments should stop the scourge of human trafficking for too many people come to the continent to spy out its good and then advance their evil business. Many blessings of the tournament take years to notice but the same goes for the problems it brings. It is within the power of the nations of Africa to allow this world event to yield the fruits they desire, but this will depend on their sharing information to combat serious economic and criminal offences. About 450 000 visitors set foot on the soil during the event and that was good news for the tourism and economic sectors.

The whole theme of, "Home", is to try to get refugees to return to their homes. Supporting refugees with education and life skills guarantees a better future for them even if they go back to their home countries. Wars and poverty are the two main causes of individuals seeking asylum. Statistically, the number of refugees who voluntarily return to the countries of their origin is low. And today, as conflicts around the world have grown more resilient, only 250 000 refugees return home annually. South Africa finds itself especially burdened by an influx of refugees from all over Africa because it is perceived as a place of economic opportunity. The records show that more refugees in the past two decades have been reluctant to return home. This means that the world's 15 million refugees will continue to live as refugees, as they refuse to return home.

Most of the time, refugees prefer to return to their home countries. When continuing or escalating conflict makes this impossible, however, it leaves the refugees with no choice but to find new homes to restart their lives. Under the banner of the United Nations High Commission for Refugees (UNHCR), we have seen better monitoring and more help reaching millions of people who need shelter, and many of their problems being solved worldwide. The main cause of asylum seekers around Africa is joblessness or endless wars that never give them an opportunity to develop and plough back into their economies. Africa has never been able to experience an easy flow of people and skills from one country to another because it is ill equipped and unprepared for such transfers. Most African countries have a high rate of illiteracy and skills shortage though this varies from one country to another. The reality at present is that the large unskilled labour workforce from poor countries is being absorbed by the wealthier ones. We see thousands of workers from Zimbabwe, Mozambique, Malawi, Congo DRC, Nigeria, with few numbers from the rest of the continent. Also Asian states have many people in South Africa and abroad.

Africa's economic management has always been different from the rest of the world. Together as a continent, it needs to erect fundamental bases to move away from the traditional economic background that has slowed down development among its own countries. If Africa is to do away with poverty and deal with its challenges squarely, it will have to allow a high level of skills cross-pollination among its people. Workers moving from low economic zones who work with those from higher economic zones produce a unified force with a successful mixture of skills. Every country on the African continent needs to strike a balance between the two economic zones before focusing on global trade. The present system benefits those already in the formal economic stream and leaves the masses by the way side, out in the cold.

Development initiatives need to be supported by everyone in order to build for the future; otherwise, only a few will be successful. The dream of Africa is to have free trade with one customs union, starting with regional blocks and extending to the entire continent. The leaders need to take into account, "the basic realities of production and trade in the areas concerned, where there are high levels of complementarities which occur in diversified economies." Many African countries are engaged in producing primary products and Intra-regional trade is "quite small". Still, the deadline of a customs union in the Southern Africa Development Community Countries was supposed to have been met by year 2010. What makes a unified Africa so difficult to achieve? Many trade experts put their trust in the leaders' vision of a "Grand free trade area", with trepidation.

The problems that the member states and the continent are experiencing are not conducive for one customs union territory. Strong policies of political reform must be in place before free trade can be implemented. We all hear excuses of what we cannot do now even when deadlines are looming by the doorstep. The simple question is, "Can we bring the goods home and make it a reality rather than just fine talk? It would have been impossible to realize the FIFA world cup if the work had not been completed on the ground. East Africa went for a free trade deal on the 01/07/2010.The region of about 126 million people was opened for free trade and the movement of residents. A milestone deal was reached to boost trade and development in five countries, which are: Burundi, Kenya, Rwanda, Tanzania and Uganda. Can this be a true sign of political change which will bring healing and economic development to these nations? Only time will tell. The truth is, Africa has reached a point of economic no-return that will force it to change its policies or sink. Most African states are sitting on a time bomb with the masses jobless youth growing restless. Revenues are getting tighter and smaller while poverty, sickness and disease increase. Sophisticated white-collar fraud is robbing the masses of a better life. And the failure to manage resources, accompanied by sabotage, has allowed the critics of independence to dictate to Africa.

The fight for economic change in Africa has brought restlessness among many politicians and their rivals. Everyone knows what needs to be done, but not everyone is willing to do the right thing. The fear is that the rich minority might be offended and push a panic button that will destroy the economies. But how long can the good keep quiet? The African economies are already collapsing from colonial residue and sabotage even when the fear of economic collapse is dealt with. Recently, we saw countries of the southern bloc going through a desperate economic overhaul phase. With the African Union trade being so small among African states, it gives little promise for future growth and raises concerns about future relations between the countries.

Botswana had the biggest layoffs of workers in the mining industry. This powerful diamond-producing nation finds itself struggling with an escalating unemployment rate. Its political stability through the years has always helped it to stay afloat despite the economic winds that blew there. Botswana suffers without words heard or known outside home. Its neighbours might be in trouble or sinking in waters, maybe much worse state of course. Zimbabwe is a weak link as it tries to recover from its economic woes, and it finds little help but rather inherits sabotage from the other states of the region. Zimbabwe has lost its educated citizens to neighbouring states and abroad. It tried to make a turnaround by introducing a black empowerment that many of its critics undermined. Hopefully, the time will come when the black empowerment will bear fruits. Many Zimbabweans are dispersed around the world leaving relatively few to build the country back up. Because such a large number of men left Zimbabwe, women had to work at mining with their young ones – not voluntarily but because of starvation. Jonathan of De Beers said that diamonds from Zimbabwe's Marange fields could not be classified as "blood diamonds".

Nevertheless, he mentioned that the mining processes there did raise concern. The responsible bodies failed to reach a consensus on whether to allow Zimbabwe to resume trading gems. The process watchdog Kimberly was deadlocked and could not come up with a clear judgment while meeting in Israel in June 2010. Thus, Zimbabwe was in limbo with regard to the diamond markets. The next meeting was to be in Russia on the 14th and 15th of July 2010 in St. Petersburg. In past years Russia has cut its diamond sales by a large percentage to Anglo America and the aim was to completely cut trading in the future and focus on new markets like China and elsewhere. The senior personnel of the Russian diamond Industry even came out boldly saying the reason for resorting to new markets was that they had been selling their diamonds like "glass". The world is at loggerheads with traditional market players who have always determined the market prices. If a buyer gets it for too cheap, as Russia perceives, terminating the supply chain is the only solution.

The government of Zimbabwe moved to bar Rio Tinto from trading its diamonds. If the government could not trade diamonds, then no one could until an agreement was reached for the state to trade its diamonds. Thus, for quite some months there were no sales of diamonds from Zimbabwe. This political hurdle put financial strains on companies. Was this a new sabotage inflicted on Zimbabwe at a time when it wanted to move forward? Zimbabwe banned all diamond exports until its controversial Marange diamonds were certified by industry regulators. Rio Tinto admitted that there had been an interruption of shipments and an impact on finances and that it was a priority to resolve the ban with the government soon. The other problem was with Chiedza diamonds, the diamond fields that were discovered in 2006 and said to have a bloody history of illegal mining. The London stock exchange had listed the company; but Africa Consolidated Resources claimed the diamonds were their stolen goods. Regardless of all these allegations, on the 5th of July 2010, the Zimbabwe government made it clear that very soon they would be selling diamonds. Would they defy the rules or wait for a certification from the regulators to sell?

Did the Zimbabwean leadership not realize the mining problems that existed there or was it because hard times had hit the country, leaving leaders with no choice but to make ends meet? Can Zimbabwe nationalize its mines or change policies in order to benefit people at the grass roots level and not politicians only? The government could pay royalties to those women who were mining with their children. The women were left with two hard choices—to work hard or die of hunger. This dilemma that leaves them with little or no options is a curse of sanctions. Schools closed down and families became dysfunctional, as men turned their backs on homes. The Diamond was in the hands of poor simple women and their children. This most sought-after commodity has provoked former colonial masters to jealousy. It made the world's controlling bodies cry foul as women and children held the stuff in their hands from their own country and land. A judge in Zimbabwe refused bail for the so-called blood diamond "whistle blower", the accused activist said to have passed false information mining violations to the international diamond control body, the Kimberly Process.

The judge, Chinembiri Bhunu, said the accusations against human rights activist Farai Maguwu justified his detention until police investigations were complete. Maguwu was arrested on the 3rd of June 2010, on charges including possessing false information and the theft of state security documents. How true were the allegations made against Zimbabwe by this man? Was it right to cause the country to lose its only export gem at that time? The allegations might have had merit but it could not be overlooked that the restriction on sales would hurt the rightful beneficiaries and subject them to even more dire consequences. The world waited to see the future of Zimbabwe diamonds. There is no doubt that the country needs a chance to make a mark on the world map again. Doing away with their currency and using standard world currencies allowed Zimbabwe to come back into world markets quickly. Its future, then, rests on its policy makers and strategists. When the allegations against Zimbabwe surfaced, the country was immediately told to stop selling diamond to the world until further notice. The diamond controlling bodies were divided concerning the sale of Zimbabwe diamonds. On the other hand, the government sales agent had about $1, 3 billion worth of unsold diamonds during its suspension of sales.

Whenever it seemed things were taking shape for Zimbabwe something seemed to drag the country down. The country has been working on a great economic overhaul that will make it hard for the enemy to have power. The way forward now could be smooth as the price has been paid, and it was a hefty one. If Africa moves in the right direction now, it will mean stability for the wrecked economies of the continent. On the 30th of June, 2010, the Zimbabwe government moved to bar agricultural imports. The local industry was said to be able to sustain the nation's needs as projected by the ministry of agriculture. The minister explained it would be unfair to let local produce rot in the markets while buying imports. Surely, if the southern block enters the free trade zone with all these problems, the region will be heading for economic collapse. Therefore, it is best for each country to be well organized before they move on together as a block or continent. The collapse of the world markets is bringing a shift in poor nations' ways of trade. Poor nations are usually the first to feel the squeeze before solutions come and the crises are managed. This is a cruel capitalist tactic that rich first world industrialists use.

On 1st July 2010, the Namibian government began pushing for mineral processing to take place within the country. The top government official said this would help them raise revenue through export tax and create more job opportunities for the people. Their lawmakers said that the benefiting entity at large, which is the government, is not in favour of the export of Namibian minerals without adding value to them. Lack of inclusion of previously disadvantaged individuals on boards and in the management of foreign companies is detrimental. Much of what the country has seen so far is window dressing and a divide-and-rule approach to employment. The entire mining sector is said to be marred with sophisticated, criminal ways of trade.

Perhaps it is time that Africa get its own new industry regulators and policy makers that are not biased but empower the citizens and benefit their nations with their own resources. It is time to go back to the drawing board and root out the scourge of poverty from this resource rich continent! It seems every country has dirty laundry hanging out. South Africa is battling with a housing backlog: the poor and middle class have difficulty finding land on which to build a house, as it is in scarcity. A new housing subsidy for low salary households is a great boost to easing the government-housing burden for its people. Hosting the World Cup has been great for the country but mainly benefited only those who were already financially established. Security guards went on nationwide strike because of greedy bosses who use people as tools for accumulating wealth. Workers at Eskom, the only power utility in the country, also threatened to put down their tools and plunge the country into darkness. Negotiations that took place before the strike gave the country victory as the management managed to have it called off at last minute.

The South African Home Affairs ministry enforced a new law on the 30th of June 2010. Cross border, drivers were told to obtain work permits in order to drive through South Africa. This caused chaos, and the move was costly to the already struggling freight industry. The industry took the department to court as trucks were jammed at all ports of entry. It was as if the ministry had no clue about regional efforts to develop a free trade customs union. The court ruled in favour of the freight industry and the law was called off until all parties could agree on certain issues beforehand. African states have a self-defeating tendency not to embrace common goals as one people. They would rather drift apart than work to find common solutions. The mining industry's failure to change is another sign of the countries' weakness and fall from the position of being the economic driving force on the continent and the world. Workers at mines, in construction and on farms not being paid has become a norm on the continent. The salaries of people in the above-mentioned industries are pathetic. These three industries have been poverty-breeding zones and need urgent attention in order to bring about transformation.

The soccer World Cup has left Africa with a winning goal. Goals of political reform have to go beyond mere promises in order to better the lives of people in Africa and the world. The cry of the poor masses of the world is to achieve justice for their cause regardless of their colour and location. FIFA taught the world to say "No" to racism and denounce some unacceptable heart attitudes. We must refuse to practise racial discrimination against others even for economic reasons. The people of the world have yet to bless their children with education and true empowerment.

An estimated 72 million children do not even get primary education, as a 2010 survey revealed. Statistics show that more than half of these children are on the African continent. FIFA president Sepp Blatter launched a One-Goal child organization right on African soil. It will be a blessing if the leaders of the world and all people put their weight behind it and make sure the idea gains traction in the future. Implementation of it would make a vast change in people's livelihoods and conditions. It is good to leave a legacy of education for generations to come that it may be their heritage. Education changes lives of people. It changes economies and causes people to dwell in harmony as resources reach everyone better when they are literate. This is what will make African leaders gain the respect of their people rather than take advantage of their political and economic ignorance. Education brings a prosperous future to all people; much credit will go to those who heed the call for a new era of world education in the third millennium. This is not an era for weapons but for good leadership in education!

The main enemy to be conquered is poverty, which is caused by many factors, but number one among them is illiteracy. Africa is quickly becoming a disease-free continent though still marred by sabotage and poverty. Only when people become educated can they break away from cultures that cause them more harm than good. South Africa has for a long time failed to have its metro and municipality towns account for financial expenditures for long. It is so bad that R7 billion has recently gone unaccounted for in just one fiscal year. Public service is very much politicised in South Africa. Therefore, cadre deployment might plunge the country into chaos if the government does not sort out and professionalise the crucial service sector soon. A clean audit can only come if they professionalise the management system rather than politicise it. The country needs good leadership in all tiers of governance, which can then unite to deliver good service to all people. The country also needs educational gurus now rather than just reward cadres in positions they do not function well in. This is one of the most testing years of the ruling party and its allies. What is the ruling party elective conferences going to bring for the future? An educated, innovative and resourceful people are the measure of the wealth of a society or nation. A good society does not look at racial colour as the code for success or innovation, but lets good work speak for itself. Fulfilled, creative people make the world a better place for all. When President Barrack Obama campaigned and said, "My heart is right," I believe he meant he would not count evil against anyone but would simply fight hard to correct what the enemies of freedom have done to derail the world for their interests.

I also quote the words of Nelson Mandela when he got out of prison. He said, "When I felt that anger well up inside of me I realized that if I hated them after I got outside that gate, then they would still have me. I wanted to be free, so I let it go." He was a man who knew too well the scourge of apartheid and how it harms a nation more than most of the citizens of South Africa. He never used the past to pin other races down, but only to justify a time for change. And he shaped the country into what they dreamt it to be during the years of struggle for freedom. The future is what drove the stalwarts not the past. Mandela said in one of his speeches, "Never, never and never again will this beautiful land be oppressed by apartheid again or people labelled by colour." The mistake of this generation is to fail to enter this rest and the beautiful land, the past being gone and the building of lives most important. The future prepared for today is more golden than our past remembered today. Blaming and fighting others about the past is wrong; that is where the youth of the land has missed it. The cause of true freedom must unite the people of the country, continent and the world. Anyway, most of the evil men and women of the past are gone. There might be a remnant of their seed among us, but, rather than destroy, we should change it and make it useful.

The entire world can join hands in a future everyone has dreamt of, through a common understanding of achieving that goal through education and determination. The hard work of a united people bears fruit for life, peace and justice. We are simply custodians of what has been entrusted to us by the Creator of all. Great leaders have come and gone and have left great inspirations for everyone to pick up and move forward. Good people both alive and gone have laid the foundation stones. Now it is time to lay every stone in its place and build toward the winning point in the age-old race of peace and prosperity for all in our world.

Epilogue

I hope and trust that you will enjoy a life that rises above cultural dogmas and racially divisive issues. ENJOY AND TEACH OTHERS HOW TO EXPERIENCE THE JOY OF

LIFE AND THE RECONCILIATION OF LOVE. Let us build up people and transform culture! If we live in truth, we will see marriages resurrected and families restored to happiness. The joy of any people is its future, embodied in its youthful generation. But widespread family breakdown is denying this generation its right to possess the future. May we create a fair platform for children without disturbing the main pillars of development. Africa must re-evaluate its cultures quickly in order to maintain relevance in a fast-changing world, and must empower its people to do the same.

There must be a true platform of gender equality, which will be source of strength, especially in promoting good governance and leadership. We will forever be grateful to all our heroes who have broken many yokes off people's necks. Their clarion call still has the power to cause all people to taste freedom and live in peace. Let corruption and wars cease from our soil. Illiteracy must become outdated as, with a new vigour, we fight to end poverty among all people. Dealing with disease and sickness must be according to modern medical science. Africa and the world must define freedom based on four pillars, which are Justice, Truth, Reconciliation (Love for humanity and life) and peace. These will bring true economic liberalization and independence.